THE

PUBLICATIONS

OF THE

SURTEES SOCIETY

VOL. 220

THE

PUBLICATIONS

OF THE

SURTEES SOCIETY

ESTABLISHED IN THE YEAR
M.DCCC.XXXIV

VOL. CCXX

NORTHALLERTON WILLS AND INVENTORIES, 1666–1719

EDITED
BY
DOROTHY EDWARDS AND
CHRISTINE M. NEWMAN

THE SURTEES SOCIETY

THE BOYDELL PRESS

First published 2016

A Surtees Society Publication
published by The Boydell Press
an imprint of Boydell & Brewer Ltd
PO Box 9, Woodbridge, Suffolk IP12 3DF, UK
and of Boydell & Brewer Inc.
668 Mt Hope Avenue, Rochester, NY 14620–2731, USA
website: www.boydellandbrewer.com

ISBN 978-0-85444-075-7

ISSN 0307-5362

A catalogue record for this book is available
from the British Library

Details of other Surtees Society volumes are available
from Boydell & Brewer Ltd

This publication is printed on acid-free paper

Printed and bound in Great Britain by
TJ International Ltd, Padstow, Cornwall

FSC
www.fsc.org
MIX
Paper from
responsible sources
FSC® C013056

CONTENTS

ACKNOWLEDGEMENTS

This volume arose from work undertaken as part of the North East Inheritance Project at Durham University. Funded by the Heritage Lottery Fund, the project began in 2006 and went online in 2010, making available a detailed index of all the probate records held by Durham University Library. A group of volunteers from Northallerton and District Local History Society travelled regularly to Durham in order to index those records belonging to that part of Allertonshire over which the Dean and Chapter of Durham held peculiar jurisdiction. The members of the group then went on to transcribe all of the wills and inventories belonging to the township of Northallerton itself. The following volunteers were responsible for the initial transcriptions published in this volume: Dorothy Edwards; Stephen Hague; Phoebe Newton; George Sutton; and Jean Thompson.

Thanks are due to Durham University Library, Archives and Special Collections, the Borthwick Institute for Archives, University of York, and The National Archives for permission to publish the wills and inventories in this volume. Particular thanks are due to Andrew Gray, who led the project, and his assistant Francis Gotto, both of Durham University Library Archives and Special Collections. Throughout the indexing and transcribing processes they dealt patiently with queries and generously supplied photocopies of the original wills and inventories which made it possible for the documents to be transcribed at Northallerton. Francis also gave willingly of his assistance and expertise during the transcription process.

Finally, thanks must go to Angus Winchester, joint general editor of the Surtees Society, for his invaluable advice, encouragement and support during the later stages of editing this volume for publication, which included preparing the Glossary.

ABBREVIATIONS

BIA	Borthwick Institute for Archives, University of York
DPR	Durham Probate Records, Durham University Library
NYCRO	North Yorkshire County Record Office, Northallerton
TNA	The National Archives, Kew
VCH	*Victoria County History*

INTRODUCTION

This collection of 153 wills and inventories from the town of Northallerton spans the period 1666 to 1719. The majority survive amongst the large collection of probate records belonging to the consistory court of the diocese of Durham, deposited in Durham University Library, Archives and Special Collections.

THE DOCUMENTS

In ecclesiastical terms, both the bishop and the dean and chapter of Durham exercised peculiar jurisdiction over the Allertonshire parishes, these being divided between the two. The parish of Northallerton fell within the peculiar jurisdiction of the dean and chapter whose probate records survive for the period 1666 to 1845. Whilst early seventeenth-century probate material survives for much of the bishop of Durham's jurisdiction, none is extant for Northallerton. One stray will in the Durham collection dates from 1585 and a handful of earlier records, from the late fifteenth and early sixteenth centuries, are deposited in the Durham Cathedral Muniments. The dean and chapter collection contains original wills, inventories and bonds from the Allertonshire parishes of Kirby Sigston, West Rounton and Northallerton, together with the latter's dependent chapelries of Brompton, Deighton, High Worsall and Romanby.[1] This volume includes only those documents belonging to the town of Northallerton.

In order to provide as comprehensive a picture as possible of the probate evidence left by the townsmen and women of Northallerton,

1 Durham University Library, Archives and Special Collections, Durham Probate Records: Dean and Chapter Allertonshire probate records, DPRI/6, 1670–1808. Two stray Northallerton wills, one dated 1585 and the other that of John Harper (d.1694), vicar of Northallerton (this volume, no. 90), found their way into the separate probate collection belonging to the bishop of Durham's Allertonshire Peculiar: Durham University Library, Archives and Special Collections, Durham Probate Records, DPRI/1, 1540–1599 and 1700–1725.

this volume also contains 13 wills held at the Borthwick Institute for Archives in York.[2] This archive includes, amongst its holdings, the general probate records of the archbishopric of York and those proved in the archbishop's prerogative court, the latter dealing with the wills of those testators holding property in more than one jurisdiction within the Northern Province. A further Northallerton will, deposited in The National Archives, has also been included.[3] The wills and inventories contained in this volume therefore represent the earliest substantial set of probate documents available for the town of Northallerton. In total the volume includes 62 wills with inventories, 37 wills without inventories and 54 inventories without wills. Five of the wills are nuncupative and two of these have an associated inventory. For the purposes of this edition, the documents have been numbered 1 to 153. These numbers are also used in this introduction in order to identify the document or the individual concerned.

The Northallerton wills, inventories and bonds from the Durham collection are all written on separate, paper documents, which have been gathered together into a folder for each individual testator. Where a will has survived, it, together with any accompanying bonds and/or an inventory, has the reference prefix DPRI/6/T; for bonds and inventories without a will the reference prefix is DPRI/6/B. The few stray documents in the main collection have the reference DPRI/1. The wills from the Borthwick Institute for Archives have the reference prefix BIA. The majority of the latter, together with the single Northallerton will deposited in The National Archives, are copies made when probate was granted.

Throughout the latter part of the seventeenth century and the early eighteenth century the number of probate bundles per decade averaged 29 to 30, with a high point of 45 in the 1680s. From the 1750s, however, figures declined with the number of Allertonshire probate bundles processed by the Durham dean and chapter in that decade falling to nine. The decline continued during the following decades, apart from a small rise, to 13, in the 1770s. Thereafter the downward trend continued with only one bundle processed in the decade before the passing of the 1857 Probate Act. A similar trend is noticeable in the bishop of Durham's peculiar jurisdictions in

2 Below, nos 4, 9, 19, 29, 34, 39, 69, 123, 124, 143, 148, 152, 153.

3 Below, no. 126. The testator in this case was a mariner, apparently based in London.

Yorkshire. Here, although greater numbers of probate bundles were processed generally, figures declined from the 1750s apart from the same, brief upward trend in the 1770s. Whether this is an indication that traditional channels of probate jurisdiction were breaking down, with more Yorkshire probates being dealt with in York, is not clear. However, this may well have been the case, possibly reflecting a wider distribution of property ownership amongst the Northallerton elite.[4] A clear decline in the number of surviving Allertonshire inventories is also apparent. In the later decades of the seventeenth century, the majority of wills were accompanied by an associated inventory but, after 1750, none have survived.[5]

Standards of literacy appear to have been relatively high amongst testators, with 50 of the deceased having signed their own names, as opposed to 32 who were able only to make their mark.[6] Of the female testators, however, only two signed, although sixteen female witnesses to wills were able to provide signatures.[7]

Of the 153 deceased, a date of burial has been identified for 136 individuals, of whom 99 left surviving wills.[8] The burial dates survive for 90 of the latter, thus enabling a comparison to be made between the date a will was drawn up and the death of the testator. The majority of these described themselves as sick or infirm, indicating that many wills were executed quite close to the point of death. Indeed, 41 testators died within 14 days and of these 13 were buried within two days of their wills being made. Nevertheless, a small number of testators describing themselves as sick or infirm did make an initial recovery. Henry Banister [**149**], for example, declared

4 Thanks are due to Francis Gotto for information on the probate figures in the later part of the eighteenth century and to Margaret McCollum for her advice regarding this issue.

5 The keeping of probate inventories within the diocese of Durham had largely ceased, except in special circumstances, by *c.*1720: J. L. Drury, 'Inventories in the probate records of the diocese of Durham', Archaeologia Aeliana, 5th series, 28 (2000), pp. 177–91. See also the discussion in J. A. Johnson (ed.), *Probate Inventories of Lincoln Citizens, 1661–1714*, Lincoln Record Society, vol. 80 (1991), p. xvi.

6 It has been suggested that the ability to sign one's name, rather than just making a mark, is not necessarily an indication of full literacy: N. Goose and N. Evans, 'Wills as an historical source', in T. Arkell, N. Evans and N. Goose (eds), *When Death Do Us Part: Understanding and Interpreting the Probate Records of Early Modern England* (Oxford, 2000), pp. 69–70.

7 See below p. xxvii.

8 NYCRO, PR/1/4–5.

in his will of June 1714 that he was infirm and weak but in the event he survived until January 1718.

It would appear that the practice of making a will whilst still healthy gradually began to increase. Between 1666 and 1699 the dates of wills and burials survive for 51 testators of whom only five (10 per cent) lived for longer than a year. However, the numbers rose to 11 out of 40 testators (over 25 per cent) in the period 1700 to 1719. Some of these individuals made no mention of the state of their health although others, such as Percival Robinson [**115**], did so: he described himself in his will of February 1695 as '... being in good health of body'. In the event, his inventory was not drawn up until September 1706, although the date of his death is not known.

THE TOWN OF NORTHALLERTON

The town, its economy and times of change

Mentioned in the Domesday survey, the manor of Allerton, in the North Riding of Yorkshire, was granted to the bishop of Durham, William of St Calais, by William II *c.*1088–91.[9] The focal point of the liberty was the small market town of Northallerton, which had, undoubtedly, long been a place of settlement, standing as it did at the centre of the pre-Conquest wapentake. Tradition suggests that a Roman encampment lay in the vicinity, although no firm evidence of this has emerged to date. Fragments of sculpture found near the parish church of All Saints suggest the presence of an Anglo-Saxon religious site in the area.[10] In its medieval form the town of Northallerton consisted of burgage properties lining either side of 'one fair long streate lying by south and north', as it was described by John Leland in the early 1540s. The medieval town had probably developed around the castle, built within the first few decades after the Norman Conquest. The castle had long been ruinous by Leland's time, although, as he noted, the bishop's manor house, or palace, erected later, stood nearby.[11] The earliest surviving documentary

9 J. Raine (ed.), *Historiae Dunelmensis Scriptores Tres, Gaufridus de Coldingham, Robertus de Graystanes, et Willielmus de Chambre*, Surtees Society 9 (1839), Appendix, p. ccccxxv.

10 *VCH Yorks*, II, p. 196; *VCH North Riding*, I, p. 418; E. Cambridge, 'Why did the community of St Cuthbert settle at Chester-le-Street?', in G. Bonner *et al.* (eds), *St Cuthbert, His Cult and His Community to AD 1200'*, (Woodbridge, 1989), pp. 382–5.

11 *The Itinerary of John Leland in or about the Years 1535–1543*, ed. L. Toulmin Smith (London, 1964), I, p. 67; *VCH North Riding*, I, pp. 418, 426.

evidence concerning Northallerton's borough status dates from 1267–68; acknowledgement of its growing prominence came in 1298 when it was granted representation in the parliament held that year in York.[12]

Northallerton was to survive the economic downturn that characterised the north-eastern economy in the later Middle Ages and the early part of the sixteenth century. As such it continued to function as the marketing, trading and administrative focal point for the 30 or so surrounding small townships and villages which comprised the liberty of Allertonshire. Its strategic position on the main thoroughfare north from York further enabled the town to benefit from the passing trade brought by the many travellers who regularly journeyed through Northallerton on their way to, or from, the North.[13] Indeed, the later seventeenth and early eighteenth centuries, the period covered by these wills, coincided closely with a time of growing economic prosperity for the town.

In terms of content, this volume complements two other published collections of probate documents from north-east England covering Darlington and Sunderland in County Durham, both of which focus upon material drawn from the first half of the seventeenth century.[14] Like Northallerton, both towns had their origins in medieval boroughs, all belonging to the bishop of Durham. Sunderland, at the beginning of the seventeenth century, still possessed many of the characteristics of a small fishing port surrounded by a rural hinterland, with its wealthiest testators being yeomen. Yet, by 1650, the town was enjoying the benefits of the burgeoning coal trade which, by the early eighteenth century, would transform it into a major national and international seaport.[15] Darlington, on the other hand, lying only some 16 miles to the north of Northallerton, provides more in the way of general comparison. There were certainly similarities between the two in terms of administration

---

12 C. M. Newman, *Late Medieval Northallerton* (Stamford, 1999), p. 5. The borough returned no further members to Parliament until 1640 when the town's right to representation was restored: *Journal of the House of Commons*, Volume 2: 1640–1643 (1802), p. 49; C. J. D. Ingledew, *The History and Antiquities of Northallerton in the County of York* (London, 1858), pp. 127–8.

13 Newman, *Late Medieval Northallerton*, pp. 91–2.

14 J. A. Atkinson *et al.* (eds), *Darlington Wills and Inventories, 1600–1625*, Surtees Society 201 (1993); J. Briggs *et al.* (eds), *Sunderland Wills and Inventories, 1601–1650*, Surtees Society 214 (2010).

15 Briggs *et al.* (eds), *Sunderland Wills and Inventories*, pp. xxxv–vi; xxxix–xl.

and economy, with the reins of local government in both held firmly by the bailiff, an episcopal appointee who supervised all aspects of the day-to-day administration of the town and organised the holding of the courts, which were presided over by the bishop's steward. There were similarities, too, in respect of local trade, for both Northallerton and Darlington were noted for their markets and fairs, especially the great cattle markets for which both were famous.[16]

As the Hearth Tax returns of 1673 indicate, Northallerton was, for the first time, beginning to overtake the neighbouring North Riding market town of Thirsk in terms of the wealth of its population and the size of its properties. Thirsk was the slightly larger of the two, being assessed on 230 households in contrast to Northallerton's 188. Nevertheless, 25 per cent of Thirsk households were deemed non-chargeable in the assessment, whereas in Northallerton the figure was only 15 per cent. Similarly, 27 per cent of Northallerton households had more than four hearths, with nine of these having seven or above, whilst in Thirsk only 10 per cent had more than four hearths, with none having more than six.[17]

The extent of Northallerton's significance as a major focal point and distribution centre for regional produce and other goods is made clear in the petition sent by the borough to Parliament in 1698, opposing plans to make navigable the Aire and Calder rivers. This complained that the proposed scheme would drain the River Ouse, thus depriving Northallerton of the means by which it exported 'great Quantities of Lead, Butter, and other Commodities [which] are daily carried from thence to Burrough-Briggs; and thence, by Water upon the River Ouze, to several Parts of this Kingdom, and beyond the Seas'.[18] The town's cattle fair, too, continued to thrive. Renowned as far back as the sixteenth century, it drew praise from the Elizabethan antiquary William Camden who described it as 'the greatest Faire of Kine and Oxen'. Daniel Defoe, writing in the 1720s, remarked upon the 'large, noble breed of oxen, as may be seen at North Allerton fairs, where there are an incredible quantity of them

16 Daniel Defoe, *A Tour through England and Wales*, vol. 2, ed. G. D. H. Cole (London, 1928), pp. 222, 247; Ingledew, *History and Antiquities*, pp. 382–4; *VCH Durham*, IV, pp. 83–5, 119–20.

17 TNA, E179/216/462, Yorkshire North Riding 1673M, analysed by The Centre for Hearth Tax Research, University of Roehampton, at <http://hearthtax.org.uk/communities/northriding/index.html>.

18 *Journal of the House of Commons*, Volume 12: 1697–1699 (1803), pp. 101–3.

bought eight times every year ...'. He noted how black cattle, too, were sold there in 'prodigious quantity'. These animals were then driven south to Lincolnshire and the Isle of Ely where they were fattened up for the London market.[19] It seems likely that a considerable number of cattle passing through Northallerton's markets originated in Scotland and two major drove roads lay within close proximity to the town. One followed the route of the main road to the North, which passed through Northallerton itself, whilst the other, still known as the Hambledon Drove Road, ran just to the north of the Allertonshire township of Osmotherley, within a few miles of the town.[20]

Writing in 1739, the antiquary Roger Gale, who represented Northallerton as Member of Parliament from 1705 to 1713, further confirmed the town's thriving economy, describing Northallerton as 'a great thorough-fare to the North with good inns for the accommodation of travellers', despite the fact that there was no 'particular manufacture carried on' there.[21] In terms of its hospitality, it seems that the town at this time was also noted for the quality of its ale. In 1697 it was remarked upon that 'North-Allerton in Yorkshire doth excel all England, nay all Europe for strong ale'. The best of this 'nectar' was said to be found 'in Madame Bradley's ... the chief house then named'. Whether this establishment had any connection with Alice Bradley **[71]**, who died in 1686, is not clear, although brewing vessels are certainly mentioned in her inventory.[22] Gale also commented, with some pride, upon the improvements taking place in the town. The 'open and spacious' high street, stretching for more than half a mile in length, was, he noted, newly paved along much of its extent, with the remaining portion soon to be completed. This, along with the 'several good houses of stone and brick erected in it', would ensure that the street would soon be 'much more beautiful and commodious than formerly'. One of these buildings was undoubtedly the 'handsome house and office' erected by authority of Parliament in 1736 for the 'registering of deeds for

19 W. Camden, *Britain* (London, 1610), p. 723; Defoe, *Tour through England and Wales*, pp. 222, 247.

20 J. Blackman, 'The cattle trade and agrarian change on the eve of the railway age', *Agricultural History Review*, 23 (1) (1975), pp. 54–5.

21 R. Gale, 'An historical account of the borough of Northallerton', in J. Nichols (ed.,) *Bibliotheca Topographica Britannica*, No. II, part II (London, 1781), pp. 209–11.

22 G. Meriton, *The Praise of Yorkshire Ale* (York, 1697).

the North Riding'.[23] Such evidence suggests that Northallerton was undergoing something an 'urban renaissance', as identified in other upwardly mobile, provincial towns across the country.[24]

In agricultural terms, this was a period of marked change in the way that the borough's fields were organised. Until the seventeenth century the borough had a large area of open field agriculture, mainly to the north-east and east of the town itself, with several large areas of grazing land. The most northerly area of this pasture was the North Moor, while to the east of the town lay Hailstone Moor and Bullamoor. In 1637 the townsfolk of Northallerton petitioned the bishop of Durham for permission to enclose their open fields and the enclosures began soon afterwards.[25] One further area, a large holding to the north of the town, was known as Wiske Moor, or 'Raker', and was the site of an early ring-fenced farm. This was not part of the medieval open field system and had always been held of the bishop by a prominent tenant.[26] In 1679 George Langley **[34]** was described as being of Wiske Moor House but his nuncupative will made no reference to an heir and the property later fell into the hands of the Kaye family, as illustrated in the will of John Kaye **[93]**.

The evidence provided by the wills adds to the hitherto rather scarce information concerning the dating of the enclosures and indicates that this was a prolonged process. It appears that North Moor was the first area to be enclosed, probably by 1641, with several of the earlier wills confirming this.[27] However, the precise location of these closes cannot be specified since those located towards the town side of the old moor continued, collectively, to be known only by the generic name of 'North Moor Closes' until at least the end of the nineteenth century. As the wills of John Wilson **[51]** and John Rymer **[118]** indicate, ring-fenced farms had been created out of the furthermost part of North Moor, with Wilson's will naming his

23 Gale, 'Historical account'.

24 See, for example, P. Borsay, *The English Urban Renaissance: Culture and Society in the Provincial Town, 1660–1770* (Oxford, 1989).

25 Durham University Library, Archives and Special Collections, CCB B/211/51 (221344).

26 In 1504 it was held by James Metcalfe, member of a prominent Yorkshire family. His father, Thomas, who held the property before him, had been the bishop of Durham's auditor for the liberty of Allertonshire: TNA, Durh. 3/68, m. 28; Newman, *Late Medieval Northallerton*, p. 50.

27 NYCRO, Beresford Peirse Title Deeds, ZBA 1/6/1, 1/8/1, 1/8/3; below, nos 12, 13, 18.

property as 'Viewly' and that of Rymer referring to his as 'Gronston Crook'. Both of these farms still exist.[28]

Hailstone Moor was enclosed at a rather later date. The will of Elizabeth Wilson [**5**], dated 1666, makes mention of her 'commons of pasture' on the moor there. By 1703, however, this land had been enclosed, as illustrated in the will of William Harrison [**112**], which mentioned his close called 'Hailstone Moore Close, alias House Close'. In his will, drawn up in 1709, William Stockdale [**121**] similarly noted his six-acre close on Hailstone Moor, this 'being formerly three common rights'. Bullamoor was a stinted pasture, held in common by 13 tenants whose rights of pasture totalled 80 beast or cattle gates. In February 1702, however, the tenants, by mutual agreement, decided to divide the moor into closes according to their respective proportions, taking account of quality, quantity and access for foot, cart and carriage. Four men from neighbouring townships were authorised to set out allotments, resulting in the hedged fields which have probably changed little to the present day.[29]

Several other closes not previously itemised in the bishops' rentals or early estate surveys were mentioned in a number of wills. These included 'Whearnhow', noted in 1671 in the inventory of Thomas Barstow [**15**]; 'Gallicarr', mentioned in 1672 in the will of Henry Powley [**18**]; 'Dunnes Close', mentioned by John Rymer [**68**] in 1685; and 'Grayson Barughs',[30] noted in the will of Isabel Flower [**73**], dated 1688. As these were in areas that had been used for arable cultivation it is almost certain that they had been created from enclosing the open fields.

The town and its governance[31]

A number of the wills included in this collection provide valuable insights into the lives and connections of those men who were instrumental in the governance of the town during the later seventeenth and early eighteenth centuries. These individuals include curates, postmasters, parish clerks and, perhaps most interestingly, members of the select vestry. While the wills pertain only to a minority of those who acted in these capacities, they are nevertheless sufficient

28 Viewly Hill (SE 355 978) and Grindstone Crook (SE 356 968).

29 NYCRO, ZBA/14/14.

30 Probably to be identified with the Grazing Bars, named on the nineteenth-century tithe map: NYCRO, MI/91.

31 This section incorporates material first drafted by George Sutton, to whom the editors wish to record their thanks.

to provide an insight not only into the lives of the individual testators, but also into aspects of the governance of the town itself.

In Northallerton the select vestry, also known as the 'four and twenty', was the main instrument of local government in this period.[32] The integration of the parish into the sphere of civil administration had developed momentum nationally during the sixteenth century, with vestries gradually acquiring further powers that had, in previous centuries, been the preserve of the manorial courts.[33] As such, in addition to the maintenance of the church and its fabric, vestries gradually assumed responsibility for matters such as the maintenance of the local highways and the promulgation of ordinances and by-laws. The vestry also became responsible for the organisation of poor relief and the setting and levying of the parish rate.[34] It is not clear when the Northallerton select vestry came into being, the earliest extant list of members dating only from 1695. In Darlington evidence concerning the 'four and twenty' dates back to the early sixteenth century, although its business, at that time, was restricted to church affairs. Moreover, members appear to have been drawn from amongst the 'more substantial and discreet inhabitants of the town', possibly the same individuals who sat as jurors in Darlington's borough court.[35]

The Northallerton churchwardens' accounts for the period 1687 to 1729 provide lists of select vestry members for the years 1695, 1706, 1715 and 1716.[36] The wills or inventories of nine named vestry members appear in this collection, these being Robert Raikes senior [**123**], James Conyers [**143**], Simon and George Meeke [**141**, **117**], George Dunn [**140**], John and Stephen Prest [**134**, **147**], Henry Whitton [**116**] and Michael Taylor [**145**]. John Harper [**90**], vicar of Northallerton from 1686 to 1694, and his successor, Charles Neile [**150**], who died in 1718, would both by virtue of their office have chaired meetings of the vestry.[37]

32 *VCH North Riding I*, p. 422.

33 W. E. Tate, *The Parish Chest: A Study of the Records of Parochial Administration in England* (Cambridge, 1946), pp. 13–15.

34 Tate, *Parish Chest*, pp. 15–19; Ingledew, *History and Antiquities*, pp. 269, 271.

35 *VCH Durham* IV, pp. 82–3.

36 Churchwardens' accounts and papers: NYCRO, PR/NO/11/1. During this period, 50 men who served as such have been identified. Of these, the names of 44 are known, the remaining 6 being illegible. However, since some of the decisions of the vestry were signed by individuals not listed alongside the 44 known members, it may be that their names are amongst those that are illegible.

37 Tate, *Parish Chest*, p. 23.

Details of the means of their appointment to the select vestry are noted in the preamble to the 1695 list. Public notice was given by the vicar, who called a meeting of the parishioners in the church porch 'for supplying and filling up the vacancy of the four and twenty men of this Parish'.[38] The names of the 'neighbours' willing to fill the posts were put forward for nomination and those subsequently chosen were appointed to the 'four and twenty'. Whether this meeting was open to all parishioners or was restricted in some way is not clear. Neither is it clear how many eligible 'neighbours' attended the meeting. The procedure may have been similar to that in the parish of Sunderland, County Durham, which was established by Act of Parliament in 1719, where those inhabitants paying 'scot and lot' (i.e. those who paid the poor rate and church dues) were called upon to choose 'twenty-four substantial and creditable inhabitants', each holding freehold estates to the yearly value of £10, to serve as vestrymen for the parish. Similar elections were to be held every three years and in the event of the death of any of the vestrymen.[39] In Northallerton, however, analysis of the surviving lists reveals many of the same names reappearing time and again, with sons often following their fathers, suggesting that the town was run by a self-perpetuating oligarchy of the middling sort. Between 1695 and 1716, the Raikes, Meeke and Prest families were represented on the vestry by both fathers and sons. In terms of their social status or occupation, the vestrymen included four gentlemen, two yeomen, four grocer/merchants, three apothecaries, a husbandman, a blacksmith, a tallow chandler, a skinner, a schoolmaster, two attorneys and four innkeepers (the latter of whom may also have had other occupations).[40]

The will of Robert Raikes senior, a gentleman, who died in 1710 [**123**], provides clear evidence of his keen eye for detail where money matters were concerned. Considered none too scrupulous in his own financial dealings, Raikes was one of the wealthiest men in Northallerton. His son Robert (1683–1753), who featured prominently in his father's will, was educated at Eton, Christ's College, Cambridge and Gray's Inn. He was elected as a Member of Parliament for Northallerton from 1710 to 1713 and went on

38 NYCRO, PR/NO/11/1.

39 W. Fordyce, *The History and Antiquities of the County Palatine of Durham*, vol. 2 (Newcastle-upon-Tyne, 1857), p. 426.

40 The occupations have been arrived at by reference to wills, occasional inclusion of occupation in the four-and-twenty lists and the burial lists of the period.

to establish the family's position firmly within the landed gentry through his marriage, in 1720, to an heiress, Mary Ellis.[41]

Of the 44 men identified as members of the select vestry between 1695 and 1717, the rateable assessments of 25 can be traced, as at March 1711.[42] The largest sum, paid by the attorney Robert Raikes junior, was £135 3s 0d. The rateable assessments of the seven vestrymen whose wills and/or inventories appear in this volume can also be ascertained. These range from the apothecary James Conyers **[143]** who paid £55 10s 0d down to the £5 paid by Michael Taylor **[145]**, a tallow chandler.

The wills and/or inventories of a number of other Northallerton vestrymen appear in this collection. Father and son Simon and George Meeke **[141, 117]** both served as vestry members. George died in 1707, his father continuing in office until his own death in 1716. In his will Simon was described as a gentleman but George, perhaps a younger son of the family, made his living as a grocer. The Meekes were related to a wide range of Northallerton families, such as those of Grimston, Flower, Barstow and Prest. As such, their names crop up in a number of the documents in this volume. Another grocer was Henry Whitton **[116]** who first appeared as a vestryman in 1695. His name reappeared in 1706 but he died soon after, in 1707.[43] Other Northallerton vestryman included the blacksmith John Prest **[134]** and his son Stephen **[147]**, a tallow chandler who replaced his father on the vestry. He was still a vestryman in 1716 but died in September of that year. The tallow chandler Michael Taylor **[145]** served as a vestryman during the same period, dying in 1717. He was replaced on the vestry by his brother-in-law, William Raine, whose wife was a major beneficiary under the terms of Taylor's will.

THE TESTATORS AND THEIR LINKS

Occupations and status

The status or occupations of 107 deceased males are given, together with those of a further 24 Northallerton residents mentioned in the documents. The status of a number of others can be surmised

41 Ingledew, *History and Antiquities*, pp. 138, 167; D. Hayton, E. Cruickshanks and S. Handley (eds), *The History of Parliament: the House of Commons, 1690–1715* (2002); online at <http://www.histparl.ac.uk/volume/1690-1715/member/raikes-robert-1683-1753>.

42 Churchwardens' accounts and papers: NYCRO, PR/NO11/1, pp. 125–30.

43 Ingledew, *History and Antiquities*, p. 200.

from their possessions (see Table 1, below).[44] Those testators who made mention of their occupation or status were often the town's tradesmen or those who described themselves as gentlemen, yeomen and husbandmen. Yeomen are mentioned most frequently although this may have been rather an indication of status, with some of these individuals following an occupation other than farming. Not surprisingly for a market town, tradesmen and craftsmen appear regularly, with seven grocers, two butchers, a mercer and two merchants as well as four tallow chandlers. Three fellmongers, two skinners, three tanners and a currier suggest a flourishing tanning industry, whilst two glovers, two cordwainers and a shoemaker represent those involved in the leatherworking trades. Weaving, too, was clearly important, with eight weavers and possibly two dyers, two of the weavers indicating that they worked with linen, one with wool, and one with silk. Horses were well catered for with three blacksmiths, a saddler, a wheelwright and a lorimer (who made straps and other accoutrements for bridles). Two innholders and a hosteller were amongst those who provided accommodation in the town, whilst a maltman provided the ale keeper with the main ingredient for beer. The building trade was, however, more generously represented in the shape of two masons, three carpenters, a plumber and glazier, perhaps adding further to the suggestion that this was a time of improvement and expansion in Northallerton. Other trades represented included those of whitesmith, barber and apothecary. Four clerks were also mentioned as was one mariner, who appears to have been working out of London rather than from the local ports.

Of the 28 deceased women, 13 were described as widows, seven as spinsters and the remainder undeclared. Women often played a major role since, in most cases when a man had a surviving wife, she was given the responsibility for the administration of his will, on occasion in conjunction with a son, but often as sole executrix. Under common law a widow was entitled to one-third of her late husband's estate[45] but in some cases Northallerton widows were left specific property and/or money in lieu of this, with the proviso that their 'thirds' should not be claimed.[46]

44 These include a carpenter, a fellmonger, a mercer, a tanner and two weavers. See Table 1.

45 For example, nos 14, 28, 44, 47, 95.

46 For example, nos 4, 37, 46, 123, 145.

Table 1: Occupation or status of testators and other named individuals[47]

Testators	No.	Others (legatees, debtors, appraisers, witnesses, executors etc.)	No.
Apothecary	1	Ale keeper	1
Blacksmith	3	Barber	1
Butcher	2	Bellman	1
Carpenter	2+1	Clerk	2
Clerk	2	Dyer	1
Cordwainer	2	Esquire	2
Currier	1	Fellmonger	1
Draper	1	Gentleman	3
Dyer	1?	Husbandman	1
Fellmonger	1	Plumber	1
Gentleman	11	Servant	6
Glazier	1?	Silk Weaver	1
Glover	2	Skinner	1
Grocer	7	Wheelwright	1
Hosteller	1	Whitesmith	1
Husbandman	3		
Inn holder	2		
Labourer	1		
Lorimer	1		
Maltman	1		
Mariner	1		
Mason	2		
Merchant	3		
Saddler	1		
Shoemaker	1		
Skinner	1		
Spinster	7		
Tallow chandler	3+1		
Tanner	3?		
Vicar	2		
Weaver	6+1		
Widow	13		
Yeoman	23		
Total	107+8	Total	24

47 The numbers prefixed with a plus sign or question mark indicate those testators whose occupations can only be surmised.

Witnesses and appraisers

Of the 99 wills included in this volume, 69 (70 per cent) had three witnesses, whilst of the remaining 30 per cent, 20 wills had four, 9 had two and 1 had five witnesses. The names of the signatories lend weight to the suggestion that kinship and social links were evident in the choices of witnesses.[48] The names of certain individuals appeared as witnesses on a number of occasions, not least those belonging to the town's more prominent families. Amongst these was Robert Raikes esquire (the father of the MP), who witnessed seven wills between 1680 and 1704.[49] William Harrison, described as a yeoman in his will [**112**], acted as both a witness and an appraiser on numerous occasions between 1695 and 1705, his own will being witnessed by Robert Raikes and his wife Ann.[50] Another well-connected townsman, Francis Kaye, younger son of the gentleman John Kaye of Wiske Moor, was a signatory to six wills, including that of his father, in the period 1696 to 1709.[51] Thomas Crosfield, named as executor in Kaye's own will [**137**], also witnessed six wills in the period 1709 to 1719, including that of the vicar, Charles Neile.[52] He also witnessed a number of other Northallerton wills at later dates. Crosfield, a solicitor by profession, married the daughter of Robert Raikes and died, aged 73, in 1761.[53] Others whose names appeared on a number of occasions included Robert Young who acted as a witness for five wills between 1711 and 1719 and several members of the Coates family who, between them, acted as both witnesses and appraisers on a number of occasions.[54] John Robinson, the parish clerk [**97**], was also called upon to witness a number of wills.[55] Although male witnesses were in the majority, 43 women were called upon to act in this capacity. Between them, these women witnessed the wills of 25 men[56] and nine women.[57]

The names of appraisers are given for 110 of the 116 inventories.

48 Arkell, Evans and Goose (eds), *When Death Do Us Part*, p. 62.

49 Nos 37, 69, 78, 95, 107, 111, 112. Raikes's wife, Ann, also witnessed the latter.

50 Nos 7, 12, 14, 31, 37, 76, 80, 82, 88, 91, 95, 106, 109.

51 Nos 93, 94, 99, 101, 114, 122.

52 Nos 121, 134, 138, 140, 150.

53 Ingledew, *History and Antiquities*, pp. 161, 165.

54 For the Coates family, namely John and James, see nos 39, 51, 62, 80, 82, 134.

55 Nos 49, 52, 58, 63.

56 Nos 9, 18, 26, 28, 30, 33, 34, 39, 40, 46, 47, 60, 66, 78, 81, 88, 109, 110, 112, 115, 128, 138, 142, 145, 146, 147.

57 Nos 2, 5, 31, 41, 71, 73, 94, 113, 122.

Of these 83 (75 per cent) had four appraisers, whilst of the remaining 25 per cent there were 14 with three appraisers, 8 with two, 4 with five and 1 inventory with a single appraiser. Some names reappeared frequently in the documents, lending weight to the theory that it was probably the case that a number of trusted individuals, especially those with expertise in business or agricultural matters, were called upon time and again to act as appraisers.[58] The above-mentioned William Harrison, for example, was called upon to act as an appraiser on 14 occasions between 1670 and 1706. Several generations of the Robinson family also acted in this capacity and were, between them, named as appraisers in over 20 inventories during the period 1671 to 1718.[59] The wills and/or inventories of eight members of the family are in this volume and these show that family members followed a variety of occupations, one being an innholder, two others linen weavers, one a fellmonger and another a maltman.[60]

Wider kinship networks

Relations of the deceased parties were fairly widespread in the surrounding villages with particularly strong links with Brompton, just to the north of the town, but surprisingly not with Romanby, situated even closer to the south-west. Some families had links as far afield as Richmond, to the west of Northallerton, and York, to the south, whilst several had friends or relations in London. Members of the select vestry are particularly notable for the extent of their interests outside Northallerton. These interests could be in terms of property or family/friend relationships. As his will illustrates, Robert Raikes senior [**123**] had extensive property interests in Yorkshire and County Durham. Simon Meeke [**141**] had property in nearby Ainderby Steeple. In terms of family connections, the apothecary James Conyers [**143**] had a brother in Yarm and a brother-in-law in Scarborough who both followed the same profession.

58 Arkell, Evans and Goose (eds), *When Death Do Us Part*, p. 293; Johnston, *Probate Inventories*, p. lxxix.

59 Nos 13, 24, 25, 32, 40, 44, 48, 49, 52, 55, 58, 62, 63, 71, 75, 77, 107, 135, 149, 152.

60 Nos 32, 59, 80, 97, 107, 113, 115, 152. The nuncupative will of Susan Robinson [113] provides a rough guide to some of the family relationships. It is not clear how closely John Robinson, the parish clerk, was related to the main branches of the family but he was one of the witnesses of Percival Robinson's will [32], suggesting that there was a connection.

STANDARDS OF LIVING

Individual wealth

Evidence of appraised wealth cannot be relied upon to give a full and accurate record of a testator's actual financial status, since inventories provide only details of personal wealth, as opposed to that from income or real estate.[61] Nevertheless, it can, perhaps, give some indication of an individual's social status and standard of living. In this collection, those with the highest levels of appraised wealth were tradesmen, undoubtedly a reflection of the town's growing economy during the period under consideration.

The inventory with the lowest valuation is that of William Dennis [**114**], a yeoman, who had goods worth only 7s 6d. Overall, eight testators were found to be in debt, once outstanding debts and bequests were taken into account, whilst another 35 had possessions worth less than £10. Only 14 individuals had goods worth more than £100. Of the latter, only one, John Kaye [**93**], was a gentleman, with goods worth £208. Three others, with valuations of over £200, were tradesmen, two being grocers and one a mercer. Of these, the grocer Henry Whitton [**116**] had goods worth £264 whilst the inventory of James Lowery [**76**], seemingly a mercer, totalled £248. By far the wealthiest, however, with an inventory total of £928, was Thomas Barstow [**15**], also a grocer. In the case of such tradesmen, their inventory totals were undoubtedly boosted by the inclusion of both household goods and merchandise.

Unsurprisingly, since all the burgage properties adjoining the High Street had common rights of pasture on the town moors, many of the deceased owned animals, even if only a single horse, two or three cows or a few pigs.[62] Animals and crops were usually the most valuable items in the inventories. William Neesome [**42**], a yeoman, had seven cows worth £11, together with other animals valued at £10 15s as well as part of a haystack worth £5. His household goods, however, were valued at only £1 14s 6d, whilst his purse and apparel had a value of only 13s 4d. The linen weaver George Robinson [**59**] had goods worth £140, of which £80 was for 85 quarters of barley and malt and a further £15 was for six horses. By contrast, items

61 See the discussions in Arkell, Evans and Goose (eds), *When Death Do Us Part*, pp. 95–102; Drury, 'Inventories in the probate records of the diocese of Durham'.

62 The early seventeenth-century wills of Darlington show a similar pattern, with some degree of farming being combined with a trade: Atkinson *et al.* (eds), *Darlington Wills*, p. 37.

pertaining to his trade (two looms and quantities of cloth) were worth just over £14. In similar vein, John Kaye [**93**], gentleman, had his purse, apparel and household goods valued at only £10 whilst his animals and crops were worth £195. Several of the tradesmen also held land. These included John Rymer [**68**], a carpenter, who, as his will made clear, held four closes. His accompanying inventory includes wheat, covering some 13½ acres, at £27, together with 7½ acres of peas and beans worth £7 10s.

A number of the documents reveal evidence of money being lent on bond between individuals. In addition to being a carpenter by trade and engaging in substantial farming activities, John Rymer [**68**] appears to have acquired some of his wealth through money-lending activities. He was owed two bonds of £5 and three of £10, together with £20 for a mortgage. He was also owed money for sheep. The inventory of Henry Banister [**149**], a mason, dated 1718, suggests that he apparently dealt at a far higher level, since he was owed the sum £400 for unspecified bonds and 'other securityes'.

While some were keen to acquire money, other testators felt the need to make some provision for those less fortunate than themselves. Fourteen wills mention bequests to the poor.[63] The merchant Thomas Barstow [**4**] left £2 10s to the poor of Northallerton, along with 10s to the poor of Brompton and 5s to those of Romanby, to be distributed amongst them before or at the time of his burial. He left a further £6 13s 4d as 'small stock' for the benefit of the Northallerton poor. The interest from this was to be distributed, at the discretion of the overseers of the poor and the churchwardens, to ten of the 'needfullest widdowes' on the eve of Easter. His mother, Jane Barstow [**29**], made a similar provision in her will, bequeathing to the poor of Northallerton £10, the interest of which was to be given to the poor each year on the anniversary of her death. She left a further £6 to be distributed to the poor at the time of her death. Others made similar bequests, often specifying one-off payments, to be made at the time of the testator's decease, as well as larger sums, of perhaps £5 or £10, to be invested for long-term poor relief.

Most of the benefactors were well-to-do members of local society, such as gentry, yeomen or businessmen, and kinship links were evident between a number of the testators, for example those of the Wilson family [**5, 7**], the Flowers [**33, 73, 124**], the Tukes [**63, 88, 106**] and, as mentioned above, the Barstows. In their case, too, religious

63 Nos 4, 5, 7, 12, 29, 33, 46, 63, 73, 88, 106, 112, 124, 150.

belief may have been a motivating factor, for the wills of both Thomas and Jane Barstow had brief but strongly religious preambles, suggesting they were following what was, perhaps, an established tradition of almsgiving.

Houses and their contents

Roger Gale noted that the 'burgage-houses' in Northallerton had been 'truly in number but 194 and a half', these being distinguished from the remaining houses by the fact that, in addition to carrying the right of election for the owners, they held right of common on the North Moor. However, by the time Gale was writing, in 1739, the number of burgages had increased to 204. He pointed out that since those that had 'crept clandestinely into this privilege' were indistinguishable from the rest, 'they are likely to retain the privilege'.[64]

From the late seventeenth century and throughout the eighteenth, the houses on the high street burgage plots were rebuilt and many of these properties survive today. As the inventories in this collection indicate, some of these were very substantial houses. That of Thomas Barstow [**15**], for example, had 15 rooms, whilst Robert Dennis's [**6**] had 14. A few inventories mention possessions without identifying rooms, whilst others appear to omit mention of rooms which contained nothing of value. The majority of the inventories do, however, provide details of the rooms, their functions and contents.

Although most usually found in the inventories, descriptions of rooms did, from time to time, appear in wills. In his will, dated 1705, William Robinson [**107**] gave precise details of the layout of the house in Northallerton which he shared with his two sons and two other named occupants. In his will, William divided the various rooms within the house between his two sons and his daughter. Elizabeth Wilson [**5**] and Helen Adston [**77**] made similar arrangements for their children.

The 'forehouse', the main living area which in some smaller dwellings was also used for cooking purposes, was regularly mentioned in inventories.[65] On occasion the term 'hall' was used instead, the inventory of Michael Pemberton [**72**], drawn up in 1687, making it clear that these rooms were generally one and the same. Most inventories mention at least one parlour, sometimes more,

64 Gale, 'Historical account', p. 209.

65 See the discussion in Johnson (ed.), *Probate Inventories of Lincoln Citizens*, p. lxvi.

while the third most regularly noted room on the ground floor was the milk house. Kitchens also featured frequently. Most of the properties had upper rooms, usually described as chambers, often identified by reference to the rooms situated directly below. Only two inventories, those of George Hudson [**132**] and John Prest [**134**], compiled in 1712 and 1713 respectively, mention a garret.

Precise locations of the properties themselves are difficult to discern from the probate evidence. Where this is mentioned, often it is only to state whether the house was situated on the east or west row of the town's one long, main street. Only two houses are mentioned by name, one known as 'Blew House', which was occupied in 1713 by Stephen Prest [**134**], and the other known as 'Jecklow', held in 1711 by John Midgley [**130**], which lay outside the town and was still in evidence in the twentieth century.[66]

Standards of living

One inventory which is particularly informative concerning the standard of living of one of the town's wealthier tradesmen is that of James Lowery [**76**], dated January 1689. It does not specify his occupation but the evidence clearly indicates that he was a mercer. As such he sold a range of good quality material such as holland (fine linen), alamode (glossy black silk), muslin and cambric for clothes, diaper and damask for table cloths, and lace, ribbons and quilting for petticoats and waistcoats. The inventory of the merchant Anthony Watson [**87**], who died in 1693, shows that he stocked even more exotic trimmings, including gold and silver thread and lace, silk and mohair fringes, gallownes (narrow trimming often of gold or silver) and callimankers (glazed wool or satin cloth for petticoats). Other goods included several types of material, such as heavy cloths, possibly used for curtains or bedding.

Lorna Weatherill's analysis of consumerism in this period, using inventories from eight dioceses, including Durham, sought to compare aspects of domestic culture in the North-East with that in other parts of the country. She focused upon the ownership of five 'key' household items: curtains, books, clocks, china and earthenware. While many of the findings of her study go beyond the scope of this discussion, light is shed on some of them by the documents presented in this collection. Weatherill suggested, for instance, that far fewer books were recorded in the North-East than in other

66 Now Jeckelow Grange (SE 351 944).

areas, while china, on the other hand, a relatively new commodity, was far more widely owned in this region than elsewhere, apart from London. Her analysis also found that social position was, for example, associated with the ownership of three of these items, namely curtains, books and clocks.[67] Curtains appear in a number of the Northallerton inventories although mostly in the context of bed furnishings, with a blacksmith, a lorimer (i.e. a harness maker) and a carpenter amongst the owners [**32**, **46**, **68**]. In three cases, however, they are specified as being for windows [**15**, **91**, **131**]. Unfortunately, the social standing of only one of these testators, the prosperous grocer Thomas Barstow [**15**], can be identified from the inventories. Books, including three bibles and one 'mapbooke', appear in seven inventories, three belonging to members of the gentry and a fourth to the local curate, William Cooper [**7**, **25**, **137**, **96**]. Of the remaining individuals, John Hudson [**22**] left 'five ould books', whilst Mary Hunton [**120**], whose goods were appraised along with those of her sister Merrial Nelson [**122**], also left a bible and 'other books'. Jane Bradley [**83**] left nine books worth 4s out of a total estate of only £8 13s. China appears in seven Northallerton inventories [**15**, **26**, **32**, **35**, **46**, **58**, **131**]. Unfortunately, the occupations of only three of these testators can be identified, a grocer, an innkeeper and a lorimer. The evidence is insufficient to add weight to the finding that ownership of this commodity was slightly higher in the North-East amongst tradesmen than those higher up the social scale. It is striking that earthenware, which was less used in this region, is mentioned little in this collection, although pewter utensils appear regularly. Clocks, evident in five documents, were, however, often owned by the gentry and professional classes as illustrated in the inventories of the gentlemen George Wilson [**7**] and Michael Pemberton [**72**], the curate William Cooper [**96**] and the well-connected tallow chandler Stephen Prest [**147**].[68] These items were almost certainly long-case clocks and probably early examples, in Northallerton, of a commodity that was to become increasingly sought after as the eighteenth century progressed, as the career of the noted local clockmaker Hugh Pannell

67 L. Weatherill, *Consumer Behaviour and Material Culture in Britain, 1660–1760*, 2nd edn (London, 1996), pp. 51–2, 63–87; L. Scammell, 'Was the North-East different from other areas? The property of everyday consumption in the late seventeenth and early eighteenth centuries', in H. Berry and J. Gregory (eds), *Creating and Consuming Culture in North-East England 1660–1830* (Aldershot, 2004), pp. 12–23.

68 Nos 7, 72, 96, 132, 147; Scammell, 'Was the North-East different?', p. 19.

illustrated.[69] Other luxury goods mentioned included leather chairs, looking glasses and feather beds. Amongst the more unusual possessions were the gaming tables owned by the gentleman Michael Pemberton [**72**] and the 'paire of virgenalls' noted in the inventory of John Hudson [**22**].

CONCLUSION

The Northallerton wills and inventories in this collection provide an invaluable insight into the nature of social and economic life in a northern market town during the late seventeenth and early eighteenth centuries. In many respects, Northallerton continued to function in this period as it had done hitherto, fulfilling its role as a small market town serving its rural hinterland.[70] As such, a significant number of townsfolk continued to engage in some degree of agricultural activity, whilst at the same time pursuing their primary occupations in trade or the professions. Yet, as the occupations mentioned in the probate records illustrate, the town had always performed more than a purely rural function, thanks to its position on one of the country's strategic trade and travel routes. Moreover, as a result of the apparent upturn in its economic prosperity, Northallerton was beginning to acquire the sophistication which, in time, was to enhance further its role as a centre of regional importance. This growing sense of confidence was evident in the urban regeneration that was taking place in the town, with its newly paved high street and handsome buildings. It was also apparent in the increasing numbers of luxury items mentioned in the wills and inventories of some of the wealthier testators, whose tastes were, undoubtedly, influenced by the growing consumerism of the period.[71] Admittedly, as the varying socio-economic fortunes of the testators covered by the probate records show, not all of its residents were as prosperous; yet, as is evident from the documents contained in this collection, many were engaged in the production of goods and services, thus adding further to the town's prosperity and its growing reputation as a prominent and attractive centre of trade.

69 For details of Northallerton's clockmakers and further information regarding the town in the eighteenth century, see D. F. Severs, *Northallerton's Clockmakers: Hugh Pannell and his Successors* (Northallerton, 1998) and idem, *A Concise Guide to the Clockmakers of Northallerton and their Clocks* (Northallerton, 2008).

70 Newman, *Late Medieval Northallerton*, pp. 100–14.

71 Scammell, 'Was the North-East different?', pp. 21–2.

EDITORIAL METHOD

The documents in this volume are presented, as far as possible, in order of death/burial rather than date of probate which, in some instances, was a considerable time after the death of the testator. The reference given at the head of each document indicates the location of the original. The dates given in these references refer to the date of probate rather than death, leading in some cases to discrepancies between the dates in the reference and those we have assigned to each document, which are dates of death and use post-1752 dating conventions. The documents are numbered from 1 to 153 for ease of reference. These are the numbers used in the Introduction to identify individuals and/or documents.

Original spelling has been retained, although punctuation and the use of capital letters have been modernised and page layout has been standardised. Abbreviations and contractions have been expanded silently, except in cases where the meaning is not clear.

Editorial conventions used:

[*signed*]	editorial comment
dec[eas]ed	abbreviated text expanded editorially
<also>	text interlined in original
~~Thomas~~	text deleted in original

Sums of money are consistently expressed in Arabic numerals in the manuscript inventories. Some use 'li' instead of '£' or have no headings to columns; entries have been standardised by inserting '£ s d' symbols in column headings. Totals have been added to inventories where necessary and interim totals omitted where original inventories cover several pages. Sum totals have also been corrected where required.

NORTHALLERTON WILLS AND INVENTORIES
1666 TO 1719

1. WILLIAM STAVELEY, 1665

DPRI/6/T/1675/S1

In the name of God, amen, March the 21th 1664 [*21 Mar. 1665*]. I, William Staveley of North Allerton being of perfecte memory and remembrance, praysed be God, do make and ordaine this my last will and testimente in maner and forme following, videlicet: First I bequeath my soule into the handes of allmighty God my maker, hoping that through the meritorious death and pashion of Jesus Christ my onely saviour and redemer to receive freparden and for giveness of all my sinnes, and as for my body to be buried in Christian buriall at the discretion of my executrix heareafter nominated. Item I give unto my brother Joseph Staveley twelve pence. Item I give unto my sister Jane six pence. Item I give unto my sister Elizybeth six pence. Item I give unto my sister Ann six pence. Item <I give> all the rest of my goods, my house and whatsoever I have I give to my wife to dispose on as she shall thinke good, she paying my legacies and make her sole executrix of this my last will and testement, revocking all other wills and testements. Wittness my hand and seale the day and yeare first above written.

William Staveley <his marke> [*sealed*]

Richard Rimer <his marke>, Edward Rimer <his marke>, George Wayre [*signed*].[1]

[1] Although this will was made in 1665, probate was not granted until 1675; hence the DPR reference. The testator is perhaps to be identified as William Stavely who was buried in Northallerton on 27 March 1665, six days after the date of this will.

2. ELIZABETH EELES, SPINSTER, 1667

DPRI/6/T/1666/E1

In the name of God, amen, the seaventh day of March 1666 [*7 Mar. 1667*]. [I] Elizabeth Eeeles of North Allerton in the county of Yorke,

of Durham, gentleman, and Marke Hall of North Allerton supervisors of this my last will and testament. In witnesse whereof I have hereunto sett my hand and seale this twelveth day of March 1666 [*12 Mar. 1667*].
Luke Cust [*signed and sealed*].[1]
Witnesses Thomas Crosby [*signed*] <juratus>, Edward Meade [*signed*] <juratus]>, Mark Hall [*signed*] <juratus>.

[1] Luke Cust was buried on 22 March 1667, ten days after after making his will.

4. THOMAS BARSTOW, MERCHANT, 1668

BIA/49/2
In the name of God, amen, I, Thomas Barstow of North Allerton in the county of Yorke, merchant, sick in body but of good and perfect memory (praysed be my God) doe make and ordaine this my last will and testament in manner and forme following. First I give and bequeath my soule to almighty God my creator, hopeing that by the merritts and mediation of the Lord Jesus Christ my redeemer I shall be one of those <to> whom my blessed saviour shall pronounce this sentence att the last day – Come yee blessed of my father, inherit the kingdom prepared for you. And my body I give to the dust to be buried att the discretion of my mother and my executor. And as for that temporall estate God hath blessed me with I give and bequeath it as followeth. Imprimis I give unto the poore of North Allerton two pounds tenn shillings to be distributed amongst them att or before my burial and to the poore of Brompton I give tenn shillings and to the poore of Romanby five shillings to be distributed as aforesaid. Item I give unto the poore of North Allerton six pounds thirteene shillings four pence as a small stock to be put forth to the use and benefit of the poore there and the increase and consideration thereof to be dealt upon Easter eaven to tenn of the needfullest widdowes there for ever by the appointment and at the discretion of the overseers for the poore of North Allerton and the churchwardens and there successors for ever. Item I give to my deare and loveing wife twenty shillings to buy her a mourning ringe. I alsoe give her my gelding. Item I give to my mother Barstowe twelve shillings to buy a ring with. To my father Snawdon twelve shillings and to my sister twelve shillings to buy each of them a mourninge ring with. And I give to my brother Christopher Barstow twenty pounds to be payd him within six months next after my death. Item whereas it is not certaine my wife be with childe or noe, and if with childe,

whether a sonne or a daughter, for which childe I am bound to make provision <as> for my two daughters already borne. I therefore will that if the childe my wife is supposed to be with be a sonne, that then I hereby give to my said sonne all my lands, tenements, heraditaments within the county of Yorke and to his heires and assigns for ever, upon the condition and provisos followinge, as alsoe the reversion and reversions, remainder and remainders thereof from and after the death of Jane my mother and Margarett my wife, provided always that my sayd sonne pay to each of my sayd daughters, if they live to accomplish the age of one and twenty yeares or be marryed, the summe of seaventy pounds, the same to be thus payd. Videlicet seaventy pounds to my eldest daughter Elizabeth, her executors or assignes, within twelve months next after the death of my mother, and seaventy pounds to Jane, my youngest daughter, twenty four months next after the death of my mother. Item in case the sayd childe my wife is supposed to be with prove to be a daughter, then I give and bequeath all the land I hold by lease or leases from and under the Right reverend Father in God, John, Lord Bishop of Duresme for tearme of three lives, unto my sayd daughters and the survivors of them, to be shared, parted and devided when they shall accomplish the age of one and twenty yeares. They in the meantime to have the profits of the sayd lands I hold as aforesaid during their minority. Item I give unto my sayd daughters, be they three or but two, and to the survivor or survivors of them (upon the condition and provisos following) the summe of two hundred and sixty pounds over and above my lease to helpe to raise them portions to be put forward for the use and benefitt, within six months next after my death until they shall respectively attaine to the age of one and twenty yeares, by such persons as hereinafter I have given the tuition of my sayd daughters unto, provided always upon the condition that in case I shall have but one daughter living att any tyme within eighteene yeares of my decease, and now issue left by my other children, that then the surviving daughter shall have all the sayd two hundred & sixty pounds with the increase thereof, shee (or in the meantime her tutors or guardians) paying forth of the same unto my brother Christopher Barstowe, his executors, administrators or assignes, the summe of one hundred pounds within twelve months of the death of her sister or sisters, my sayd surviving daughter being by God's permission likely to enjoy a fair estate and good portion beside the hundred pounds aforesaid. And upon this further provisoe & condition that in case both my daughters now living, and that which my wife is but supposed to be with, shall all happen to dye before they accomplish the age of one and twenty yeares or be marryed leaveing no issue, that then I will that Jane (the wife of Richard Lumley, my sister) shall have a full moity of the sayd two hundred and sixty pounds with the increase thereof by reason my brother Christopher will be then my heire att law. Item I desire my deare and loveing mother, by whose care and God's blessing, shee having beene left a widow in the flower of her youth and soe continued, to her great credit of her and hers, that small estate my father left hath beene much increased, that shee will continue a loveing grandmother to my children and give them yearly during her life, forth of the lands in Romanby shee now holdeth as her thirds forth out of my father's estate, which I hereby confirme unto her and her assignes for the tearme of her naturall life, shee paying yearly forth of the same the reserved rent to the cheefe lord of the fee thereof as above, all the overplus over and above tenn pounds yearly. And the sayd reserved rent, which shee shall from yeare to yeare let the sayd land in Romanby, for and during her life to my daughters to helpe towards there education, it being intended that my sayd mother shall onely receive forth of the sayd lands tenn pounds per annum dureing her life and the reserved rent. And that the surplusage be by her payd to my daughters as aforesaid. And I doe herebye intreate my deare and loveing wife to take example att my sayd mother and if God give her the guift of continency that shee continue my widdow dureing the minority of my children. And that shee will be content to accept of fifty pounds in lieu of her thirds forth of my personall estate. And that shee will be carefull of the education of my children whose tuition I give them dureing her widdow hood, desireing that they may be brought up in learning and instructed in the nurture, feare and admonition of the Lord and in decent apparrell cloathed and not otherwise. And if my sayd wife be married then I give from that day forward the tuition of my sayd children to Jane Barstow my mother and Edmund Barstow my uncle and I give my sayd uncle twelve shillings to buy him a ring with in remembrance of me. Item I doe make Robert Snawden my brother in law, Richard Lumley, Thomas Staines and John Pybus, my well beloved friends, supervisors of this my last will and desire them and the survivors of them to advise and counsell my mother, wife and children and perform a good understanding amongst them to prevent all differences that may arise which God in his mercy prevent. And for there care and paines I give unto every one of them twelve shillings to buy every of them a ring with in remembrance of me. I also desire my sayd loveing wife to give my daughters for there education free untill

they come to twelve yeares of age, the better to advance there portions, which, untill after my mother's and my sayd wive's death, will otherwise be but small, and for the rest of my goods and chattells, movable and immovable, my debts and legacies being first payd and funerall expences discharged, I give to be equally devided betwixt my two daughters now borne and I hereby make Margarett my loveing wife sole executrix of this my last will and testament, to whom I give my ring to keepe in remembrance of me, in testimony and confirmation whereof I have hereunto sett my hand and seale the thirteenth day of March in the twentieth yeare of the reign of King Charles the second, annoque domini one thousand six hundred sixty seaven [*13 Mar. 1668*].
Thomas Barstow.
The words (or be married)[1] were interlyned and afterwards sealed, signed and published in the presence of Edmund Barstow, Thomas Crosby, James Slinger, John Snawden, Thomas Waide.

[1] Here and in other witness clauses the brackets are as in the original.

5. ELIZABETH WILSON, WIDOW, 1668

DPRI/6/T/1668/W1
In the name of God, amen, I, Elizabeth Wilson of North Allerton in the countie of Yorke, widowe, being sicke & weake in body but of good & perfect memory, laud and prayse be unto God, doe make & ordaine this my last will & testament this 15th day of June anno domini 1666 in manner and forme followeing: First I bequeath my soule into the handes of allmightie God my mercifull creator hopeing that by & throughe the meritts & sufferrings of Jesus Christ my onely saviour & redeemer to receive a full & free pardon for all my sinnes; and my bodie to the dust to be buried in the west end of North Allerton church yeard neer unto the place wheere my husband was buried. Item I give unto the poore of North Allerton fortie shillings. Item I give unto my grand childe Dorothy Browne, wife of James Browne junior, of North Allerton aforesaid twenty shillings and to her deaughter Jaine Browne ten shillings. Item I give unto Ann Jefferson, my grand childe, ten shillings yearely for foure yeares. Item I give unto my daughter Isabell Flower ten shillings and to every one of her children twenty shilling apiece. Item I give unto my sonne in law Francis Pye twenty shillings to buy a ring & every one of his children twenty shillings. Item I give unto my daughter Ann Pye & her two children the summe of three poundes six shillings

eight pence yearely for four yeares. Item I give unto my sister Dorothy Staines ten shillings and to my sonne Michaell Jefferson ten shillings. Item I give unto my sonne George Wilson and his heires for ever all that the middle part of my nowe dwelling house scituate and being on the West Rowe in North Allerton aforesaid with all & singular profitts of common & commons of pasture whatsoever with the appurtenances theirunto belonging lying & being on North Allerton East Moore otherwise called Hailstone Moore conditionally that he the said George shall and doe pay & discharge all my debtes and legasyes whatsoever. Item I give to my cousines Christopher Snawdon and Thomas Staines either of them five shillings, whom I appoynt as supervisors of this my last will & testament. And all the residue of my goods & chattles whatsoever unbequeathed, my debts paid & funerall expences discharged, I give and bequeath unto my sonne George Wilson whome I make and ordaine my sole executor of this my last will & testament. In witness wheerof I have heerunto sett and putt my hand & seale the day and yeare before mentioned & expressed.
Elizabeth Wilson her marke [*sealed*].[1]
Witnesses heereof, Thomas Staines [*signed*] <juratus>, Dorothy Staines <her marke>, Isabell Flower <her marke>.

[1] Elizabeth Wilson was buried on 22 March 1668, almost two years after making her will.

6. ROBERT DENNIS, 1670

DPRI/6/B/1671/D1
The inventory of the goods and chattles of Robert Dennis late of Northallerton deceased; was prised by William Harris[on], John Hudson, John Hebden & Robert Harrison the 19th day of October 1670.

	£	s	d
His purse & apparrell with the household goods	07	05	04
Item leather, barke, & tubs & other implements	15	00	00
	22	05	04

Prised by John Hudson [*signed*], John Hebden [*signed*], Thomas Pickerin his marke, Robert Harrison [*signed*].[1]

[1] Robert Dennis was buried on 10 October 1670.

7. GEORGE WILSON, GENTLEMAN, 1670

DPRI/6/T/1670/W1

In the name of God, amen, the last day of October in the yeare of our Lord one thousand six hundred & seventy. I, George Wilson of North Allerton in the County of Yorke, gentleman, being sicke in body but of good & perfect memory (praised be God) doe make & ordaine this my last will & testament in manner & forme following. First I committ my soul into the hands of almighty God my creator & my body to be buryed in the churchyard of North Allerton, and for my temporall estate which it hath pleased God to bestow upon me I dispose thereof in manner following. First I give and bequeath to my niece Elizabeth Flower the summe of fifty pounds of lawfull money of England. I give to Jane Browne, (daughter of James Browne), twenty pounds & to James Browne & Elizabeth Browne, (children of the said James Browne), to each of them tenne pounds. I give and bequeath unto Anne Jefferson my niece the summe of fifteene pounds. Alsoe I give to each of my brother in law Francis Pye's foure children tenne pounds & to the two children of my sister Anne Pye tenne pounds apiece. Also I give to the poore of North Allerton forty shillings to be distributed at my decease. Alsoe I give to my servant William Franckland three pounds, to my servant Isabell Flower three pounds & to my servant Anne Squier forty shillings. I give to Dorothy Staines & Elizabeth Lumley twenty shillings apiece to buy them rings & to my kinsmen Thomas Staines & Christopher Snawden each of them ten shillings to buy them rings. I give to my brother in law Francis Pye & to my sister Pye each of them twenty shillings to buy them rings. All the rest of my goods & chattells rights and creedits my debts legacyes and funerall expences being satisfyed and discharged I give & bequeath unto my sister Flower. And I constitute & make the said Thomas Staines & Christopher Snawden joynt executors of this my last will & testament. In witnesse whereof I have hereunto sett my hand & seale the day & yeare first above written.

Geo: Wilson [*signed and sealed*].[1]

Sealed signed & published in the presence of Rich: Conyers [*signed*] <juratus>, Tho: Grasonn [*signed*], William Frankland, his marke <juratus>, Thomas Waide [*signed*].

An inventory of the goods & chattells which were of George Wilson late of North Allerton in the county of Yorke, gentleman, deceased made & apprysed the fifth day of November in the yeare of our

Lord 1670 by Richard Conyers, William Harrison, Thomas Grason & Thomas Waide.

	£	s	d
In primis, his purse & apparell	10	00	00
In the forehouse			
two tables, three chaires, two fourms, a chopping block & two planck fourms	00	15	00
two clocks, one jake, three little buffet stools, one paire of bellows, one paire of tongs, one fire shovell, two reckons, one watering pott, two tiffeneys, one glasse case & other emblements	02	00	00
In the south great parlour			
two standing beds, two feather beds, two mattrices with all other furniture & one empty truckle bed	06	05	00
one long table, a litle table, two buffett fourms, one planck fourme, foure chaires, a long settle, a livery cupboard, one trunck, nyne cushions, two carpets, one paire of tongs & other emblements	03	00	00
In the great chamber over the great parlour			
two standing beds, two feather beds, two mattrices with all other furniture & one empty truckle bed	08	10	00
seven chaires, seven stools, two tables, one fourme, one paire of tongs, one fire shovell, six cushions, three carpets, one looking glasse & other emblements	03	15	00
In the chamber over the litle parlour			
two standing beds with their furniture, one table, one fourme, one close stool, one carpet & an old chaire	02	10	00
In the litle back parlour			
one standing bed with furniture, one truckle bed with a mattrice & a blanckett, one table, one fourme, three chaires, three cushions & a carpett	02	10	00
In the milke house			
one kimling, one tub & fifteene bottles & other emblements	00	15	00
In the buttrey			
nyne silver spoons, two salts & a large silver cup all weighing thirty ounces & a halfe	06	17	03
thirteen pewther flagons, five cans, twelve candlesticks, a quart pott, eleaven chamber pots, eleaven large pewther dishes, eleaven pewther dishes of a lesse size, sixteene litle dublers, three pye plates,			

twelve sawcers, three salts, three porringers, a mustard pott & two brasse candlesticks	08	15	00
one cupboard, one presse, one table, one dresser table, three stools, two chests, three voyders, one churne, six doozen of trenchers, one brasse mortar & pestle, one smoothing iron & shredding knife, two shelves, one paire of jibs & other emblements	02	02	06
In the Northe fore parlour			
one standing bed with furniture, one truckle bed, one chaire, two chests, one cupboard & cushion, one table & carpett, one planck, one cushion, one Bible, one mapbooke & other emblements	04	00	00
one caske of cutt tobacco containing 80 lb ½ at	04	00	06
one caske more best Virginia containing 77 lb ½ at 22d per lb	07	02	01
In the parlour joyneing on the forehouse			
two beds with their furniture, one cupboard, one presse, one pannell chest, one board chest, one warmeing pan, one paire of garden sheers & other emblements	02	15	00
In the Scott chamber			
one standing bed, one truckle bed with furniture, one table & carpett, one fourme, one planck, foure chaires, one liverey cupboard, one stool, one paire of tongs, one fire shovell with other emblements	06	05	00
In the closett chamber			
two standing beds with furniture, one table, one chaire, one stoole & three cushions	05	00	00
In the entry chamber			
two beds with furniture & one chest	01	00	00
In the cellar			
nyne hogsheads, two tubs, three stands, two paire of gantrees	01	10	00
In the buttrey			
two tubs, three barrells & other emblements	00	12	00
In the kitchin			
nyne spits, two paire of tongs, two paire of racks, three dripping pans, one broyling iron, two beefe forks, with other iron emblements	01	10	00
foure brasse pots, foure brasse kettles, eight pans, one scummer, three ladles	03	15	00

foure pailes, foure woodden dublers, one bushell, one flackett, one tray, one swill with other woodden emblements	00 10 00
In the brewhouse	
one lead, one maske fatt, three coolers, one cheese presse, two swine tubs, three sacks, one stand, one woodden bowle with other brewing emblements	03 10 00
In the meal chamber	
one boulting tub, one dough trough with other emblements	00 05 00
In the colehouse coles there	02 10 00
In the stables racks and mangers, two ladders & other emblements	01 00 00
Linnen in severall truncks & chests, sheets thirty two paire, twenty six pillows, twelve table cloaths, six doozen of napkins, ten towells	18 18 00
In widow Flowers kiln thirty two bushells of malt	04 00 00
Corne in the barnes	18 04 08
In the rye flats one stack of hay & fifteene stack barrs	15 00 00
In the yarde & stable broome	01 00 00
Stones on the backside	01 00 00
Compost at the doore	00 10 00
One bore, two sowes & seven other swine	04 10 00
One old gelding	01 00 00
	167 02 00
Booke debts due to the deceased by severall persons whereof a great part are desperate	32 14 00
In all	199 16 09

Richard Conyers [*signed*], William Harrison [*signed*], Thomas Grasonn [*signed*], Thomas Waide [*signed*].[2]

[1] George Wilson was buried on 2 November 1670, two days after making his will. He was the son of Elizabeth Wilson [5].

[2] At the head of the following page: 'Debts due to the deceased', followed by four names and sums of money, all heavily erased and largely illegible. The names of the debtors appear to read: 'Sir Richard [....]ter'; 'George [.........]; 'Luke Cust' and '[........ ....] dec[ease]d'.

8. ROBERT DIXON, 1671

DPRI/6/B/1670/D1

A true and perfect inventory of all the goodes and chattelles of Robert Dixon of North Allerton late deceased taken and appraised by

Thomas Coulson, Thomas Grason, John Savile and John Lickus the one and thirtith day of January 1670 [*31 Jan. 1671*].[1]

	£	s	d
Imprimis, his purse and apparell	03	00	00
In the fore howse			
one table, three chaires, three stooles with other implements	00	13	04
Item one cubbard	02	06	08
Item one brasse pott, one iron pott, two ketles, two pannes & one brasse bason	01	00	00
Item tenne pewter dublers, two flaggons, one quart, one candlesticke, one salt, two cupps with other implements	01	05	00
Item two recons, one pare of tonges, one fire shovell with other implements	00	05	00
In the parlour			
one chare, one stoole, one beddestead with one chaffe bedde and furniture	01	05	00
Item one sett of drawers	00	05	00
In the chamber over the howse			
two halfe headed beddes with furnniture, two chestes, one drippin panne, one kimlin, one tubbe with other implements	02	00	00
In the shoppe			
two beddesteades, one cubbard, one chest and one litle cubbard	03	10	00
Item the workeing tooles there	01	10	00
Item boardes and railes in the chamber over the shoppe	04	00	00
In the stable planke & beddsteades with railes, jeystes and other timber	08	00	00
In the backe shoppe			
six hundred and forty peice of timber att	24	00	00
In the feilds one blacke cowe and some hay there	03	00	00
five paire of course sheetes, one paire linne sheetes, four pillowers with some other linnen	01	05	00
Somme is	57	05	00
Debtes oweing by the deceased			
for rent due att May Day	02	03	00
to John Lickus	05	00	00
to William Garbutt	01	00	00
to Francis Barker	01	10	00
funerall expences	01	10	00

11 03 00

John Lickis [*signed*], John Savill [*signed*], Thomas Coulson [*signed*], Thomas Grasonn [*signed*].

[1] Robert Dixon was buried on 11 November 1670.

9. EDMOND BARSTOW, GROCER, 1671

BIA/52/225

In the name of God amen, I, Edmond Barstowe of North Allerton in the county of York, grocer, being sick of body but of sound and perfect minde & memory praised be to allmighty God for the same doe make this my last will and testament in manner and forme following. And first I commit my soule to allmighty God my creator and my body to be buryed in the church of North Allerton aforesaid. And as concerning my temporall personal estate wherewith it hath pleased allmighty God to blesse me withal, I dispose of it in manner and forme followeing, my debts and funerall expences being first payd and discharged. To every one of my daughters Eliz Barstowe, Jane Barstowe and Issabell Barstowe I give and bequeath the summe of two hundred and fifty pounds to be payd by my executors hereafter named out of my said estate moneys goods and chattells when they shall respectively come to their severall ages of twenty one yeares or shall respectively marry as shall first happen. And in case any of them to dye before she shall attaine the age of twenty one yeares or shall marry then the part of her soe dyeing shall goe to the survivor or survivors of them, equally to be divided, which said two hundred and fifty pounds soe given to each of them as aforesaid shall be in full satisfaction of their severall and respective children parts and portions. Item I give to each of them a full part of my household goods, utensills and plate the whole in fower parts to be devided and one part thereof being already secured to my sonne Thomas Barstowe of deede. Item I give to William Stephenson as a legacy forty shillings. Item to Elizabeth Lambe senior I give as a legacey tenn shillings. To my executors hereafter named to each of them as legacy twenty shillings to buye a ringe. Item I bequeath the tuition of all my said three daughters, till they shall come to their respective ages of twenty one yeares or respectively marry, to my beloved sonne Thomas Barstowe and to my good freind Edward Place of Well in the county of York, whome I desire to take upon them the trouble, and to see their severall and respective portions aforesaid put forth into good hands and them carefully maintained and religiously educated with the interest money thereof comeing, as also the said portions as above limitted to see carefully payd. And the overplus of my said estate, the several summes above mentioned being accordingly payd, equally to devide amongst my said three children Elizabeth, Jane and Issabell. And [I] doe make the said Thomas Barstowe, my sonne, and Edward Place executors of this my last will to whome I committ the management of this affaire hopeing they will see it carefully executed. In witnesse whereof I have set my hand and seale the first day of January anno domini one thousand six hundred seaventy [*1 Jan. 1671*].

Edmond Barstowe.[1]

Memorandum that these words (hereafter named) and these words (moneys goods & chattels) were enterlined and this signed sealed and delivered and published to be his last will in presence of us Thomas Metcalfe, Richard Lumley, Elizabeth Lambe her marke.

[1] Edmond Barstow was buried on 9 January 1671, eight days after making his will. He was the father of Thomas Barstow [15].

10. MARK HALL, YEOMAN, 1671

DPRI/6/T/1672/H1

In the name of God, amen, I, Marke Hall of North Allerton in the county of Yorke, yeoman, being weake in body but of good & perfect memory (praised be God), doe make & ordaine this my last will and testament in manner & forme following. First I commend my soul into the hands of almighty God my creator & my body to the earth from whence it came. And as for my temporall estate I doe dispose thereof as followeth. First whereas upon a former settlement made by mee about the tyme of my first marriage three messuages burgages or tenements with their appurtenances in North Allerton aforesaid are likely to descend and come unto my daughter Elizabeth which is a great part of my estate, & more then would have fallen to her (if the same settlement had not been made), I doe therefore give and bequeath unto my said daughter Elizabeth the summe of five shillings of lawfull money of England in full of her filiall parte or childes portion that shee can or may have or clayme out of my personall estate. Alsoe I doe give and devise unto my deare and loveing wife Anne Hall her heires & assignees for ever all and singuler other my messuages burgages lands tenements & hereditaments whatsoever with their & every of their rights members & appurtenances scituate lying & being within the towne precincts

fields and territoryes of North Allerton aforesaid in the said county of Yorke and all my estate, right, title, interest, revertion & revertions, remainder & remainders, clayme & demaund whatsoever of in and to the same and every or any of them. Alsoe I doe give and bequeath unto my said wife Anne Hall all and singular my goods and chattells moveable and immoveable, rights and creedits whatsoever (my debts legacyes and funerall expences being satisfyed and discharged[)]. Alsoe I doe constitute make and ordaine my said wife Anne Hall <iuratus> sole executrix of this my last will & testament. In witnesse whereof I have hereunto putt my hand and seale the seventh day of January in the yeare of our Lord one thousand six hundred and seventy [*7 Jan. 1671*].
Mark Hall [*signed and sealed*][1]
Sealed signed and acknowledged in the presence of Richard Smith [*signed*] <juratus>, John Abbott [*signed*] <juratus>, John Hebden [*signed*] <juratus>.

[1] Mark Hall was buried on 9 January 1671, two days after making his will.

11. DOROTHY STEVENSON, SPINSTER, 1671

DPRI/6/T/1670/S2
In the name of God, amen, I, Dorothy Steevenson of North Allerton in the county of Yorke, spinster, being sicke of body but of good and perfecte memory (praysed be God) doe make my last will and testamente in manner and forme following. First I give my soule unto almighty God my maker and into the hands of Jesus Christ my soole saviour and redeamer and my body to be buried in the parrish church yard in North Allerton. Item I give and bequeathe unto Jane Dennis and hir sonne fower pounds. Item I give unto Dorothy Flower ten shillings. Item I give unto Margret Bilton tenn shillings. Item it is my will that my brother John Steevenson and my sister Elezabeth Steevenson be my soole executors revooking all other wills I formerly made. In witnesse whereof I have set to my hande and seale the nynteene day of January in the yeare of our Lord God one thousand six hundred & seaventy [*19 Jan. 1671*].
Dorothy Steevenson hir marke [*sealed*].[1]
Sealed & delivered in the presence of John Coats [*signed*], Edward Hutchinson [*signed*] <juratus>.

An inventory of the goods & chattells of Dorothy Stevenson late of

North Allerton deceased and praysed by us whose names as under written the 6th day of Aprill 1671.

	£	s	d
Imprimis, hir purse and hir apperrell	1	10	0
Item 1 bedd & furnitory to it	2	10	00
Item in bonds & bills & debts	10	00	00
Item more in debts	2	00	00
Summa totalis	16	00	00

Robert [....]her [*signed*],[2] Edward Hutchinson [*signed*].

[1] Dorothy Stevenson was buried on 22 March 1671, two months after making her will.

[2] Surname partly illegible.

12. JOHN SNOWDON, YEOMAN, 1671

DPRI/6/T/1671/S1

In the name of God, amen, the third day of Februarii 1670 [*3 Feb. 1671*]. I, John Snowdon of North Allerton in the county of Yorke, yeoman, doe make and ordaine this my last will and testament in manner and forme followinge. First I commend my soule into the hands of God my creator and to Jesus Christ my redemer, and my body to the earth to be buryed in the church yard of North Allerton wheere my father did ly. Item I give unto the poore of North Allerton thre pounds ten shillings to be paid imedieately after my death. Item I give unto the poore of Brumton ten shillings to be given as aforesaid. Item I give unto the poore of Romanby ten groats to be given as aforesaid. Item I give unto each of my daughters forty shillings a peece. Item I give unto Elesebeth Barstow, my granchild, fower pounds to be paid her when she shall come to the age of one & twenty years or be marryed. Item I give unto Jane Barstow my grand childe fower pounds to be paid her when she shall come to be one and twenty years of adge or be marryed. Item I give unto my sonne Snowdon, my sonne Hall and my sonne Lends chilldren everie one of them forty shillings apeece. Item I give unto Alse Smith, daughter of Thomas Smith of Brunton, forty shillings. Item I give unto my wife Dorythy one close called Foxton Flats and one close called North Moore Close and one house wheerein Ellinge Buttre and Richard Spence now liveth, for her naturall life and affter her decease unto my sonne Robert Snowdon and his heires for ever. Item I give unto my sonne Robert Snowdon all my housses and lands unbequeathed, in North Allerton and Brunton and elsewheere to him and his

spinster, being sicke in body but of good and perfect memory praised be God doe make and ordayne this my last will and testament in manner and forme following. First I give and bequeath my soule to almighty God my maker hoopeing and assuredly trusting through the meritts, death and passion of my allone savior Jesus Christ to have full remishion of all my sinns. As for my bodie I committ to the ground from whence it was taken and to be buryed in the church yard of North Allerton. As for my temporall goods I give and bequeath them in manner and forme following. Imprimis I give and bequeath unto Nicholas Prist and Elizabeth his wife theire heires and assignes for ever one messuaige house in Kirby Wiske with the little garth on the backe side with all other appurtinances belonging to the said premisses which is now in the tenure and occupation of one Simon Curle as by my assignemente. And alsoe one barne on the south end of the said garth. And all the rest of the said goods movable and immoveable I give unto Elizabeth Prist, the wife of Nicholas Prist, who I make my soole executor of this my last will and testamente revocking all other wills and testaments. In witness whereof I have set to my hande and seale the day and yeare above written in the presence of
Elizabeth Eeeles hir marck.[1]
Wittnes our hand, Richard Atkinson [*signed*] <juratus>, Alles Attkinson hir marck <juratus>, Richard Cape [*signed*].

[1] Elizabeth Eeles was buried on 15 March 1667, eight days after making her will.

3. LUKE CUST, GENTLEMAN, 1667

DPRI/6/T/1666/C1
In the name of God, amen, I, Luke Cust of North Allerton in the county of Yorke, gentleman, sicke of bodie but of sound and perfect memorie (blessed bee God), doe make my last will and testament in manner and forme following. First I give and bequeath my soule to almighty God hopeing to bee saved by his mercies and by the merits of Jesus Christ my saviour and redeamer and by [*sic*] body to bee buried in the church next to the bodye of my late deseased wife; & I doe give unto my daughters Jane & Alleson, (my debts and funerall expences discharged), all my goods and chattells moveable and imoveable whatsoever to bee equally shared betwixt them; and I doe make my brother in law Lancelott Taylor of the city of Durham, pewterer, my sole executor in trust for the use and on the behalfe of my said daughters; and I doe constitute and apoint Francis Crosbye

heires for ever. Item I give unto my daughter Barstow whatsoever househould goods my wife intended for her. Item the residue of all my goods and chattels moveable and unmoveable whatsoever not bequeathed, my debts paid, legases deducted and funerall expences discharged, I give unto my wife Dorithy and [my] sonne Robert Snowdon (he payinge unto my said wife fower pounds ten shillings per year dureinge her naturall life) who I doe make executors of this my last will and testament. In wittnesse wheereof I have heereunto sett my hand and seale the day and yeare aforesaid.
John Snowdon [*signed and sealed*][1]
Witnesses William Harrison [*signed*], Thomas Smith [*signed*].

A inventary of all the goods & chattells moveable & unmoveable of John Snawdon of North Allerton deceased praised by Richard Lumley, Thomas Barston, William Harrison & Thomas Smith the 11th day of May 1671 as followeth.

	£	s	d
Inprimis, his purse and apparrell	10	00	00
Item in the hall			
2 tables with carpitts, 9 chaires, 5 stooles, one firme, sixe quishons, one little cubbert, one jack, two reckons, one iron randle balke, 2 shelves with other small implements	03	08	00
In the greate parlour			
2 trunkes, one chest, 6 stooles, one cubbert with cubbert clothes, one warmeing pan, one close stoole with pan, one voider, one cabbinett, two land irons, one iron balke, nine paire of sheetes, 12 pillovers, 18 napkins, 15 table clothes & three hand towells	05	04	00
Item in the best chamber			
one table & carpett, one cubbert and cloth, one coverlitt, one paire[2] of blanketts & one rugg	01	06	08
In the chamber over the house & little chamber adjoyneing			
one teaster bed with feather bed and all furniture belonginge to itt, one little bed with furniture, two chaires, one stoole, one chest, 8 furdeeles with other small implements	03	15	06
Item in the little parlour			
two beds with furniture, one stoole, one firme & little table	02	05	00
Item in the buttery			
one flagon, one quart pott, 2 pewther cupps,			

2 candlestickes of brass and one of iron, one cubbert table, one salt, one hogshead, 3 barrells, two shelves with other implements	00	19	02
Item in the milke house			
45 milke bowles, 10 shelves, 3 stands, one tray with other small implements	01	02	00
Item in the kitchin			
9 dublers, 5 saucers, one poringer, one cullingder, 24 trenchers, 3 brass kettles, 3 brass potts, one fryeing pan, 3 pewther chamber potts,1 paire of iron rackes, one brasing morter, one dripping pan, two spitts, 2 reckons, 2 chaires, one cubbert table with other implements	04	00	00
Item in the milne house			
one hand milne, 4 furdeels with other implements	02	06	00
Item in the bouting house			
one beefe tub, one meale tub, 1 broyle iron, one paire of jarsey combs, one paire of garding sheares, 1 bras pan, 1 fire shovle, 2 paire of tongues with other implements	01	03	04
Item in the chamber over the seller			
one bedstead and bedinge, 6 teames, 4 shackles, 2 paire of plough irons, two dikeing spades, one gavelacke, 3 axes, 2 hay spades, 5 ends of new iron and old iron together	03	04	08
Item in the seller two chirnes, 3 tubs & one milke paile	00	10	00
Item in the wood house and the yard wood new and old	01	04	00
Item in the barne & hay house			
corne threshed & unthreshed, one paire of new unbound waine wheeles, 4 harrowes, 2 ploughes, 3 oxe yoakes, one paire of horse geere with hay & other implements	07	00	00
Item in the fould 3 waines or cowpes with some small implements	02	15	00
Item malt in the garners & the kilne & one grate with some other implements	34	00	00
Item 4 oxen, 4 horses, 8 kine, 3 younge beasts, 22 sheepe with 18 lambes	66	13	04
Item corne on the ground, 5 acres of wheate, 9 acres of beans & oates & 6 acres of barley	40	00	00
Item in the feild 31 stackbars	02	10	00
Item three swine	01	10	00

Summa	194 16 08

[1] John Snowdon was buried on 28 April 1671, three months after making his will.
[2] The phrase 'one paire' repeated in MS.

13. JOHN SURBERT, TALLOW CHANDLER, 1671

DPRI/6/T/1671/S2

In the name of God, amen, the nyneth day of May in the yeare of our Lord one thousand six hundred seventy one. I, John Surbert of North Allerton in the county of Yorke, tallow chandler, being weake in body but of good & perfect memory (praised be God) doe make this my last will & testament in manner & forme following. First I committ my soul into the hands of almighty God my creator & my body to the earth from whence it came. And for my temporall estate I doe dispose thereof in manner following. And first in case my wife be with childe I doe give & devise unto such childe & the heires & assignees of such childe all such messuage burgage or tenement with the appurtenances in North Allerton & all my close lying on the North Moore of North Allerton aforesaid. Alsoe I doe give & devise all the estate reall & personall which I gott with my wife unto my said wife. Alsoe I give & bequeath unto every of my owne brethren & sisters & their children five shillings apiece and the remainder of my personall estate I doe give & bequeath unto such childe as aforesaid and in consideration of the guift aforesaid to my said wife my mynde & will is that incase shee be with childe shee shall educate such childe till it attaine to the age of foureteene yeares. And notwithstanding the guift aforesaid my mynde & will is that my father & mother shall enjoy the forehouse & parlour & chambers over them, the stable & halfe of the garden for their naturall lives & the longer liver of them, but in case my wife be not with childe I doe give and devise my said messuage or tenement with th'appurtenances unto my father & mother for their naturall lives & the longer liver of them and after the decease of the survivor of them I doe give & devise the same unto my brother Richard Surbert his heires & assignees for ever but upon this condition that they pay unto my wife yearely & every yeare for her life foure pounds of lawfull money of England upon the eleaventh day of November & the third day of May by equall portions. And alsoe that my said brother Richard shall within six moneths next after the decease of the survivor of my father & mother pay to my brother Robert the summe of thirty pounds if hee be then liveing & in case

hee be dead then to such childe or children as my said brother Robert shall then have liveing equally to be devided amongst them. And in caise there shall happen any failer of payment of the said yearely summe of foure pounds or of the said summe of thirty pounds it shall be lawfull for the partyes aforesaid to whom the same shall be due respectively to enter into the premisses & the same to hold & enjoy till full payment be made. Alsoe I doe give & devise unto my owne sister Mary Surbert her heires & assignes for ever all that my close lying on the North Moore of North Allerton aforesaid with th'appurtenances (the crop of corne now sowne thereon excepted). Alsoe I doe give & bequeath to my brother Cuthbert Surbert three pounds, to my brother Robert three pounds, to my sister Margarett three pounds & to my sister Jane three pounds. Alsoe I give to my wife all my household goods (the utensills & worke geere belonging my trade excepted) which said severall guifts & legacyes to my said wife is to be in full of all demaunds in or to my whole estate. And in case any difference, ambiguity or doubt arise touching this my last will or any clause matter or thing herein conteined the same shall be referred to George Robinson of Borroby & George Dunn of North Allerton whom I desire to order & determine the same. All the rest of my goods & chattells rights & creedits (my debts, legacyes & funerall expences being first satisfyed & discharged) I doe give & bequeath unto my brother Richard Surbert <iuratus> whom I make sole executor of this my last will & testament. Witnesse my hand & seale the day & yeare above written.
John Surbert [*signed and sealed*].[1]
Sealed, signed & published in the presence of Thomas Crosby [*signed*], George Dunn [*signed*], Cuthbert Hall <juratus> his marke, Thomas Robinson, junior, juratus, 2° Junii 1671.

A true & perfect inventory of all the goods and chattalls moveable and immoveable of John Surbert of North Allerton late deceased taken & appraised by Cuthbert Hall, Thomas Marshall, Thomas Robinson & Thomas Grasonn the 30th day of May 1671.

	£	s	d
Inprimis, his purse and apparrell	03	00	00
Item in the shop			
one chest, fower stone of towe, sixe stone of candleweeke, two paire of brass scailes, one large wooden beame & scailes with other implements	05	05	00
Item in the workehouse			
one brass kettle, two chopinge troughs, one candle			

case, fower tubs, one swill, three bowles, one tallow pres, sixe dozen of broashes with other implements of his trade	08	13	04
Item eight stone of tallow	02	00	00
Item two acres & a halfe of barley on the ground	03	10	00
Summa	22	08	04
Debts oweinge to the deceased			
Inprimis, by John Abbott	04	00	00
Item by John Hebden	02	06	00
Item by John Hudson	02	06	00
Item by Jane Dennis	00	10	00
Item by Thomas Cape	00	13	06
	09	15	06

1 John Surbert was buried on 13 May 1671, four days after making his will.

14. JOHN HUDSON, YEOMAN, 1671

DPRI/6/T/1671/H1

In the name of God, amen, I, John Hudson of North Allerton in the county of Yorke, yeoman, being sick in body but of good & perfect remembrance (praised be God), doe make & ordaine this my last will & testament in manner & forme following; first I commit my soul to almighty God my creator & my body to the earth whence it came. Alsoe my minde & will is that after my debts & funerall expences are satisfyed & discharged my wife shall have a third part of all my personall estate. And as for the residue of my whole personall estate I doe give & bequeath the same amongst my six children equally to be devided amongst them. And I doe make Elizabeth <juratus> my wife sole executrix of this my last will & testament. And likewise doe grant the tuition of all my said children unto my said wife, desireing that shee may take the advice & direction of my cousin Thomas Barstow whom I make supervisor of this my last will & testament and I doe desire him to be assistant unto my said wife in any thing touching the execution of this my will. In witnesse whereof I have hereunto sett my hand & seale the three & twentyeth day of September in the yeare of Our Lord one thousand six hundred seventy & one.

John Hudson [*signed and sealed*].[1]

Sealed signed & published in the presence of Rob Stouteville [*signed*], William Cooper [*signed*], Robert Booth, junior.

An inventary of the goods, cattells, debts and rights of John Hudson of North Allerton in the county of Yorke late deceased praised the third day of October anno domini 1671 by Leonard Wass, William Harrison, John Blakelocke and Thomas Crosby.

	£	s	d
Imprimis, his purse and apparrell	02	00	00
In the fore house			
two tables, one cubbert, one long settle, one chaire, one press, one glas case, two paire of tongues, one fire shovle, one paire of bellowes, 3 reckons, one gallow balck with other implements	01	04	10
In the back parlour			
one table, one buffett forme, one pannell chaire and other 4 chaires, fower covered stooles, one cubbert, one standing bed with beding, 5 quishons, one voyder and one warmeing pan	02	12	08
In the seller chamber			
one table, two stools, 2 chaires, one bedstead with hangings	00	11	00
In the greate chamber			
one table & a carpett, one buffett forme, one little table, 6 chaires, one cubbert frame & cloth, one seeing glass with other implements	01	06	08
In the servants chamber one standing bed	00	06	08
In the chamber over the house			
one old table, two old chests, one truncke, one standing bed with beding & one truckle bed	00	13	04
In the yellow chamber			
one table, one buffett forme, 2 standing beds with furniture, one pannell chest with lining, 2 greene chaires & one close stoole with pan	05	18	04
In the greate parlour			
2 tables, one buffett forme, one liverey cubbert, 4 chaires, one standing bed with furniture, one pannell chest, 2 pewther candlestickes with other implements	02	15	00
In the buttery			
16 pewther dishes, one pye plate, 3 pewther candlestickes, 2 porringers, 4 sawcers, 3 quart potts, 6 pint potts, 2 gills & 2 half gills & 6 flaggons	02	08	06
In the seller			
one hogshead of beare, 5 gallons wine & 4 empty hogsheads	02	02	02
In the kitching			

2 brass kettles, 5 brass panns, 3 brass potts, one posnet, 2 driping pans, one fryeing pan, 4 spitts, one paire of racks, 4 table tubs, one teirce, one barrell, 2 pales with other iron implements	03 01 08
In the milke house	
one teirce, milk bowles, one cheese press with other implements	00 10 00
One old horse	01 00 00
One cowe	02 00 00
Fower young swine	01 00 00
Debts oweinge to the deceased	
By Roger Talbott esquire by bond	70 00 00
Oweing by the executors of my brother Barstow, and by the executors of my cozen Barstow	07 16 00
	[*total* 107 06 10]
Debts demanded and alledged to be due by the deceased.	
To Elizabeth Tod by bond	09 00 00
To Mr Edward Thompson	60 00 00
To the executors of my brother Barstow and my cozen Barstow for malt & shop goods	20 06 05
To William Harrison for malt	02 10 00
To Thomas Lashells esquire	03 10 00
To the postmaster for malt	01 10 00
To John Blaickelock	10 18 04
To Jane Barstow	01 10 00
To Richard Sudbert	02 06 00
To Thomas Waide	01 10 00
To Thomas Crosby	00 15 08
To William Robinson	03 00 00
To John Carver	03 00 00
For servants wages	03 00 00
Funerall expenses	07 10 00
	[*Total of debts owed* 130 06 05]

[1] John Hudson was buried on 25 September 1671, two days after making his will.

15. THOMAS BARSTOW, GROCER, 1671

DPRI/6/T/1671/B1

In the name of God, amen, I, Thomas Barstow of North Allerton in the county of Yorke, grocer, being weake in body but of good

& perfect memory (praised be God), doe make this my last will & testament in manner & forme following. First I committ my soul into the hands of almighty God my creator, & my body to be buryed in the church of North Allerton. Also I doe give & bequeath unto my three sisters all my household goods equally to be devided amongst them (such goods as are in the great fore chamber excepted which I give to my sonne, & five large puther dishes which I give to my mother Metcalfe). Alsoe I give to my said three sisters out of my estate soe much as will make each of them three hundred & fifty pounds with that which my father left them to be in full of all which they can clayme as well by my father's will as myne besides the aforesaid household goods. And in case my personall estate will not extend soe farr above the payment of my debts I desire the same may be payed out of my lands. Alsoe I doe give & bequeath unto my sonne one large silver bowl & a doozen of silver spoons in case hee attaine to the age of foureteene yeares. And in case it please God hee dye before the said age of foureteene yeares I doe give & bequeath the same bowl & spoons to my sisters then liveing. Also I give to the postmaster of North Allerton twenty shillings to buy him a ring. Alsoe I give to every one of my ant Hudson's childrens forty shillings a piece, to be payd them as they respectively come to the age of one & twenty yeares, & to every one of my now household servants five shillings a piece. Alsoe I give & bequeath unto Marke Nelson soe much of haberdashers wares & groceryes out of my shopp as shall be worth tenne pounds, & to my uncle William twenty shillings. Alsoe I doe grant the tuition of my sonne unto my father in law Mr George Metcalfe, & give him power to receive the rents & profits of my lands for my sonn's use untill hee shall attaine to the age of sixteene yeares, & and I desire hee may be carefully educated. And my minde & will is that my said father Metcalfe & my cousin Richard Lumley stand tutors for my three sisters in my place. And in case anything remaine of my personall estate after the payment & discharge of my debts & legacyes <& funeral expenses> I give & bequeath the same to my sonne. Also I give & bequeath to my said father Metcalfe & cousin Lumley twenty shillings apiece to buy them rings and doe make my said father Metcalfe & cousin Lumley joynt executors of this my last will & tetament. In witnesse whereof I have hereunto sett my hand & seale the one & twentyeth day of October in the yeare of our Lord one thousand six hundred and seventy one.

Thomas Barstow [*signed and sealed*].[1]

Sealed signed & published in the presence of Thomas Crosby [*signed*] juratus, Marke Nelson [*signed*].

I was present at the publishing of this will. Thomas Metcalfe [*signed*] juratus.

A true and perfect inventary of all the goods & chattells of Mr Thomas Barstow late of North Allerton deceased taken & appraised the 30th day of October 1671 by Leonard Wass, Matthew Morley, Thomas Crosby & Thomas Grayson as followeth.

	£	s	d
Inprimis, his purse & apparrell	20	00	00
Item in the shop cloath stuff and other goods	340	15	06
Item in the fold garth 6 oxen & 2 heiffers	30	00	00
Item in the feild three kine	08	10	00
Item in the stable two geldings & 2 maires	18	00	00
Item in the Chappell Garths one stack of hay	02	00	00
Item in Whern How one pike of hay	05	00	00
Item barley in the barne	18	00	00
Item wheate & mashleion there	36	00	00
Item beanes & oates there	10	00	00
Item in the helme			
3 waines, 2 plowes, 3 horss harrowes, one paire of oxe harrowes, 4 teames, 2 plowes, one cart, five yoakes, one old waine with other implements of husbandry	09	00	00
Item 3 stand heckes	00	03	00
Item compost in the feild and aboute the house	03	00	00
Item corne sowen in the feild	07	10	00
Item in the yeard one swine	00	16	00
Item att the garth end two stickes of wood and one old sawe horse	00	10	00
Item in the low stable sixe plowe beames and five axle trees	01	01	06
Item in the lime house 4 horse load of lime	00	05	00
Item in the fold garth 4 swine troughs & 5 stones	00	06	00
Item in the hay barne sixe load of hay	02	00	00
Item in the ware house one cheese press, one lead candlecase with some old tubs	00	17	00
Item in the malt chamber & kilne			
2 cha<u>lder of malt, 2 bushells one halfe bushell, one malt grate, 3 shovles, one kilne haire, 7 sackes, one windring cloth, one lead cistern & trough, 2 skuttles, one paire of tongues with other implements	17	00	00
Item in the coale house & kilne coales	05	10	00

Item att the well two stone troughs, one stone with some slates	00	03	00
Item in the milne house one hand milne, two chests, one ladder with other implements	03	00	00
Item in the stable three ladders, bridles & sixe wain felfs	01	03	00
Item 37 stack bars	01	15	00
Item in the helme 8 bars, 9 planckes, one paire of coupe stanges & other old wood	00	13	04
Item on the backside of Thomas Grayson's in the garth & barne there some old timber	01	06	08
Item in the fore house two tables with carpetts, one dresser, one pannell chaire, one wand chaire, 2 leather chaires, two covered chaires, one child chaire, two buffett stooles, one paire of bellowes, 4 iron reckons, two smothing irons, 2 brass laddles, one scumer, one baister, two paire of snuffers, one fire shovle, one paire of tongues, one cole rake with other implements	02	14	00
Item fower brass candlestickes	01	00	00
Item five large pewther dishes	03	06	00
Item one hollow dish, one pie plate	00	06	00
Item 14 trencher plates	01	05	00
Item one seeing glass	00	02	06
Item one fowleinge peece	00	08	00
Item one iron jacke	00	05	00
Item in the buttery three flagons, three cans, one dozen of pie plates, one dozen of trencher plates, two possett bowles, five porrengers, ten pewther dishes, 2 chamber potts, one large salt, one glass case, 3 dozen of wooden trenchers, 2 paire of iron rackes and other implements	04	13	0
In the milke house one beefe cisterne	03	00	00
Item one press, one saife, & one cubert	00	15	00
Item 7 shelves, one firme, 18 wooden bowles, 4 cheese fatts & other implements	00	14	00
In the parlour one table & carpet, one french table & carpet & sett worke chaires, one child's chaire, one wand chaire, sixe covered stooles, one wood cisterne, one paire of tongues with other implements	05	00	00
In the parlour closett			

5 dozen of trenchers, one cheyney dubler, 7 custard potts, 7 glass potts, 6 salts, one candle chest with other implements	01	10	00
In the entry one pike, one halbert, one glass case with some glasses	00	10	00
In the chamber over the house			
one standing bed with hangings & furniture, one pannell chist, one long settle, one shelfe & other implements	04	00	00
In the maid's chamber			
one standing bed with hangings & furniture, one truckle bed with furniture, one chist & some implements	04	10	00
In the far chamber			
one standing bed with hangings & all furniture, one truckle bedstead, one liverey cubbert, one round table, one paire of drawers, two chaires, sixe stooles, one boxe, one chist, one trunck & tongues with other implements	09	06	08
Item one oyle press	00	06	08
Item in Marke chamber			
one standing bed with hangings & furniture, one truckle bed with furniture, two old chaires, one trunke, one chest, one skreene, one stoole & some implements	04	00	00
In the greate chamber			
one standing bed with curtaines & furniture, one dozen of covered chaires, one long stoole, one hanging shelfe, two tables & carpetts, two window curtaines, 2 cushnetts, one other cushnett, one large seeinge glass, one wand baskett, one wand chaire, one bason, one chamber pott with some other furniture	20	00	00
Item in the chist there one paire of 20ty yeards sheetes	02	05	00
Item two paire of 15 yeards sheets	02	00	00
Item three paire of 10 yeards sheetes	01	10	00
Item two damask square clothes	01	10	00
Item two fine square clothes	01	00	00
Item one dyaper square cloth	00	04	00
Item two lin square clothes	00	05	04
Item 15 pilloevers	01	10	00
Item one long cloth, one square cloth & 12 fine huggaback napkins	01	05	00

Item one little dyaper cloth & 11 little napkins	00	10	00
Item one little dyaper cloth & 5 napkins	00	10	00
Item 5 little huggaback napkins	00	02	06
Item 2 huggaback towels & 1 dyaper towell	00	04	00
Item 20 yeards of fine huswife cloth	02	04	00
Item 11 yeards of fine huswife cloth	01	02	00
Item 10 yeards of course huswife cloth	00	12	06
Item 4 yeards of huswife cloth	00	06	08
Item 6 yeards of course huggabacke	00	03	00
Out of the chist one paire of wide sheetes	00	16	00
Item two paire of theire owne bed sheetes	00	13	04
Item one greate linn cloth & 11 napkins	01	10	00
Item one greate square cloth, one little square cloth & 15 fine huggaback napkins	01	02	00
Item nine pillovers	00	13	06
Item one greate square cloth, one little square cloth & 12 course huggaback napkins	00	17	00
Item one large dyaper cloth & 7 napkins	01	01	04
Item 2 huggaback napkins & 2 linn towells	00	04	00
Item one large fine elwide sheete	00	07	00
Item 20 yeards of Hamburgh cloth	00	06	08
Item one square linn cloth	00	02	08
Item in the kitchin one leade	02	10	00
Item three brass kettles	02	10	00
Item fower brass pans	00	06	08
Item one large brass pott & 2 dripping pans	01	00	00
Item two little brass potts	00	06	08
Item one old cubbert & one old call	00	03	04
Item one maskefat, one cooler, one guile fatt & one salt tub with salt	01	06	08
Item five spitts, 1 chane, 1 buffett stoole, 2 cheese troughes, 1 daugh trough, 2 haire tempses, 1 paire of racks & one galley balke & one reckon	00	17	00
Item one chirne, 1 swill, 2 flasketts, 2 bowles, 3 pailes with other implements	00	10	00
In William parlor & the chamber one servants bed, one old table, two old chaires, two hogsheads, one close stoole & pan, one meale tub, one pewther still, one chirne, 1 screw press, two feather tubs, one bagg of feathers & other implements	02	00	00
Item in the drinke butterie 3 hogsheads, one large kimlin & one large chirne	00	10	00

Item 2 lb 3 oz haberdupoize of plate att 4s 4d	07	11	08
Item 1 lb 7 oz more att	04	19	08
Summa totalis	660	16	06
Item booke debts & other debts oweing to the deceased	267	19	11
In toto	928	16	05

[1] Thomas Barstow was buried on 27 October 1671, six days after making his will. He was the son of Edmond Barstow [9]: C. J. D. Ingledew, *The History and Antiquities of Northallerton in the County of York* (London, 1858), p. 196.

16. THOMAS SQUIRE, 1672

DPRI/6/B/1671/S1

February the 17th 1671 [*17 Feb. 1672*]

An appraisment of the goods of Thomas Squire late of North Allerton deceased praised by John Skelton, John Unthancke, Thomas Dennis and Christopher Hunton as followeth[1]

	£	s	d
Imprimis, his purse and apparrell	03	06	08
Item money oweing to him by John Harwood	01	03	00
Item more oweing to him by George Smith of Ripon	04	14	00
Item more oweing to him by Tom Richardson	00	14	00
Item more oweing to him upon bond	10	00	00
Item more oweing to him upon bond	10	00	00
Item utensalls of house pewther	00	13	04
Item one cubbert, one pannell chist and one settle att	01	06	08
Item two tables, one firme	00	08	00
Item three chaires three stoole & two clog stooles	00	05	00
Item 18 spoones, a plate flaggon, a plate candlesticke, one lantron, one brasse and one grator	00	02	6
Item putter[2] vessell & wooden vessell	00	04	00
Item fifteene quishons	00	07	00
Item one brass pott & three brass pans & one brass laddle	00	05	06
Item one spitt, one reckon, one fire shovle, one paire of tongues & one paire of bellowes	00	03	00
Item materiall things in the milke house	00	05	00
Item one hogshead one kimlin and one tub	00	08	00
Item coales prised att	00	08	00
Item one glass case	00	00	6
Item two bedsteads and beding belonging thereto	01	06	8
Item the things belonging to the whole chamber	00	02	00
Summa	36	02	10

Debts oweing by the deceased			
for rent	01	00	00
oweing to Thomas Buttery	01	00	00
given to his brother Ralph Squire	05	00	00
funerall expences	05	00	00
Summa	12	00	00

[1] Thomas Squire was buried on 13 February 1672.

[2] Reading of second letter uncertain; the meaning is presumably 'pewter'.

17. THOMAS LENG, 1672

DPRI/6/B/1672/L1

A true & perfect inventary of the goods & chattells of Thomas Leng late of North Allerton in the county of Yorke deceased & apprized the eleaventh day of Aprill 1672 by those men whose names are hereunto subscribed videlicet,

	£	s	d
Imprimis his purse & apparrell	01	00	00
Item a house & garth	20	00	00
Item money	35	00	00
Summa totalis	56	00	00

The apprisers' names. John Tarran, William Raper, John Calvert, William Rowth his marke.

18. HENRY POWLEY, YEOMAN, 1672

DPRI/6/T/1674/P1

In the name of God, amen, the last day of February in the yeare of our Lord one thousand six hundred seventy one [*29 Feb. 1672*]. I, Henry Powley of North Allerton in the county of Yorke, yeoman, being sick in body but of good & perfect memory (praised be God) doe make this my last will & testament in manner following. First I commit my soul into the hands of almighty God my creator & my body to be buryed in the churchyard of North Allerton. I give and devise to my loveing wife Anne Powley the house wherein I live for her life & after her decease I give & devise the same house with th'appurtenances unto my sonne Henry Powley & to the childe which my wife shall next bring forth their heires and assignes for ever. Alsoe I give unto my said wife two closes lying on the North Moore of North Allerton aforesaid untill such tyme as my youngest childe shall attaine to the age of foureteene yeares. And after I give & devise one of the said closes (to witt) that joyning on Richard Stringer unto my sonne James Powley his heires and assignes for ever, hee paying to my daughters Anne & Elizabeth three pounds a piece within twelve moneths next after the same shall fall to him. And in case hee fail to pay the same it shall be lawfull for my said two daughters to enter into the said close & hold the same till the severall summes be payd to them. Alsoe I give & devise to my sonne William Powley his heires & assignes the other close called Gallicarr with th'appurtenances. All my goods & chattells I give unto my said wife after the payment of my debts & funerall expences & doe make my said wife sole executrix of this my last will & testament. Witnesse my hand & seale the day & yeare above written.

Henry Powley [*signed and sealed*].[1]

Sealed, signed & published in the presence of Jane Rimers marke, Thomas Smelt <iuratus> [*signed*], Darathy Dunne hir marke, Ellenor Buttery hir marke <iuratus>.

An inventory or praysment of the goods & chattell of Henry Powley deceased by us whose hands are underwritten, Aprill 18, anno domini 1672:

	£	s	d
Imprimis, his purse and his apparell	00	13	00
Item a bed in the parlour, a table and chest, a press & a forme	00	13	00
Item a chaffe bed, a paire of sheets, and a blankett	00	03	00
Item in the chamber over the house one standing bed, & a truckle bed, a chest, a coffer, a livery cubbert & one glasse case	00	10	00
Item in the chamber over the parlour, two tables, two formes, a chest, a cradle, a wanded chaire	00	10	00
Item in the work-house a kettle, two panns & a pott, a cubbert, a churne, a kimlinn & two barrells	01	10	00
Item a loame & that which belongs to it	0	10	00
Item a truckle bedd	00	01	06
Item in the milk-house 14 boules, 9 shelves	00	04	00
Item in the forehouse nine pewter dishes, a flagon, three pewter cans, two candlesticks, and two salts, three pewter cupps, ten pewter spoones	00	10	00
Item a voydor & two chaires with two spitts	00	02	00
Item one paire of coarse sheets	00	02	00
Item one black cow	01	13	04
	07	01	10

The debts of the said Henry Powley which he owed were these:

Imprimis, to Robert Banks	03	00	00
To Mistress Jane Barstow	00	09	00
To John Skelton	00	12	00
To William Robinson	00	10	00
To Dorothy Knowdon	00	06	08
To Robert Heardman	00	10	00
Item owen to Thomas Kirby	00	19	00
To the schoolmais[t]er	00	10	00
To Ellenor Buttery	00	05	00
To James Whittons	01	01	00
[*Total of debts owed*	08	02	08]

George Wayres [*signed*], Richard Rimer [*mark*], Edward Rimar [*mark*], John Rimar [*signed*].

[1] Henry Powley was buried on 8 March 1672, a week after making his will.

19. GEORGE MILLER, GLOVER, 1672

BIA/54/23 [probate copy]

20 May 1672

George Miller of North Allerton, sonne of Thomas Miller late of Stainely Rachners, deceased, in the parish of Stainely in the countye of Yorke.[1] The aforesaid George Miller of Northallerton in the countie of Yorke, glover, being sicke in body but of a good and perfect memorie doe for the peacable and quiet settlinge and disposal of my temporall estate make this my last will and testament in manner and forme following. First I doe make and appoint John Wells, my now master, executor of this my last will and testament and therefore doe give and bequeath unto him all my personall estate with all goods and chattels, rights, credits, my debts and legacies being paid and funeral expenses beinge discharged, and with legacies being as followeth. Imprimis I bequeath my soule to God who gave it and my body to be buried in the church yard of Northallerton. Item I give to my father in law and mother in law two shillings. Item I give to my uncle Frances Miller two pounds. Item I give to my brother William Miller tenne shillings. Item I give to my brother Thomas Miller tenne shillings. Item I give to my brother Robert Miller tenne shillings. Item I give to my brother Francis Miller tenne shillings. Item I give to my brother Christopher Miller tenne shillings. Item I give to my sister Margrett Miller tenne shillings. Item I give to my sister's sonne John

[…][2] five shillings. Item I give to my master's sonne Edward Wells five shillings. And all the rest and remainder, if any be, I give and bequeath unto my master John Wells as aforesaid whome I doe make executor of this my last will and testament. In witnesse whereof I have hereto sett my hand and seall the day and yeare first above written.

George Miller his hand and marke

Sealed and delivered in the presence of Cuthbert Surbat his mark, Christopher Lasenby, John Skelton.

Note that my master John Wells is not to pay these legacies to any of my brethren and sister until within one twelve months after that they come to the age of one and twentie years and if any dye the money to rest and remaine in the hands as due to my master John Wells. Note that this [was] written before the sealing and deliverie hereof.

1 South Stainley, Yorkshire West Riding (SE 30 63).

2 Surname illegible.

20. WILLIAM STAINES, 1672

DPRI/6/B/1672/S1

An inventary of the goods and creditts cattalls and chattalls of William Staines late of North Allerton deceased which were not administred by Katherine Staines his widdow and Bridgett Staines his daughter, administratixes of the goods & chattells of the said deceased.

	£	s	d
Inprimis, a lease of 10[1] certaine grounds in North Allerton called Appleegarthes for nine yeares yett to come valued att	50	00	00

John Skelton [*signed*], Henry Flower [*signed*].

1 Reading uncertain. The word 'of' has been repeated, then partly erased and modified, perhaps to read '10'.

21. SAMUEL MERINTON, 1673

DPRI/6/T/1673/M1

A true and perfect inventary of all and singuler the goods, chattells, rights & creditts, which were of Samuell Merinton late of North Allerton in the county of Yorke deceased made and apprized the 29th day of May 1673 by George Metcalfe, George Meriton, Marmaduke Flower and George Drybrough as followeth.[1]

	£	s	d
Inprimis, his purse and apparrell	05	00	00
In the hall			
Item one longe table and firme	00	06	08
Item one square table	00	02	06
Item one little square table	00	01	00
Item two pannell chaires and one wrought	00	02	08
Item two buffett stooles and one covered	00	01	00
Item one shelfe and one warmeing pan	00	02	06
Item eight pewter flaggons	00	12	08
Item two pewter chamber potts	00	01	08
Item nine pewter dishes and sixe plates	00	12	04
Item one possett bason and three pottingers	00	01	08
Item five quishons & one paire of bellowes	00	02	06
Item one gallybalk, fire shovle and tongs	00	02	06
Item one cubboard in the chimney corner	00	01	06
Item one chopping knife and one skimmer	00	00	06
Item one smoothing iron	00	01	00
In the streete parlour			
Item one table and firme	00	15	00
Item one pannell chaire and one covered	00	02	00
Item two throwne chaires	00	00	06
Item one covered stoole and three footed stooles	00	01	00
Item one carpett and five quishons	00	05	00
Item one greate cupboard	00	15	00
Item five pewter dishes and three candlestickes	00	14	08
Item three salt sellers & one houre glass	00	02	00
Item one iron candlestick	00	00	06
In the low parlour			
Item one long table and firme	00	09	00
Item one pannell chist & one old cupboard	00	05	00
Item one standing bedstead and curtaines	00	12	00
Item one feather bed & yellow rugg	00	17	00
Item one three footed stoole & one chaire	00	00	06
Item one square table	00	01	06
Item one <old> bedstead and one chaff bed	00	04	00
Item one reckon and one paire of tongs	00	02	00
In the kitchinge			
Item two brass kettles and one pan	00	16	00
Item one brass pott & two other kettles	00	16	00
Item one little kettle, one pot & one pan	00	05	00
Item one reckon and one paire of pothookes	00	01	00

Item one paire of iron rackes and one spitt	00	04	00
Item one driping pan and one table	00	03	00
In the milkehouse			
Item two dozen and an halfe of milke bowles	00	08	00
Item seaven cheese fatts and one kimlinge	00	07	00
Item one doughtrough & one firme	00	02	00
Item three shelves, one chirne & 3 pales	00	05	00
Item one cheesetrough and one fish pan	00	03	06
Item one maske, 1 cooler, & 1 halfe barrell	00	04	00
In the buttery			
Item 15 pewter dishes	01	08	00
Item two pewter pye plates & 4 runletts	00	05	04
Item two pewter candlestickes & two sawcers	00	01	04
Item one hogshead & one barrell	00	05	00
Item one guilefatt and one little box	00	01	00
In the parlour chamber			
Item one long table & firme	00	03	00
Item one chaire & one covered stoole	00	01	04
Item one liverey cupboard	00	04	00
Item one carpett & two quishons	00	01	00
Item two standing bedsteads & curtaines	01	13	00
Item two feather beds & fower bolsters	01	05	00
Item two blanketts, one rugg & one coverlett	00	10	00
Item three rugs & one shelfe	00	01	06
In the hall chamber			
Item one square table and one lookeing glass	00	04	00
Item one pannell chest and one box	00	04	00
Item fower covered chaires	00	03	00
Item one standing bed, curtaines & vallance	00	10	00
Item one feather bed and one bolster	00	10	00
Item two pillowes & one blew rugg	00	02	00
Item one pannell chest & one trunck	00	03	00
Item three little boxes	00	01	06
In the entry chamber			
Item one bedstead and one flock bedd	00	04	06
Item three pillowes and one blanckett	00	01	06
Lynnen			
Item sixe paire of lynnen sheetes	01	10	00
Item 5 paire of harden sheetes	00	05	00
Item nine pillowbeares	00	09	00
Item one huggaback table cloth	00	02	06
Item one dozen of huggaback napkins	00	06	00

Item one little lynnen table cloth	00	06	00
Item one dozen of lynnen napkins	00	03	00
Item one harden table cloth	00	02	06
Item one dozen of harden napkins	00	02	00
In the malt chamber			
Item 124 bushells of malt	11	00	00
Item one dusting malt grate	00	03	04
Item one bushell and one peck	00	01	06
Item one shovle	00	00	04
In the kilne			
Item 79 bushells of malt	07	00	00
Item one haire, one shovle and one paire of tongs	00	06	00
In the stable			
Item one saddle and two pannells	00	02	00
Plough geare			
Item three carts & two waines	09	00	00
Item three teames & two paire of horse geere	00	10	00
Item one spade & one forke	00	00	06
Cattell			
Item eight mares and geldings	20	00	00
Item two oxen and fower cowes	16	00	00
Item one sow and two piggs	01	05	00
Corne on the ground			
Item eight acres of barley	12	00	00
Item three acres of wheate & rye	08	00	00
Item three acres of oates	01	10	00
Item one silver cupp	00	06	00
Debts oweing to the deceased			
In good debts	60	13	10
In desperate debts	18	18	00
Summa totalis	195	17	06
Debts oweing by the deceased			
In debts to severall persons	99	03	06

[1] Samuel Merinton (or 'Meriton') was buried on 18 July 1673.

22. JOHN HUDSON, 1674

DPRI/6/B/1673/H1

An inventory of the goods & cattles, debts & rights of John Hudson of Northallerton in the county of Yorke late deceassed & of Elizabeth his late wife deceassed, praised the seaven and twentyth day of

January anno domini 1673 [*27 Jan. 1674*] by us whose names are here under written.

	£	s	d
Inprimis. In the greate parlour.			
One long table, one firme, one standing bedstead & seates againste the windows	01	00	00
Item in the <back parlour>			
One paire of virgenalls, one buffett firm, one bedstead with curtains & vallance and one wainscott chaire	02	00	00
Item in the fore house			
Two tables, one jack, one gallow balk & doggs, one cubbarte, two shelves, one glasscase, two cubbarts in the chimney corner, two wainesscott window leaves	01	12	00
Item in the great chamber			
One long table, one buffett firme, one bedstead, one cubbart frame & firms	01	13	04
Item in the servant's chamber			
One bedstead with curtains and vallance, one table, one trunck, one chest & one great cheste	01	06	08
Item in the chamber over the house one bedstead	00	03	04
Item in the cellar chamber one bedstead, one table & one counter cubbert	00	15	00
Item in the yallow chamber one table & firme, one little table, one pannell chest, two standing bedsteads	03	00	00
Item in the kitchin one dresser board, one gantrey, one ould tubb with other implements	00	03	04
Item in the stable			
18 firr deales, one rack, one manger, 3 poles, one cheese presse, one gantry	01	01	00
	12	14	8
In the kitchin chamber			
Item two fetther bedds of 5 stone weight, one boulster, six chaires & six stooles, three brass kettles, three brass potts, three brass pans, one brass skellet with other implements	06	00	00
Item in the servant's chamber			
In the trunk one box with some peices of laces, five ould books, two hatts with hat casses, one paire of green searge curtains & vallance & other implements	02	00	00
Item in the chest in the servant's chamber			

Eight paire of sameran sheets, eleaven pillow beares, twelve napkins, two towells, one cubbart cloath, one long table cloath of huggaback, one of diber, one square huggaback table cloath	05	04	00
	13	04	00
[*Total*	*25*	*18*	*08*]

George Thompson [*signed*], William Neesome <his marke>, Richard Smith [*signed*], Edward Hutchinson [*signed*].

23. ROBERT HIRDMAN, CORDWAINER, 1674

DPRI/6/B/1674/H1

The inventory of all the household goods and chattells belonging unto Robert Hirdman of North Allerton cordiner late deceased, prazed by us whose names are underwritten the twentyth day of March in the yeare of our Lord God 1674, and alsoe debts owne unto the deceased and debts owne by the deceased as followeth.[1]

	£	s	d
Imprimis. His purse and apparrell	03	00	00
Item leather in his house broken and whole	08	00	00
Item shooes and boots withall the working gear	04	00	00
Item the brass and puder in the house and kitching	01	10	00
Item in the forehose one cubboard, tables, chares, stools, woodden vessell and imploment things	01	10	00
Item in the parler one bedstead and bedding to it belonging	00	10	00
Item linin in the house, that is to say 2 payre of lin sheets, 2 payre of sammaran sheets with there pillows and one dozen of table napkins & one table cloath	01	00	00
Item for funerall expences	04	00	00
Debts owne unto the deceased in one debt book of desparate debts	02	00	00
Owne unto the deceased	20	00	00
Debts owne by and for the deceased	29	00	00

John Abbott [*signed*], Rechart Mose [*marke*], Hennery Cleff [*marke*].

[1] Robert Hirdman was buried on 3 March 1674. The sum of his inventory is £41 10s 0d. His debts and funeral expenses total £33 0s 0d.

24. CUTHBERT SURBERT, 1674

DPRI/6/B/1674/S1

A true and perfect inventary of all and singuler the goods, cattells, rights and creditts which were of Cuthbert Surbert late of North Allerton in the county of Yorke deceased. Apprised the fifth day of September 1674 by George Robinson, Cuthbert Hall, Cuthbert Surbert and Thomas Waide as followeth.[1]

	£	s	d
Inprimis, his purse and apparrell	05	00	00
Item in the fore house			
two tables, one long settle, three chaires, one firme, 3 little buffett stooles, three other stooles, one cubbert, one glass case, one salt pye and one voyder	02	00	00
Item pewter in the fore house	03	00	00
Item two reckons, fower paire of tongs, one fire shovle, three spitts, 4 brass laddles, three brass scummers and other implements of brass & iron	00	13	04
Item 4 brass kettles, three brass potts, one iron pott, one iron pan, three pans, two driping pans, one paire of rackes and other implements in the kitching	02	10	00
Item in the kitching and buttery, brewing vessell, and in the milke house, bowles and other wood vessell	00	15	00
Item in the parlour			
One feather bed, bedstead and furniture, one cubbert & two tables, two chaires, fower stooles & other implements	02	10	00
Item in the chamber			
Two beds with furniture, one table, two firmes and other implements	03	10	00
Item in the chamber over the kitchinge			
Two beds & bedsteades with furniture & one counter	02	00	00
Item in the chamber over the entry			
Two beds with furniture	01	00	00
Item in the fore chamber			
Two <beds>, bedsteads and furniture, one livery cubbert, one table, fower chaires, one firme, sixe quishons, one carpet and other implements	10	00	00
Item in the same roome one chest with linnen	03	10	00
Item in the field three kine, two calves and fower sheepe	12	00	00
	48	08	04

[1] Cuthbert Surbert was buried on 17 May 1674.

25. PATRICK OGILBY, GENTLEMAN, 1674

DPRI/6/B/1674/O1

An inventary of the goods and cattells of Patrick Ogilby late of North Allerton in the county of Yorke, gentleman deceased. Apprised by Thomas Waide, J. Robinson and J. Slinger the last day of July in the yeare of our Lord 1674.[1]

	£	s	d
Inprimis, his purse and apparrell	02	00	00
Item one saddle bridle and a paire of bootes	00	12	00
Item bookes	00	10	00
	03	02	00
Due upon bond to the deceased	30	00	00
Summa totalis	33	02	00

[1] Patrick Ogilby was buried on 27 July 1674.

26. EDWARD HUTCHINSON, 1674

DPRI/6/T/1674/H1

September the 8 1674. A note of Edward Hutchinson mind that he did declare as followeth unto Flurance Douglas and William Hutchinson. I give unto my eldest daugter Ellisabeth Hutchinson all that of the east side of the house & malt kill and all the goodes moveable & unmoveable within & with out, two key & a hores & a stack of heay, paying unto my sonne Edward Hutchinson tenn poundes.
Witnes our handes, Flurens Douglas <hir marke>, William Hutchinson <juratus> [*signed*].

Imprimis a true & a perfect praisment of Edward Hutchinson goods & chattells lately deaseased moveable & unmoveable

	£	s	d
Imprimis his purss and apparell	01	00	00
Item 7 paire curss sheets	0	10	06
Item 3 cubards	01	15	00
Item 12 table napkins	00	04	00
Item one feather bed & one bolestar & one pillow & one blankit & a rugg & a struell beed & one chist & 2 spining wheels & one bedstead	03	00	00
Item one table & one furme & one chaire	00	10	00
Item 2 carping cloath	00	03	00
Item one teaster beed & one halfe beed & one trunell beed & beed cloats with curtings	01	10	00

Item one table & 5 stouls & a chest	00	10	00
Item foure score yarne	00	05	00
Item one gould ring & a silver ring	00	05	00
Item one beedstead & a feather beed & two pillows & one boulstar & paire sheets & a cuferlit & a blankit	01	00	00
Item one deske & two strunks[1] & two chests	00	10	00
Item two tables & 1 furme & a chaire	00	05	00
Item one stand with ale in it	00	06	08
Item two stemses & a meale box & a chease strough[2]	00	03	00
Item two dozsen table napkins	00	04	00
Item twentie puder dublers & 9 quart flagons	01	10	00
Item 16 sacers & 5 salts & 8 puder candlesticks & 3 puder chamer potts & 3 cups	00	12	00
Item one silver cupp	00	08	00
Item 12 spowns	00	00	08
Item 3 tables, 2 furms, a long settle & 2 chares & foure stouls	01	00	00
Item 12 quishings	00	10	00
Item 4 ketles & 2 pans	02	10	00
Item two brass potts & one iron pott & brass morter	00	12	00
Item one warming pan	00	02	00
Item 2 brass candle sticks	00	01	06
Item one paire racks, two speets & a drepin pan & 3 paire tongs & a fire shovle & paire gibs & fryin pan & a candlestick	00	05	00
Item two reckings & one iron chafein dish & two paire pott croks	00	02	06
Item 1 brass skummer & two brass ladles & iron beafe forke & a chomping knife & a shreding knife, a smothing iron & 3 heeters	00	02	06
Item 7 cheney dublers	00	01	06
Item paire tables & a seeing glass & 1 oure glass & custard plate & kase knifes	00	05	00
Bearhouse			
Item 1 bead steed & one feather beed, 3 paire lin sheets, one paire blankits, 2 cuferlits & one rugg, 2 boulsters & 2 pillows & 3 curtings	07	00	00
Item wood vessell belonging to milkness & brewing	00	10	00
Item five lin sheets & 3 lin table cloats & other litle implements belongin to the house	00	10	00
Item foure swine & seven geese	00	10	00
Item one stacke of hay	02	00	00

Item two kass & a horse	05 10 00
Item one bee hife & five stack barrs	00 07 00
	33 10 10

Praysed by us whose names are heare under writing, William Hutchinson [*signed*], Symon Taylor [*signed*], Thomas Butcher [*signed*], Marke Nelson [*signed*].

[1] 'trunks' is probably meant.
[2] 'trough' is presumably meant.

27. ANNE THOMPSON, WIDOW, 1675

DPR/6/T/1675/T1

In the name of God, amen, the eighteenth day of December in the yeare of our Lord one thousand six hundred seventy four, I, Anne Thompson of North Allerton in the county of Yorke, widow, being weake in body but of good & perfect memory (praised be God), doe make this my last will & testament in manner & forme following. First I committ my soul into the hands of almighty God my creator and my body to be buryed in the churchyard of North Allerton. And for the temporall estate which it hath pleased God to bestow upon me I doe dispose thereof as followeth. First I give and bequeath unto such children as my sonne in lawe John Robinson now hath or thereafter shall have by Elizabeth his wife the summe of fourty pounds of lawfull money of England to be equally devided amongst the said children, and the increase thereof to goe forward for the use & benefitt of the said children, and the whole to be devided amongst the said children by equall shares and proportions as they shall respectively attaine to the age of one & twenty yeares, provided alwayes that if my said daughter Elizabeth Robinson shall fall into decay or need, it shall be lawfull for my executor hereafter named to give & dispose such part of the said moneys unto my said daughter as to him shall seeme meet & convenient, and her receipt in writing under her hand shall be a sufficient & good discharge unto my executor against the said children for soe much as shall be payd unto her (anything herein before conteined to the contrary notwithstanding). All the rest of my goods & chattells, rights and credits (my debts, legacyes & funerall expences being first satisfyed & discharged) I doe give and bequeath unto my said daughter Elizabeth Robinson. And I give and bequeath to my sonne George Thompson <iurat> twenty shillings and make him sole executor of this my last will and

testament. In witnesse whereof I have hereunto sett my hand and seale the day & the yeare first above written.
Anne Thompson her marke.[1]
Sealed signed and published in the presence of Cuthbert Hall <his marke> iuratus, George Thompson [*signed*].

[1] Anne Thompson was buried on 27 February 1675, two months after making her will.

28. THOMAS CAPE, SKINNER, 1675

DPRI/6/T/1675/C1
In the name of God, amen the fourth day of June in the year of our Lord 1675. I, Thomas Cape of Northallerton in the county of York, skinner, being sick & weak in body but of good & perfect memory (praised be God), doe constitute & make this my last will & testament in manner & forme following. First I commend my soule to allmighty God my creator, beleeving to be saved by the precious death & merits of my saviour & redeemer Christ Jesus, and my body to the earth to be buried in such decent manner as to my executors hereafter named sall be thought meet & convenient, and such worldly estate as the Lord in mercy hath lent me my will & meaning is the same shall be imployed & bestowed as hereafter by this my will is expressed & declared. Inprimis I give unto my eldest daughter Jane one cottage house now in the occupacon of George Scot with one chamber on the back side of John Trewitt with seven sheep pens on the fore front of the said John Trewitt, with a stable belonging to the aforesaid cottage house. Item I give unto my daughter Anne one cottage house now in the occupacion of Elizabeth Walker the fore house buttery & parlor & two chambers thereunto belonging, and my will is that she shall not enter on the said housing till five years after my decease. Item I give unto my wife <iuratus> during her life one free burrow house now in the occupacon of Thomas Marshall & Grissell Race with three sheep pens thereunto belonging & after her decease unto my son Christopher for ever. Item I give unto George Langley and Henry Danby full power & authority to dispose of & sell my now dwelling house a free burrow house in Northallerton with the common right joyning on William Hebdon's lands on the North Moore belong<ing> to the aforesaid burrow with one acre of land more or lesse lying in Toullerton fields for the satisfying & paying William Lumley of Upper Ousegate in York the summe of ten pounds yearly & every yeare for the terme of seven years by such equall proporcions as is declared

by writing. And my will is that the remainder and overplus moneys (when the said burrow right in Northallerton & lands in Toullerton fields are sould & the said debt satisfyed & paid) be equally divided in<to> three parts, two parts thereof for my two sons, & the third parte for my wife; & my will likewise is that the said George Langley & Henry Danby shall (for their security) have the said three parts and summe of moneys remaining after the payment of the aforesaid debt in their disposing untill their be a legall assignement made of the burrow & lands aforemencioned by my wife, and my two sons Christopher & Thomas when they shall accomplish the age of one and twenty years. Item all my personall estate movable and immoveable (my debts paid & funerall expences discharged) I give & bequeath unto my two sons Christopher & Thomas whom I make joynt executors of this my last will & testament. In wittness whereof I have hereunto sett my hand & seale the day & yeare above written. Thomas Cape.[1]
Sealed signed & declared in the presence of Cicily Harrison mark, Thomas Gamble [*signed*], George Langley <juratus> [*signed*].

The invature of Thomas Cape late deseased the 18 June 1675: mayd by these foure men whose names are heare under writen.

	£	s	d
Imprimis, his purse & apparrill	01	00	00
Item 20 duson of shepe leather	02	00	00
Item in the littill chamber a bed & 2 chests & other imelments	00	08	02
Item in the greate chamber a leveray coubertt & a loung table & a beed with other impellments	02	03	04
Item in the kiching a hougshead & a great cimling with other impellments	00	13	00
Item a gray hors & a cow	04	10	00
Item in law house 2 cettells with other impelments	01	18	08
Item in the milkehouse vshewles[2] with other impellments	00	04	00
Item in the parlor a coubart & a pannell chest with other impell[ments]	02	07	08
Item in the fore house a cubartt & tow tables with other impellment	04	13	00
Item for woole	05	04	10
Item in the worke house leleaven hors skines, 2 swine skines with other impellments belounging to the trad	00	17	04
Item a cartt & foure wheeles	00	13	04
	26	13	04

William Flowere [*signed*], Henry Danby marke, Christopher Hunton [*signed*], John Welles marke.

Dorithy Cape accompt of hir husband's funerall	£	s	d
Mary Harrison 2 dus[en] b[read][3]	00	02	00
Flarunce 1 dus[en] halfe	00	01	06
Mary Ad:St[4] 2 d[usen]	00	02	00
Eleseabeth Walker sad	00	01	00
Bess Walker	00	01	00
Peg Loftis 1d[usen]	00	01	00
John Welles for chese	00	02	02
Surberts for c[heese]	00	04	08
for coffin	00	08	04
Ringers	00	02	06
Mary Harrison 5 & ha[lf]	00	05	06
Nan Wetherll 1 d[usen]	00	01	00
Mary Jo: 1 d[usen]	00	01	00
Nane Abat for drink	00	02	06
Ral[ph] Gren	00	02	03
for table drinke	00	00	09
	01	19	02
for a lone veale			
Matthew Coverdill: 0 1s 2d for another lone veale	[00	01	02]
[*Total of funeral expenses*	02	00	04]

[1] Thomas Cape was buried on 8 June 1675, four days after making his will.

[2] Reading uncertain; perhaps 'utensils' or 'vessels' is intended.

[3] The abbreviations have been expanded on the assumption that they record the widespread practice of distributing doles of bread and cheese at funerals: see David Cressy, *Birth, Marriage and Death: Ritual, Religion and the Life-Cycle in Tudor and Stuart England* (Oxford, 1997), pp. 443–5.

[4] The surname is probably Adston. There were other Adstons in Northallerton at this time (e.g. Helen Adston, below [77]).

29. JANE BARSTOW, WIDOW, 1675

BIA/56/260 [probate copy]

In the name of God amen, the first day of December in the yeare of our Lord, six hundred and seaventie five I Jane Barstow of Northallerton in the county of Yorke, widow, being sicke of bodie but of good and perfect memorie, praise be God, doe make this my last will and testament in manner and forme following. First I committ my soule into the hands of almighty God, my creator, and my bodye to be buried in the church of North Allerton aforesaid. And as for my temporall estate which God hath been pleased to bestowe upon me I do order and dispose thereof as followeth, that is to say, I doe give and devise to my sonne in law Richard Lumley his heires and assignes forever, all those my two closes lying on Hailston Moor within the townshippe of Northallerton aforesaid with there and every of there appurtenances. Also I give and bequeath to the fower children of my said son in law Richard Lumley fiftye pounds apeece to be payd to them as they shall respectively attaine to the age of one and twenty yeares. Alsoe I give to the three servants of my sayd son in law Richard Lumley tenn shillings apeece. Alsoe I give and bequeath to the poore of the towne of Northallerton tenne pounds, the interest whereof shall be yearley distributed amongst the said poore the same day of the month I shall dye, and I give six pounds more to be distributed to the poore at my decease. Alsoe I give to my daughter Jane Lumley all my malt, malt stocke, barley and debts in my malt booke. All the rest of my goods and chattells, rights and creditts, my debts, legacies and funerall expenses being satisfied and discharged, I doe give and bequeath to my sayd son in law Richard Lumley whom I make sole executor of this my last will and testament. Alsoe I give to my daughter in law Margrett Barstowe five pounds, and my minde and will is that notwithstanding anything herein before expressed, the two daughters of my said son Thomas Barstowe shall not receive their respective legacies of fifty pounds apiece unless they or there heires shall, at the request, costs and charges of the said Richard Lumley or his heires, well and sufficiently convey and assure to the said Richard Lumley and his heires all there and every of there estate right by the interest and demand whatsoever of, in and to the sayd two closes on Hailston Moore and every part and parcell thereof. Alsoe I give to Jane Trewman, wife of Marmaduke Trewman, ten shillings to buy her a ring, and to Rachell Barugh, Jane Bell, Rachel Bell, Richard Staines, John Staines, Rachell Staynes, Ann Pybus the yonger, Ann Parker, Elizabeth Meeke, Jane Barstowe and Isabell Barstowe ten shillings apeece to buy them rings and to Ann Pybus the elder and James Pybus ten shillings apeece for to buy them rings. In witnesse whereof I have heareunto sett my hand and seale.

Jane Barstowe hir marke.[1]

Sealed, signed and published in the presence of Symon Meeke, Francis Rymer and James Slinger.

[1] Jane Barstow was buried on 26 January 1676, almost two months after making her will.

30. RICHARD MERITON, YEOMAN, 1676

DPRI/6/T/1676/M1

November the 22th 1676.

I, Richard Meriton of Northallerton in the county of Yorke, yeoman, being sicke of body but of perfect memory doe make this my last will and testament as followeth. Item I give devise and bequeath unto my sonne Francis Meriton my two closess called the Halfe Maske Flats to him and his heires for ever, he paying out of them the summ of ten pounds as a legacy to my sonn John Meriton within one year after the proveing of this my will, and I make my sonn Francis Meriton <iuratus> executor of this my last will.

In witness of: Christoper Barnes <his marke> iuratus, William Best <his marke>, Ann Wright <her marke.>[1]

An inventary of the goods and chattells of Richard Meriton late of North Allerton deceased.

	£	s	d
His purse and apparrell and other things	06	06	08

[1] Richard Meriton was buried on 4 December 1676, two weeks after making his will.

31. DOROTHY SNOWDON, WIDOW, 1677

DPRI/6/T/1677/S1

August the first 1677.

I, Dorothy Snowdon of Northallerton in the countie of Yorke, widdowe, beinge sicke of bodie but of good & perfect memorie, praised be to God, doe make this my last will & testament in manor and form following. First I give unto every one of my grand children twentie shillings. Item I give unto my daughter Mergret Bastow one brass ketle & one iron pott. Item I give unto my sonn Robert Snowdon and Ann Lund and Mergret Bastow all the rest of my goods and chatles and houshold stufe and all debts, biles, bonds due and belonging unto me equelly to be devided amonst them, they paying all my debts & funerall expences, whome I make jo[i]ntly my sole executor and executrix of this my last will and testament.

Dorathy Snawdon <hir marke> [*sealed*][1]

(Witnes my hand and seale the day and yeare above writen)
Wittnesse. Ann Squire <her marke>, Dorothy Wilson <her marke>.

September the 24th 1677. An inventary of all the goods and chattells moveable & unmoveable of Dorothy Snowdon of North Allerton within the county of Yorke widdow deceased as followeth.

	£	s	d
Inprimis, her purse and apparrell	20	00	00
Item nineteene ewes & ten lambes	13	10	00
Item two <fatt> kine and one bull	11	03	04
Item more five kine	15	00	00
Item two calves	01	10	00
Item 200 bushells of malt	24	00	00
Item 8 quarters of barley	08	00	00
In the chamber two bedsteads with theire furniture and one press	03	10	00
In the parlor eight stooles, 6 chaires, two little tables, two bedsteads and two brass candlestickes	02	13	00
In the kitchen			
5 pewter dishes, two flaggons, 4 kettles, two panns, 4 reckons, one iron balk, one iron pott, one plate, one basin, one forke, two spitts, one paire of iron rackes, one fire shovle, one paire of tongs, one table, two chaires with other implement things	04	00	00
In the milke house two chirnes, 13 bowles, two cheesefatts	00	10	00
In the seller one bedstead furnished	00	10	00
Item the mill with iron gavelock	01	03	04
Item silver tumbler with two spoones	01	10	00
Item two swine	01	06	08
	108	06	04

Praised by us, Thomas Smith, William Harrison, John Unthank.

	£	s	d
Funerall expences	22	00	00

[1] Dorothy Snowdon was buried on 9 September 1677, five weeks after making her will. She was the widow of John Snowden [12].

32. PERCIVAL ROBINSON, INNHOLDER, 1678

DPRI/6/T/1678/R1

In the name of God, amen, the seventeenth day of June in the yeare of our Lord one thousand six hundred seventy eight. I, Percivell Robinson of North Allerton in the county of Yorke, inholder, being

weake in body but of good & perfect memory, praised be God, doe make and ordaine this my last will & testament in manner following. First I committ my soul unto the hands of almighty God my creator and my body to be buryed in the churchyard of North Allerton. And for my temporall estate I doe dispose thereof as followeth. First I doe give & devise unto Mary Robinson my wife, and Christopher Robinson my eldest sonne <& Thomas Waide of North Allerton, yeoman>, theire heires & assignes forever all that my messuage, burgage or tenement, two kilnes with the cesternes therein, one barne with all stables, houses, edifices, buildings, orchards, gardens, yards, backsides, profits, commodityes, priviledges, advantages, hereditaments & appurtenances whatsoever thereunto or unto any part or parcell thereof belonging or in any wise apperteining or now used or enjoyed therewith. And also one close of meadow ground conteining three acres or thereabouts lying on Hailston Moore within the territoryes of North Allerton aforesaid upon this speciall trust & confidence & to the intent & purpose that they, the said Mary Robinson <iuratus>& Christopher Robinson <& Thomas Waide> or the survivor of them or the heires of the survivors of them, shall make sale of the premisses, and with & out of the purchase money ariseing by such sale satisfy, pay & discharge all my just debts. And the overplus, if any such be, shall be equally devided amongst my said wife, eldeste sonne & the rest of my youngest children by equall shares. And the premisses till sale shall be assetts in the hands of my said trustees. Alsoe I doe give unto my wife tenne pounds out of my goods & chattells. All the residue of my goods & chattells I doe give equally amongst my said wife & children. And I doe make my said wife sole executrix of this my last will & testament, and doe hereby revoke annull & make voyd all & every other will or wills by mee formerly made, published or declared. In witnesse whereof I have hereunto sett my hand & seale the day & yeare above written.
Percivell Robinson [*signed and sealed*].[1]
The words (& Thomas Waide of North Allerton yeoman) (& Thomas Waide) were enterlyned & afterwards sealed, signed & published in the presence of John Robinson [*signed*], James Slinger [*signed*] juratus, George Thompson [*signed*].

Northallerton. July the fourth 1678. An apraizment made of the goods of Porsivell Robinson of Northallerton late deceased as followeth.

	£	s	d
Inprimis, his purse and apperill	02	00	00
In the parler next streett			

one bedd stead with bedding & courtings	01	10	00
Item 6 chaires	00	14	00
Item one cubbert, 1 cloth & 2 quissions	00	07	00
Item one table & firme	00	06	08
Item one warmeing pann	00	03	00
In the back parler			
2 bedd steads with bedding & courtings	03	10	00
Item 3 chists	00	15	00
Item one trunke & frame	00	03	00
Item one long settle, one table & buffitt firme	00	15	00
Item two shelves	00	00	08
In the milke house			
one bedd steade & bedding	00	06	08
Item one safe, one chease trough, one lanthorne, 2 shelves & 1 firme	00	05	00
In the celler			
3 hogsheads, one gilefatt, one tearse, 3 gantrees, one shelfe, one kimlin & 1 runll	00	12	00
In the forehouse			
three tables, one buffitt firme, one long settle, one buffit stoole, one chaire, one little chare, one firme	00	15	00
Item one jack & weights	00	10	00
Item reckings	00	01	00
In the read chamber			
one bedd steade with bedding, courtins & ballons	04	00	00
Item 6 chaires	00	15	00
Item one great chare	00	03	04
Item one table, 2 firmes & carping cloth	00	15	00
Item one trunler bedd with bedding and one standert	00	05	00
Item one leavery cubbert & cloth with a white possit pott	00	10	00
Item 3 picktures	00	00	09
Item one iron range & tongs	00	01	06
In the white chamber			
three bedd steads & bedding with courtings & hingings	05	00	00
Item one frame & cloth with a chyny doubler	00	02	06
Item one table, one firme & one chiste	00	06	08
In the buttery chamber			
three halfe headed beddsteads with bedding	01	10	00
Item one pannle chiste & 1 little table	00	08	00
Item one trunling bedd steadde	00	01	06
In the greene chamber			
six greene chaires	00	12	00

Item one large chaire	00	03	04
Item one table & firme with a carping cloth	00	10	00
Item 5 picktures	00	01	03
Item one iron range	00	00	09
Item one screene & one close stoale	00	08	00
In the buttery			
2 cubberts	00	05	00
Item 3 shelfes, 2 meall skeyls & 1 box	00	01	02
Item 2 chists, 1 drusser table, 1 kneeding trough & 1 block	00	04	00
Item one morter & pestle	00	06	00
Item one shredding knifes & boarde	00	00	08
Item one voyder	00	00	10
Item 17 peices of pewther	01	14	00
Item 12 plates of powther	00	06	00
Item 6 chamber pots powther	00	04	06
Item 17 peices of small pewther	00	07	00
Item 12 flagons	00	18	00
Item 5 pewther cans	00	04	00
Item 4 dosen of trenchers	00	04	00
Item 1 glass case	00	00	04
Item 2 candle sticks of pewther	00	02	00
In the kitching			
Item 2 brass pots	00	05	00
Item 3 large brass candle sticks	00	04	06
Item one iron pott	00	03	06
Item 3 little candle sticks	00	01	06
Item 2 brass scummers	00	01	00
Item 1 brass laddle	00	00	06
Item 2 kettles	01	05	00
Item 5 pans	00	10	00
Item 4 speetes, 1 paire iron rackes with one iron dreaping pan	00	12	00
Item 1 gibbit	00	00	09
Item one frying pan, one salt pye, 1 pare bellice one chafeing dish & one chopping knife	00	02	06
Item 2 reckons, 2 paire tongs & 1 fire shovle	00	04	00
Item one old peck & a riddle	00	00	06
Item one leade, one stone trough, one old bush[el]le	00	10	00
Item two skealls & one traye	00	01	10
Item 4 tubs	00	03	00

Item two silver tumblers, one wine cupp & 6 spoones: 228 oz.	04	00	00
Item four dosen & ½ hugaback napkins at 7s 0d	01	11	06
Item four hugaback table cloths	00	10	08
Item one plaine table cloth	00	02	00
Item four hugaback towels at 10d	00	03	04
Item 3 plaine towels at 6d	00	01	06
Item 11 paire linn sheetes	04	02	06
Item 2 paire sammron sheetes	00	11	00
Item 1 paire hardon sheets	00	04	00
Item one sheete	00	02	06
Item 16 coddwars at 10d	00	13	04
Item 1 dosen course napkins	00	06	00
Item 3 table cloths	00	04	06
Item 3 course codwars	00	02	00
Item 3 caurse napkins & one towell	00	01	06
Item in coales	00	13	04
Item one chease priss, 4 cheasfats, 2 sinkers & one dosen boales	00	08	06
In the garner			
A spining wheall & a craddle	00	03	06
Item a grate	00	04	00
Item a line wheall	00	01	06
Item a meall tubb	00	00	06
Item a blinde maire & a carte	03	00	00
Item a cowe	03	10	00
Item an old sew & 4 pigs	00	10	00
Item one sew & one hogg	01	00	00
Item 6 little pigs	01	00	00
Item one paire old cart weales	00	02	00
Item 4 question & one tempse	00	01	10
Summa totallis	61	03	02

George Robinson <his marke>, Timot[hy ...]urst [*signed*], James C[....] [*signed*], [.....] Robinson [*signed*].[2]

Depts owne by the deceased			
Item one hundred & seaventy poundes	[170	00	00]

[1] Percival Robinson was buried on 26 June 1678, nine days after making his will.

[2] The foot of the page is torn and parts of the signatures are missing.

33. GEORGE FLOWER, YEOMAN, 1679

DPRI/6/T/1679/F1

In the name of God, amen, I, George Flower of North Allerton in the county of Yorke, yeoman, being sicke in body but of good & perfect memory (praised be God), doe make this my last will & testament in manner and forme following. First I committ my soul into the hands of almighty God my creator & my body to be buryed in the churchyard of North Allerton. And for my temporall estate I doe dispose thereof as followeth. First I doe give, will & devise unto my mother Isabel Flower her heires and assignes all that my messuage, burgage or tenement with the appurtenances in North Allerton aforesaid wherein shee now liveth. And all that my oxegang of old land with the appurtenances lying & being within the fields & territoryes of North Allerton aforesaid given & bequeathed unto mee by Thomas Flower, my late father deceased. Alsoe I doe give & bequeath unto my brother William Flower five pounds as a legacy, to my sister Jane Flower as a legacy five pounds, and to my nephew George Meeke sonne of Simon Meeke five pounds as a legacy to be payd to them respectively by my said mother out of the messuage & premisses to her devised within six moneths next after my decease. Alsoe I doe give & bequeath unto the poore of North Allerton three pounds. And to every one of my cousin William Flower's children five shillings apiece & to everyone of my cousin James Browne's children five shillings apiece & to my cousin Anne Jefferson five shillings to be payd likewise by my said mother out of the premisses aforesaid. All the rest of my goods & chattells, rights & credits, my debts, legacyes and funerall expences being satisfyed & discharged, I give unto my said mother Isabel Flower <iuratus>, and doe make her sole executrix of this my last will & testament. In witnesse whereof I have hereunto sett my hand & seale the one & twentyeth day of February in the yeare of our Lord one thousand six hundred seventy and eight.

George Flower [*signed and sealed*].[1]

Sealed, signed & published in the presence of Tho: Staines [*signed*], Richard Lumley [*signed*] <juratus>, Thomas Waide [*signed*], Jane Lumley [*signed*].

An inventory of the goods & chattells, rights & credits which were of George Flower late of North Allerton in the county of Yorke deceased. Apprysed the fifth day of May in the yeare of our Lord one thousand six hundred seventy nyne by us whose names are subscribed.

	£	s	d
Inprimis his purse & apparell	07	10	00

Appryzors. Richard Lumley, Thomas Waide.

[1] George Flower was buried on 15 March 1679, some three weeks after making his will.

34. GEORGE LANGLEY, YEOMAN, 1679

BIA/58/400

Memorandum that upon or aboute the ninth day of May in the yeare of our Lord God one thousand six hundred seaventy nine, George Langley of Wiske Moore House in the parish of North Allerton in the county of Yorke, yeoman, being at the house of his habitation or dwelling at Wiske Moore House aforesaid, where he had lived and beene resident for many yeares before, and sick of the sicknesse whereof he dyed but of perfect minde and memory, and having a full intent and meaning to make his last will & testament, did in the presence of divers and sundry credible witnesses then and there present, whome he bid and desired to beare witness thereof, nuncupatively and by word of mouth publish and declare the same in these words. Videlicet I desire that my body may be buried in Yafforth church and I give unto Anne Langley my wife all my estate, goodes, chattells, rights and creddits; and I make her and institute her sole executrix of my last will and testaments, and desire that my cozen Robert Langley and my brother Jerome Robinson will be assistants to my said wife and endeavour that none should wrong her.

Then and there being present Richard Whetherell, John Gibbon and Mary Sayer.[1]

[1] George Langley was buried on 6 June 1679, almost a month after making his nuncupative will.

35. THOMAS GRASON, 1679

DPRI/6/B/1679/G1

December the 5th 1679.

An inventory then made of the goods & chattells of Thomas Grason late disceased by us whose names are hear under written: videlicet

	£	s	d
Imprimis. In the fore house			
one long setle, two chaers, one warming pann, one fryin pan, one paer of tonges, one reckin, one paer			

of bellowes, one glas caise, one chafein dish, six trenchers & six piggines, one flock bedd and one pillow at	0	10	0
Item in the fore chamber			
one standing bedd, two lether chaers, one litle cubberd & one box	0	12	0
Item in the chamber over the entry			
one table, one low bedd, thre owld chists, one owld fether bedd, one coverlit and one blankitt	0	6	8
Item in the buttre			
fower flaggins, one salt, one dubler, one woden tra, one tablecloth, two napkines and one chyney dubler	0	8	0
Item in the sellar two hogsheads, two barrells, two guile fatts	0	8	0
Item in the kitchin			
one paer of tonges, one reckin, one drippin pan, one bras ketle, two spitts, one mash fat, one cooler, one tearse, one bras pann, two wash tubbs, one gallone piggine & one table	1	0	0
Item in the foreparler			
one standing bedd, one truckle bedd, one fether bedd, one bowlster, one codd, one rugg, one blankit, one coverlit, one chaff bedd, thre curtins, two carpitts, one wood chaer & one iron rainge	2	0	0
Item one iron jack, two sowes & thre pigs	1	13	4
Sum is	6	18	0

Prased by us, Marke Nelson [*signed*], Marke Adston [*signed*], Jo[hn] Whiteheade [*signed*], William Chapman <his marke>.

36. JOHN RAPIER, SADDLER, 1679

DPRI/6/B/1679/R1

A perfect inventory of the good and cattells of John Rapier of Northallerton, sadler, deceased the 18th instant, by us whose name are underwritten this 24th day of July 1679.[1]

	£	s	d
Inprimis his purss and apparell	02	10	00
Item in the fore house			
one cupboard	01	00	00
Item more two tables, 3 chaires, 4 stooles, one forme	01	06	08
In the buttrey			
2 kettles, one brass pott, 2 frying pans, 3 other pans	01	06	08

Item more 14 pewter dishes, 3 flaggons, 2 candlesticks, 3 salts, 4 pottingers, 4 sausers	01	10	00
More one chafing dish, one driping pann, 2 recon, one spitt and racks, 2 pair of tongs, a fire shovell, one smothing iron, one pair of bellowes	00	10	00
Item 2 paire of sheets, 2 pair of sheets and 12 table napkins	00	12	00
In the chamber over the house 2 bed steds and the beding thereto bellonging	01	10	00
In the other chamber 2 bedds and bedding, one chaire and 2 coffers	01	10	00
Item goods in the shopp	01	10	00
Item in the milk house 2 skeiles, 12 boules, 18 trenchers and other things	00	08	00
Item 3 cowes	06	00	00
Item in the little parlor one beddstead and bedding, one chaire and table	02	00	00
	21	13	04

John Greene [*signed*], Thomas Dinnis [*signed*], Richard Smith [*signed*], John Skelton [*signed*].

[1] John Rapier (also spelt Raper) was buried on 19 July 1679, the day after his death.

37. MARMADUKE FLOWER, 1680

DPRI/6/T/1680/F1

In the name of God, amen, I, Marmaduke Flower of North Allerton being weake in body but of perfect memory do make this my last will and testament in manner following. That is to say first I will and devise that that all my just debts shall bee discharged and satisfied out of my lands and tenements in North Allerton. And I do give and devise my messuage, lands and tenements as well freehold and leasehold unto my sonn Thomas Flower his heires and assignes for ever, chargable neverthelesse and upon this condition that hee shall forth of the same pay and satisfy as well all my just debts as all portions, payments and other bequests hereafter mencioned in this my will. Item I give, devise and bequeath unto John Flower my sonn the summe of fourty pounds to bee paid unto him if hee shall <come> into the countrey personally to demand itt within six months after such demand, but in case hee never come to demand itt my mind and will is that the said fourty pounds shall be equally devided

amongst my children Thomas, Frances and James and the survivors of them. Item I give, devise and bequeath unto my sonn James the summe of fourty pounds to bee paid when hee shall attaine the age of one and twenty years. Item I give, devise and bequeath unto my daughter Frances the summe of thirty pounds to bee paid when shee shall come to the age of one and twenty yeares. And my mind & will is that in case either my sonn James or my daughter Frances shall dy before theire respective ages of one and twenty yeares then theire said portions or my bequests shall bee equally divided amongst such the surviving of my said children John, Thomas, Frances and James, and I do declare that such payments, summe and summes of money hereby given & bequeathed shall bee in full of theire and every of their filiall or child's portions. Item I give unto my daughter Ann Jackson the summe of ten pounds in money and as many household goods (agreeable to and with the discretion of my executor and my loving wife) as shall bee worth other tenn pounds, to bee paid and given unto my said daughter Ann within one yeare next after my decease in full of her child's part or portion. Item my mind and will is and I do hereby give and devise unto my loving wife the yearely summe of ten pounds to bee paid her during her naturall life in liew of her dower and thirds or any other her claime of, in or to my lands and tenements, goods or chattells, and my mind & will is that in case my said wife will not bee content with such yearely payment in full of her thirds according to the true meaning of this my will, that then such my guift and devise unto her shall bee voyd. And my mind and will further is that in case my said sonn Thomas shall faile to pay and satisfy such my guifts and bequests and payments unto my said <wife and > children as they shall come respectively due to bee paid, that then it shall and may be lawfull for my said <wife and> children, or such off them them who shall so want such theire portions <or payments> according to this my will, to enter into my said lands and tenements and to have and hold the same untill such theire portions <and payments> bee only paid or received by them or such of them out of the rents, issues and proffitts thereof. And I do hereby give all the residue of my personall estate unto my said sonn Thomas who I hereby make my sole executor of this my will and testament. And I do hereby revoke all former wills and testaments. In witness whereof I have hereunto sett my hand and seale the nineteenth day of December in the yeare of our Lord one thousand six hundred seaventy and nine.
Marmaduke Flower [*signed and sealed*].[1]

Signed, sealed and published in the presence of William Harrison [*signed*] juratus, John Hall [*signed*], juratus, R. Raikes [*signed*].

A true and perfect appraizment of the goods & chattles movable and unmoveable of Marrmaduke Flower of Northallerton in the county of Yorke, late deceased. February the 7th 1679 [*7 Feb. 1680*].

	£	s	d
Inprimis his purse and and apparell	05	00	00
In the forehouse			
Item two tables, 2 firmes, one longe settle, one cubbert, one glass case, 3 buffett stooles, 1 chaire, 1 dreaping pan, one reckon, 1 pare of bellice, 1 powther dish, 3 flagons & 1 tankard with other implements	02	05	00
In the house parlour			
Item 2 bedd steades with bedding & courtins, one table, 2 chaires			
Item 2 chests, 1 press, one powther dish, 2 candle sticks & 2 quessions & pannle chest, 1 line spining wheale	02	04	04
In the white chamber			
Item 1 bed, beding & curtins, one table, 1 pannle chest			
Item 1 dosen linen napkins, 2 pare linen sheetes, 5 pare harden sheets			
Item ½ dosen linen pillivers, 3 table cloths, ½ dosen course napkins			
Item 3 course pillivers	03	06	08
In the buttery			
Item 6 powther doublers, one possitt boole, 1 chamber pott of powther			
Item one powther bason & other implements with 3 salts, 3 brass candlesticks & 1 flagon	00	10	06
In the milke house			
Item one dosen & ½ of bowles, 2 skealles, 2 chirnes & 10 little shelves & one planke table	00	06	08
In the low parloure			
Item one cubbertt, 2 tables, 1 chaire, 1 buffitt stoale, one trunnle bedd	00	18	00
In the kitching			
Item 3 little kettles, 3 pans, 2 potts, 1 pare racks			
Item 2 speetes, 1 reckon, 1 saddile & 1 pillion seate			
Item one spining wheall, 2 old tubs & one spade & one halbott & one axe	01	15	06

In the coale house			
Item in coales	00	10	00
In the stable			
Item in sheepe pens, 3 stees, 1 rack & manger	01	10	00
In the helme			
Item 2 waines & a caridge, 2 ploughs, 2 pare horrowes, 2 pare coupe swoole, 3 yoakes, 3 teames, 2 shakles & boolts & horse geare	04	00	00
In the yarde			
Item seaven bee hives	01	10	00
In the barne			
Item 8 stoukes of weate, 20 stookes barly, 8 stoukes rye			
Item beanes & pease one loade			
Item 2 riddles, one hopper, 2 scottles	03	05	06
In the food garths			
Item 8 oxen	20	00	00
Item 3 stand hecks	00	02	00
Item 6 milke kine	12	00	00
2 stotts	01	00	00
Item 3 calfe	01	04	00
Item 19 sheepe	05	00	00
Item 3 horses	05	00	00
Item corne on the grounde	15	00	00
Item 2 pykes of hay	04	00	00
Item one swine	00	10	00
	91	18	02

This appraisment made by us whose names are underwritten, William Harrison [*signed*], George Dunn [*signed*], George Tuke [*signed*], Richard Smith [*signed*].

1 Marmaduke Flower was buried on 10 January 1680, three weeks after making his will.

38. CUTHBERT TOMSON, 1680

DPRI/6/B/1680/T1

A true & perfecte inventory of all the goods & chattels of Cudbertt Tomson of Hemerdell[1] deceased, the 19th day of March 1679 [*19 Mar. 1680*]. Apprised by us George Bowre, William Bowre, Thomas Bowre & Isacke Rountry as followeth.[2]

	£	s	d
Imprimis his purse and aparill	2	10	0
Item in the fore house			

one cubbertt, two tables, one glase case, two chares, two buffitt stoules, one buffitt firme, ten peices of puther, one flagine, one candlesticke with other implements to the value of	3	6	8
Item in the fore parler			
one bed with hangings, one panill chest, one chare with other implements to the vallue of	1	10	0
Item in the backe parller			
one bed with hangings, one table, one chare, two bufitt stouls with other implements to the value	1	15	0
Item in the kitchinge			
thre kettles, two potts, two speets, two pans with other implements	2	0	0
Item in the milke-house			
thre kirnes, fowre skeeles, two dussan & a halfe of bowles, two stands, one cheese trough with other implements	1	10	0
Item in the chamber over the parler			
thre beds, two chares, two stouls, one chest with other implements to the vallue of	3	13	4
Item in the chamber over the house			
winnowed wheate, two speininge wheeles, one chare, one bushell with other implements	1	6	8
Item two pare of lin sheete, thre pare of course sheetes, thre pillowvers, one dussan of table napkins, one table cloath	1	6	8
Item one wane, one cart, harrows, plues, yokes & teames with other husbandry geere to the value	4	0	0
Item oates in the barne unshreshed to the value of	0	10	0
Seaven oxan to the vallue of	21	0	0
Item three horses to the vallue of	6	0	0
Item in the Ings five kine, six sturkes	15	10	0
Item in the Layers one dun cow, one bull and five younge bease to the vallue of	10	10	0
Item forty and five sheepe to the value	16	0	0
Item for harde corne on the earth	20	0	0
Item for ware corne on the earth	20	0	0
Item six pigs to the vallue of	0	12	8
	133	00	00

Debts due by the deceased as followeth:			
Item due to Mrs Scarlett	10	00	00
Item due to George Tomson	20	00	00

Item due to John Wilkinson	20	00	00
Item due to Mrs Snawdan	10	00	00
Item due to William Sheppertt	9	00	00
Item due to Ann Neysom for her portion	30	00	00
Item due for rente	21	10	00
And for funerall expences	4	00	00
Item due to Mr Richard Lumley	7	00	00
	114	10	00
	[*recte* 131	10	00][3]

1 Helmersdale (SE 389 923), south-east of Northallerton.

2 Cuthbert Tomson was buried on 16 March 1680.

3 The debts owed to Mrs Scarlett and Mr Richard Lumley, of £10 and £7 respectively, appear to have been added later, in a different hand, and were not included in the original inventory total.

39. GEORGE DUNN, GROCER, 1680

BIA/58/36 [probate copy]

In the name of God, amen this two and twentieth day of April in the yeare of our Lord one thousand, six hundred and eighty, I, George Dunn of North Allerton in the county of York, grocer, being sicke in body but of good and perfect remembrance, praised be God, doe make this my last will and testament in manner and forme following. First I commit my soule into the hands of almighty God my creator, and my body to be buried in the church yard of North Allerton, and for my temporall estate I doe dispose thereof as followeth. First I doe will, give and devise unto my sonne Thomas Dunn, his heires and assigns for ever, all that my messuage or tenement with thappurtneances in Thryntofte[1] in the said county of Yorke, and two oxgangs of land thereto belonging, now in the tenure or occupation of Sampson Loftus, my tenant, and which I purchased of Sampson Hopwood. Also I doe will, give and devise unto my said sonne Thomas all and every the rents, yssues and profits of all and singular other my messuages, lands, tenements and heraditaments with their appurtenances in Thryntoft aforesaid until such time as my sonne George shall attaine to the age of one and twenty yeares, in full of his filial part or child's portion. Alsoe I doe give and bequeath unto my cozen, Elizabeth Surburt, tenn peeces of gold and tenn poundes in silver; to my servant, John Dagget, five poundes and unto my nephew, Thomas Driffeild, five poundes to put him to an apprentice. To my sister, Anne, three poundes, to my servant, Elizabeth Loftus, forty shillings. Alsoe I doe give and bequeath unto my cozen, Elizabeth

Surburt, my sister, Dorothy Coates, to my loveing friends, Leonard Wass, William Harrison, and to my brothers, John Coates and Thomas Coates, each of them ten shillings to buy them rings. Alsoe I doe give and bequeath unto my daughter, Anne Dunn, five hundred poundes to be paide out of my personall estate in full of her filiall part or childes portion. All the rest of my goods and chattels, rights and credits (my debts, legacies and funeral expenses being satisfied & discharged), I doe give and bequeath unto my sonne, George, and I doe make the said Leonard Wass, William Harrison, John Coates and Thomas Coates executors of this my last will and testament in trust for my said sonne, George, til he attaine to the age of one and twenty yeares. And I doe make, constitute and appoint the said Leonard Wass, William Harrison, John Coates and Thomas Coates tutors and guardians to my said three children, their landes and portions till they shall respectively attaine unto the age of one and twenty years, and in case my personall estate will not satisfy the said five hundred pounds & all my debts & other legacies, then I doe order, will and devise that the same be paide out of the landes descending to my sonne George. And I doe will and devise that the said trustees shall have all theire charges allowed them in & aboute the management of this my will. Alsoe my mind & will is that the five hunred poundes given to my daughter, Anne, shall be paide to her when she shall attaine to the age of twenty years and in the meantime shall she shall have twelve poundes yearely allowed unto her for her education and mainetenance. In witnesse whereof I have hereunto set my hand and seale the day and yeare above written.
George Dunn.[2]
Sealed, signed & delivered in the presence of Thomas Coates, Ann Flint, John Dagget, Thomas Coates,[3] John Starr.

[1] Thrintoft (SE 32 93), three miles to the west of Northallerton.
[2] George Dunn was buried on 30 April 1680, eight days after making his will.
[3] Reading of surname uncertain.

40. JAMES HORNER, 1680

DPRI/6/B/1680/H1

An apraisement made of the goods and chattell of James Horner lately disceased.[1]

	£	s	d
Item his purs & apparell	02	00	00
Item barley valued to	03	00	00

Item beans praised to	00	06	08
Item 2 cows & a calfe praised to	03	00	00
Item 14 sheepe praised to	01	15	00
Item 1 ould hors praised to	00	05	00
Item 1 sow & 7 pigs praised to	00	11	00
Item 7 gooses praised to	00	04	00
Item 8 puter dishes praised to	00	05	00
Item 2 flaggons, 2 candlesticks, a tankerd can p[raised]	00	03	00
Item 1 cubbert praised to	00	06	08
Item 2 tables praised to	00	05	00
Item 1 firme & 2 shelves & one buffet stoole	00	01	06
Item 3 ould chaires praised to	00	02	00
Item 1 glascase praised to	00	01	00
Item 2 pots & 2 pans praised to	00	05	00
Item 1 creddele praised to	00	01	06
Item 3 quishins praised to	00	00	06
Item 6 bowles & 1 kirn & 1 sile	00	02	00
Item 1 spit & 1 paire of racks, 2 reckons & a paire of tongs with other small things	00	03	00
Item 1 litle bed & beding belonging to it	00	04	00
Item 1 pannell chist & another litle chist, 1 coffer	00	07	00
Item 1 litle table	00	01	06
Item 2 tubs & 1 leaven tub	00	02	00
Item 1 spinning wheele & 1 temps	00	01	00
Item 2 sheets, 1 table cloth, 3 napkins, 2 pillevers	00	08	00
Item 1 persell of yarne	00	14	00
Item 1 loome and worke geare belongin to it	00	10	00
Item coales praised to	00	04	00
Item 1 litle pike of hay	00	15	00
Item aples & peares praised to	00	03	04
Item 1 row web in the loome unwrought	00	05	00
Item the money which James Horner had owne	00	03	06
Item to James Horner more	00	02	06
	[*16*	*18*	*08*][2]
Item James Horner oweing to his brother Thomas Horner liveing at Sober Hill[3]	16	00	00
Item and oweing to John Phenick	03	10	00
Item unto Marke Calvertt	05	06	00
Item unto William Rymer	05	00	00
Item unto Michaell Meeke	03	00	00
Item unto William Harrison	00	08	00
Item unto George Dunn	00	10	00

Item unto Francis Foster	01 19 06
Item unto Henery Bell	08 00 00
Item unto Dorothy Bland	04 07 00
Item unto Elizabeth Coates	03 03 00

Wee who are praisers have subscribed our hands: George Tuke senior [*signed*], Mark Calvart [*signed*], George Robinson [*signed*], Henery Harrison [*signed*].

1 James Horner was buried on 29 September 1680.
2 Inventory total before the deduction of debts which totalled £51 3s 6d.
3 Sowber Hill (SE 353 894) in Newby Wiske, three miles south of Northallerton.

41. ELEANOR BUTTREY, WIDOW, 1680

DPRI/6/T/1680/B1

In the name of God, amen, this twoe and twentieth day of September anno domini 1680. I, Ellynor Buttrey of North Allarton in the county of Yorke, widdowe, being sick and weake in body but of perfect memory, praised bee God, doe make this my last will and testament in manner followeing. First and principally I committ my soul into the hands of almighty God my maker hopeing & assuredly trusting in, by and through the merritts and mediacion of Jesus Christ my saviour & redemeer to receive pardon & forgivenes of all my sinnes and transgressions, my body I doe committ to the earth to bee decently buryed att the discretion of my executrix hereafter named, and for that smale estate wherewith God hath beene pleased to blesse mee I doe order & dispose the same as followeth. First I give and bequeath unto my three sonnes Christofer Buttrey, John Buttrey and Thomas Buttrey to each of them the summe of five shillings apeece in full of theire partes & shares of what they or any of them can or shall lawfully clayme forth of my estate. All other my goods, money, silver plate, household goods, utensills of houshold or other personal estate whatsoever whereof I shall dye possessed I give & bequeath the same and every parte thereof unto Jane Buttrey my daughter in requitall of the dutifull care and true paines she hath taken for mee from time to time. And lastly I doe make her the said Jane Buttrey <iuratus> my daughter full and sole executrix of this my last will & testament, hereby revoaking all former wills & testaments by mee heretofore made and this onely to stand & bee my last will and testament. In witnesse whereof I have hereunto sett my hand & seale the day and year first above written.

The marke of Ellen Buttrey [*sealed*].[1]
Sealed & declared as the last will & testament of the above named Ellynor Buttrey in presence of us. The marke of Richard Rymer, Grace Pleasaunce [*signed*], Forster Pleasaunce [*signed*] <iuratus>.

An inventary of the goods & chattells late of Ellenor Buttrey of North Allarton in the county of Yorke widdowe deceased, taken and appraized this eight day of December 1680 by us whose names as are hereunder written. As followeth, videlicet

	£	s	d
Inprimis her purse & apparell	02	00	00
In the kitchen			
one old dresser table & one old forme	00	02	06
Item the breweing vessell with a breweing kettle thereunto belonging	01	02	06
Item one iron pott & twoe little brasse pannes with some other smale iron, & one spitt & an old iron dripping panne	00	10	00
In the parlor			
Item one old longe table & an old forme	00	10	06
Item twoe standing bedsteads & with matts & cords	00	15	00
Item one large chest very old & an old coffere	00	04	00
Item twoe old fether beds, twoe boulsters with coverlidds & blanketts thereunto belonging	02	10	00
In the chest in that roome			
Item fowerteene paires of sheets, 14 pillowebeares, three table cloathes, twoe doozen and halfe of napkins, three hand towells	02	10	00
In the forehouse			
one old longe table & one old forme, sixe chares, twoe little old stooles, one old salt pye & and one paire of bellowes	00	16	00
Item nyne pewter flaggons, ten pewter dishes, fower pewter candlesticks & fower brasse candlesticks, twoe pewter chamber potts, twoe little pewter salts & fower saucers & three pewter plates & one doozen and halfe of pewter spoones	02	10	00
Item one iron reckon & twoe spitts, one beefe forke, a tosting iron & one shredding knife, twoe fire shovells & twoe paire of tonges	00	08	00
In the chamber			
Item three standing bedsteads with matts & cords &			

old curtaines and vallans. Item three little tables & fower old chaires	03	05	00
Item twoe old fether beds & twoe bolsters with coverlidds & blanketts to them, one caffe bed & bolster & six feather pillowes	02	10	00
In the coalehouse			
Item coales there	01	00	00
In the back chamber			
Item twoe old tables & twoe formes	00	13	04
	21	06	10

Fo[rster] Pleasaunce [*signed*], Georg Drybrough [*signed*], the marke of Richard Rymer, John Rimer [*signed*].

[1] Eleanor Buttrey was buried on 24 November 1680, two months after making her will.

42. WILLIAM NEESOME, YEOMAN, 1680

DPRI/6/B/1680/N1

A true & perfect inventory of the goods & chattells, rights and credits of William Neesome of the North Moore in the parish of North Allerton in the county of Yorke, yeoman deceased, and apprized by us whose names are here subscribed, December the 7th 1680.[1]

	£	s	d
Imprimis his purse & apparrell	00	13	04
Item in the forehouse one cupbourd, one table, two chaires, one cheese trough, three pewter dishes with other implements thereto belonging	00	13	04
Item one pot, one kettle, a recking crook, one pair of tongs, one spitt	00	06	08
Item one bed in the parlour	01	00	00
Item seaven cowes	11	13	04
Item six storks & a bull storke	06	00	00
Item three calves	01	00	00
Item one old horse	01	00	00
Item one little stagge	01	10	00
Item tenne lambs	01	05	00
Item part of a hay stack & two little pikes	05	00	00
in all	30	01	08
To pay for Martinmass rent	11	15	00
Item for May Day rent next	11	15	00
in all	23	10	00

Debts owing by the party above named deceased as followeth:

Imprimis oweing upon bond to Richard Walker of Brompton	03	00	00
Item oweing to widdow Langdale upon bond	02	00	00
Item oweing in trifles	06	00	00
in all	11	00	00

Witnesses. John Jackson [*signed*], Symon Taylor [*signed*], John Blakie his marke, Christo: Robinson [*signed*].

1 William Neesome was buried on 26 November 1680.

43. URSULA COATES, WIDOW, 1681

DPRI/6/T/1681/C1

In the name of God, amen, I, Ursula Coates of North Allerton in the county of York, widdow, being sick in body but of perfect memory do make this my last will & testament in manner & forme following. First I give my soule into the hands of almighty God who gave itt and my body to the earth to bee buried in decent manner according to the discretion of my executor hereafter named. And as for my temporall estate I dispose thereof as followeth. First my mind and will is that my just debts shall bee satisfied out of my estate. And from and after the payment of my debts & discharge of my funerall expences I give all the remainder of my goods & chattells, rights & creddıtts unto Cuthbert Hall <juratus> of North Allerton aforesaid who I make sole executor of this my last will and testament. In witness whereof I have hereunto sett my hand & seale this seaven & twentieth day of January in the yeare of our Lord one thousand six hundred and eighty [*27 Jan. 1681*]

Ursula Coats hir marke [*sealed*].[1]

Signed, sealed, declared & published in the presence of Francis Beckwith [*signed*], George Tuke [*signed*] juratus, John Rimer [*signed*].

An inventory of the goods & legacies due to Ursula Coates widow late of North Allerton deceased.

	£	s	d
Inprimis her pursse & apparell	01	00	00
Item a legacee given to the said Ursula by Christopherr Coates her son deceased	15	00	00
Total	16	00	00

1 Ursula Coates was buried on 30 January 1681, three days after making her will.

44. RICHARD WAIDE, WOOLLEN WEAVER, 1681

DPRI/6/T/1681/W1
In the name of God, amen, I, Richard Waide of Bankhead in the county of Yorke, woollin weaver, haveing in my eye the mortallety attending mankind and for the better ordering of my estate and for the disposing there of do make this my last will and testament in manner and forme following. First I give unto my wife Ann Waide the third part of all my kine, oxan, young catle, horses, sheepe or any other goods that can be properly calld mine, as also the third part of all my moneys and household goods after all debts, legecies and fewneral expences is discharged. I doe give unto my son Samewell Waide eleavin pound of lawfull money of England, and to my grand child Richard Waide five shilings. All the rest of my money, kine, oxan, young catle, horses, sheepe or any other goods properly belonging to me. Alsoe the two thirds of my household goods, after my debts, legecies and fewnerall expeces is discharg I do give unto my son Thomas Waid, my sonne James Waide, my son Abraham Waide, my sonne Isaac Waid and my daughter Rebeca Waid equally to be devideed amongst them, And I do make my son Thomas <juratus> and my son James <juratus> executors of this my last will and testament. In witness hereof I have set my hand and seal this 23 day of Desember in the yeare of our Lord one thousand six hundred and eighty.
Richard Waid [*signed and sealed*]
Sealed in the presents of Charles Greensid [*signed*], Thomas Slumer his marke juratus.

An apprysment of the goods and chattells which were of Richard Waide of Banckhead in the county of Yorke wollen weaver deceased, made and apprysed the 26th day of March anno domini 1681 by Charles Greenside, Ralph Hodgson, George Robinson and Robert Pecock

	£	s	d
Imprimis his purss and apparell	05	00	00
Item in the forehouse one table, one cubbard, two chares, one forme, thre buffit stooles and other implements	01	10	00
Item in the parlor one cubbord, two bedds, two chists, two coffers, one kimlin, one table, one arke with other implements	08	00	00
Item in the chamber thre beds	01	00	00
Item in the milkehouse two churns, bowles, chese trough, skeles and other implements	01	10	00

Item woll	00	13	04
Puter and brass and one iron pott	02	00	00
Item tenters, lumes and other things belonging to the trade	07	00	00
Item two oxan	09	00	00
Item eleavin kine, foure stirkes and foure calfes	39	00	00
Item ten sheepe	03	10	00
Item six horses	18	10	00
Item wane and plougs with other things belonging to husbandry	06	00	00
Item corne in the barne and stacks	04	00	00
Item corn on the ground	04	10	00
Item two swine	01	00	00
In all	112	03	04
Debts owing by the deceased	26	00	00
Rests	86	03	04

Geo: Robinson [*signed*], Charles Greenside [*signed*], Raphe Hodgson [*signed*], Robeart Peacock [*signed*].

45. JOHN HARDESHE, WOOLLEN DRAPER, 1681

DPRI/6/B/1681/H1

A true and perfect inventary of all and singuler the goods & chattells, rights and creditts which were of John Hardeshe at the time of his death late of Northallerton in the county of York woollen draper deceased, taken and apprised the fifteenth day of Aprill 1681 by George Metcalfe, Thomas Meriton, James Appleby & John Hopton.

	£	s	d
Imprimis his purse & apparrell	01	00	00
Debts oweing to the intestate			
Imprimis by Richard Peirse esquire	05	00	06
Item by Daniell Lascells esquire	02	07	06
Item by Leonard Wass gentleman	02	05	05
Item by Caleb Hawkeswell	01	03	11
Item by Peter & Richard Hird	03	03	00
Item by James Slinger	02	02	10
Item by Shadrack Dinning	01	00	06
Item by Allen Sigsworth	01	01	00
Item by Richard Smith	00	19	00
Item by Phillip Westland	00	14	11
Item by Ann Hall widdow	00	12	01
Item by Dorothy Loftus widdow	00	04	06
Item by Matthew Morley	00	01	04

Item by Mary Neesome widdow	00	11	01
Item by Christopher Catterick	00	04	00
Item by John Kirkby	00	01	06
Item by Reynold Anderson	00	06	08
	22	19	09
To be deducted for funerall expences	02	10	00
Rests	2[0]	09	09

46. JOHN BLAKELOCK, LORIMER, 1681

DPRI/6/T/1681/B1

In the name of God, amen. The twentyeth day of July in the yeare of our Lord one thousand six hundred seventy seven. I, John Blakelocke of North Allerton in the county of Yorke, lorrainer, being sicke in body but of good & perfect memory (praised be God), doe make & ordaine this my last will & testament in manner & forme following. First I committ my soul into the hands of almighty God my creator & my body to the earth whence it came. And for my temporall estate I doe dispose thereof as followeth. First I will that all my just debts be payd and satisfyed out of my personall estate soe farre as the same will extend & the residue out of my reall estate. Alsoe I give & devise unto my loveing wife Margaret Blakelocke the annuall or yearely summe of eight pounds to be payd her yearely out of my house & lands in full of her thirds or other clayme out of my estate. And the residue of my estate I doe give & devise unto my daughter Jane, her heires & assignes for ever. And in case my said daughter dye without issue I doe will & devise that my brother Anthony Blakelocke & brother in law William Robinson or the survivour of them or the heires of the survivour of them shall make sale of my house & lands in North Allerton & the money ariseing by such sale to be equally devided amonst the children of the said Anthony & William, saveing that my neece Dorothy Blakelocke shall have five pounds more then any of the rest. And that I give to the poore of North Allerton out of the money ariseing by such sale ten pounds lawfull money the consideration whereof to be payd yearely. And I doe make my said wife sole executrix of this my last will & testament. Witnesse my hand & seale the day & yeare above written.

John Blakelocke [*signed and sealed*]

Sealed, signed & published in the presence of Richard Smith [*signed*] juratus, Robert Harrison [*signed*] juratus, Mary Smith her marke, Jane Blakelocke her marke.

A true and perfect inventary of all and singuler the goods and chattells, rights and credits which were of John Blakelock late deceased of North Allerton in the county of Yorke, made and apprized the twentieth day of May in the yeare of our Lord God 1681 by us Thomas Cottingham, Henry Carleton, Richard Surbert, John Jackson.

	£	s	d
Inprimis his purse and apparrell	05	00	00
Item in the fore house			
one bed with all the furniture, two tables, one cupboard, one glass case, two wanded chaires, two litle chaires, two buffet stooles, one lookeing glass, one hanging candlestick, two brass candlesticks, 2 brass standrers, five quishiens, 2 brushes, <one paire of bellows, 2 reckons,> one jack, one paire of tongs, one bible, one cheney jugg, six cheney plaites, one porringer, two gownes, two petticoates, one riding hood, one safeguard, one pillion cloth and pillion seate and one cradle cloth with other implements	10	10	08
Item in the buttery			
3 flaggons, two pewter candlesticks, 3 salts, 2 tankerds, 2 porringers, 10 pewter dishes, six pewter plaites, a dozen & a halfe of trenchers and one tray with other implements	02	10	00
Item in another place one iron pot, 3 paire of pott crookes, one frying pann, one brass pott, two litle kettles, 2 panns with other implements	01	00	06
Item in the chamber over the shop			
one standing bedd, one rugg, one blankett, one boulster, vallance & curtaines, one table, one forme, one carpett, five chaires, one warming pann, one hanging shelfe with other implements	03	10	00
Item in the chamber over the fore entry			
two chests and other small implements	00	05	00
Item in the chamber <over the fore house>			
two beds with all theire furniture, 3 coffers, one panell chest, <one old chest>, one table and carpett, one buffett stoole, one trunck, 2 paire of sheets, one huggaback table cloth, one dozen of napkins and a towell, 2 boxes, one shelfe, one voyder with other implements	04	10	00

Item in the chamber over the kitching one old bushel & one wheele & other implements	00	02	06
Item one paire of racks, one spitt, one pale and one pewther dish	00	04	00
Item one raper	00	06	08
Item more in the fore shopp two chests and other hard ware goods and commodities	09	18	02
Item in the back shop one paire of bellows and one anvill & other work geere	01	00	00
Item 1368 latts	00	19	00
Item the corne sowne downe	08	15	00
Item one litle stack of hay in the Mill flatt & another little rooke of hay in another place	04	00	00
Item corne in the barne	06	05	00
Item wheat	00	03	00
Item straw	00	11	00
Item one brass morter and a pewther chamber pott and a cupboard cloth and some weareing linnen & a pound and a halfe of jarsay	00	18	00
Item 4000 of nailes & an old cart	00	13	00
Item in the debt book oweing by severall c:[1] men	04	03	04
	65	04	10

[1] The significance of this abbreviation is not clear.

47. JOHN WHITEHEAD, YEOMAN, 1681

DPRI/6/T/1681/W2

In the name of God, amen, the second day of May in the yeare of our Lord one thousand six hundred eighty one. I, John Whitehead of North Allerton in the county of Yorke, yeoman, being sicke in body but of good and perfect memory (praised be God), doe make this my last will & testament in manner & forme following. First I committ my soul into the hands of almighty God my creator & my body to be buryed in the church yard of North Allerton. And for my temporall estate I doe dispose thereof as followeth. First I doe will, give & devise unto Christopher Baine of Kilburne in the county of Yorke gentleman & James Baine of the city of Yorke gentleman their heires & assignes for ever all that my messuage, burgage or tenement in North Allerton aforesaid in the said county of Yorke wherein I now live with all & every the rights, members & appurtenances thereunto belonging or in any wise apperteining (the dower or thirds of the

same belonging or to belong to my wife excepted) upon this speciall trust & confidence neverthelesse & to the intent & purpose that they the said Christopher Baine & James Baine or the survivour of them or the heires of the survivour of them shall make sale of the premisses & with & out of the purchase money ariseing by such sale satisfy, pay & discharge such part of my just debts as my personall estate will not extend to discharge & pay. And the residue of the said purchase money I desire & my minde & will is may be equally devided amongst my wife & children, save onely that I desire my eldest sonne Thomas may have five pounds more then any of the rest. All the rest of my goods & chattells, rights & credits I doe give & bequeath unto the said Christopher Baine & James Baine upon the trust & to the intent & purpose aforesaid, they haveing their reasonable charges & expences allowed them in & about the premisses. And I doe make & constitute the said Christopher Baine & James Baine <juratus> joynt executors of this my last will & testament. In witnesse whereof I have hereunto sett my hand & seale the day & yeare first above written.
John Witeheade [*signed and sealed*].[1]
Sealed, signed & published in the presence of Thomas Lascelles [*signed*] juratus, James Conyers [*signed*], Mary Conyers [*signed*], Thomas Waide [*signed*].

A true and perfect inventary of all and singuler the goods and chattells of John Whitehead late of North Allerton made by George Tuke, Robert Welbanck, John Prest and Robert Nelson.

	£	s	d
Inprimis his purse and apparrell	05	00	00
Item in the forehouse one table, pewter and other materialls	02	05	00
Item in the back parlor one bed & beding with other household stuffe	01	10	00
In the chamber over the parlor one bed, table and other materialls	02	00	00
In the chamber over the back parlor one bed and other stuff	01	00	00
In the chamber over the forehouse one bed, table and other materialls	01	10	00
In the buttery pewter & other implements	00	15	00
In the kitching brasse & brewing vessells	00	18	00
In the celler sixe barrells	00	10	00
Swine	00	07	06
Plate	02	15	00
Lynnen	03	00	06

One horse, briddle and saddle	05 00 00
Summa totalis	26 11 00

[1] John Whitehead was buried on 4 May 1681, two days after making his will.

48. JAMES AND DOROTHY GRANT, 1681

DPRI/6/B/1681/G1

A true inventorie of the household stuff of James Grant & Dorathy his wife lately deceased.[1]

	£	s	d
Imprimis in the low parlour, one pannel chest, one planke with other utensils	00	10	00
With purse & apparrell	01	00	00
In the great parlour one bed and bed steed, two coverings & two blanketts	01	17	09
Item nine puter dishes, two tankerds, two candlesticks	00	10	08
Item 2 brass pots, one iron pott, 2 kettles	00	12	03
Item three brakes & one table	00	04	02
In the fore house one table, two planks & two chares	00	06	08
[*Total*	*05*	*01*	*06*]

Witness our hands this seventeenth day of May anno domini 1681. John Carver his marke, John Prest [*signed*], John Robinson [*signed*].

[1] James Grant was buried on 13 May 1681 and his wife, Dorothy, two days later on 15 May.

49. SAMUEL ELLA, 1681

DPRI/6/T/1681/E1

I Samuel Ella of North Allerton in the county of Yorke being weak & sick but of perfect memory, praised be God, I do here make this my last will & testament. Inprimis I give and bequeath to Robert Ella, his wife & two daughters six pence a piece. Item I give to Ann Ella the elder six pence. Item to John Ella of Old Brough & his two sons six pence a pice. And last of all I give to Joan my wife all my personall estate, making her my sole executrix of all my goods & chattell whatsoever. Witness my hand and seal this seventeenth day of May anno domini 1681.

Samuel Ella his marke [*sealed*][1]

Sealed & delivered in the presence of Christopher Stevin his marke juratus, Robert Jackson his marke, John Robinson [*signed*] clerk.

A true inventory of the houshold goods of Samuel Ella of North Allerton in the county of Yorke late deceased, valued & esteemd by John Unthanke, Christopher Stevin & Robert Jackson praisers.

Imprimis his purse & apparrell	one pound one shilling eight pence
Item in the fore house	one pound
Item in the parlour	fifteen shillings
	[*Total: £2 16s 8d*]

Witness our hands this twenty third day of May anno domini 1681. John Unthanke [*signed*], Christopher Stevin his marke, Robert Jackson his marke.

[1] Samuel Ella was buried on 18 May 1681, the day after making his will.

50. ANN HORNER, 1681

DPRI/6/B/1681/H2

November the fift 1681. An apraisement then maide of the goodes of the laite deseased An Horner of North Allerton as followeth.[1]

	£	s	d
Inprimis in the fore house	0	13	4
Item in the parler	1	0	0
Item in the milke house	1	0	0
Item in the worke house p^{e}[2] on lome	0	6	8
Item haye & korne	2	0	0
Item one little cow & a stirke	2	0	0
Item one swine	0	5	0
Item 5 sheepe	1	0	6
	8	5	6

Christo: Richardson [*signed*], Thomas Horner [*signed*], John Greene [*signed*], Simon Prist [*signed*].

[1] Ann Horner was buried on 12 July 1681.
[2] Reading uncertain. Perhaps an abbreviation for 'piece'.

51. JOHN WILSON, 1682

DPRI/6/B/1681/W1

January the 10th 1681 [*10 Jan. 1682*]

A true and perfect inventary of all the goods and chattells of John Wilson of Vewly[1] in the parish of North Allerton late deceased. Apprized by Francis Kay, Simon Prest, John Whitfeild, William Prest, John Coates.[2]

	£	s	d
Imprimis his purse and apparrell	02	04	00
Item in the forehouse 1 cupboard, 1 table, 1 forme, 1 shelfe, 1 recken, 1 peel, 1 horse lock & other implements	00	17	00
Item in the parlour 1 chaire, 3 stooles, 1 heckle, 4 quishions, 1 line wheele	00	03	04
Item linnen, 1 paire of linn sheets, 3 paire of harden sheets, 6 napkins, 1 table cloth, 2 towells, 1 linnen codware	00	13	06
In the little closett 1 iron teame & old iron	00	03	00
Item in the <chamber over the> parlour 10 cheeses, 2 bushells of rye, 1 wane axeltree, wooll, tow & line and other implements	00	18	00
Item in the chamber over the house 7 bushells of oates, 1 chest, 1 coffer, 1 craddle, 1 basket & other implements	00	17	00
Item in the milk house 1 kettle, 1 frying pan, 22 bowells, 2 skeels, 1 cheesefatt, 1 kirne, 1 trough, 1 sincker & other implements	01	06	00
Item in the little parlour 1 bedstead with beding, 1 old chest, pewther	00	16	00
Item harrowes	00	02	06
Item 5 kine, 1 ox, 1 bull, 2 steeres, 1 heffer, 2 twinters, 3 yearing calves	16	11	08
Item 20 sheep	05	10	00
Item 1 horse	02	10	00
Item hay in Sinnemire[3]	03	06	08
Item 1 swine, 4 geese	00	12	00
	36	07	08
	[*recte* 36	*10*	*08*]

[1] Probably Viewly Hill (SE 355 978).
[2] John Wilson was buried on 4 January 1682.
[3] The name is preserved in Cinnamire Farm (SE 359 976).

52. RALPH LENG, WEAVER, 1682

DPRI/6/T/1682/L2

January the seventh one thousand six hundred eighty one [*7 Jan. 1682*].

In the name of God, amen, I, Ralph Leng of North Allerton in the county of Yorke, weaver, being sick & weake but of perfect memory, praised be God, I do make this my last will & testament in manner & forme following. Imprimis I bequeath my soul to God that gave it &

my body to be desently buried at the discression of my executors in the church yard of North Allerton. Item I give to my wife Grace one house adjoyning to the bridge on the West Row now in the tenure or occupation of George Skelton, Jane Browne, widow, & Thomas Broadley, and after my eldest sonne Edward come to age to him & his heires for ever. Item I give to my daughter Mary fifteen pounds to be paid out of my stock when she shall come to the age of twenty one yeares. Item I give to the childe in the mother's womb fifteen pounds, that is tenn pounds out of the stock & five pounds to be paid by my eldest son if the said childe shall accomplish the age of twenty one years. Item I give to my brother Ralph Bell two pounds. And last of all I constitute & ordaine my said brother Ralph Bell and Grace my wife joint executors of this my last will & testament & to receive all such debts as to me apperteineth or any wise belongeth. In witness hereof I have hereunto sett my hand & seal this seventh day of January 1681.
Ralph Leng his marke [*sealed*][1]
Sealed & delivered in the presence of Richard Bell his marke, Ralph Bell [*signed*] juratus, John Robinson [*signed*].

1 Ralph Leng was buried on 11 January 1682, four days after making his will.

53. JOHN MILBURNE, HUSBANDMAN, 1681

DPRI/6/T/1682/M1
In the name of God, amen, this three & twentieth day of May 1681. I, John Milburne thelder of North Allerton in the county of Yorke, husbandman, being very sicke & weake in body but of perfect mind & memory, praised bee God, & not knoweing howe soone it may please God to call <mee> forth of this world, being desireous to settle my wife & children in peace & quiett after my departure hence, I doe therefore make this my last will & testament in manner following, hereby revoakeing & making voyd all former wills & testaments heretofore at any time by mee made & this to stand for my last will & testament. First & principally I committ my soule into the hands of God almighty my maker hopeing & assuredly trusting in, by & through the merritts & mediacion of his blessed sonne Jesus Christ, my saviour & redeemer, & by the assistance of his blessed spiritt, to receive pardon & forgivenes of all my sinns and a joyfull resurreccion at the last day of judgement. My body I committ to the earth from whence it came to bee decently buried at the discretion of my executrix hereafter named. And for those smale goods & personall

estate wherewithall it hath pleased God in much mercye to blesse mee I give & dispose the same as followeth. First I give & bequeath unto my twoe sonnes William Milburne & John Milburne the summe of sixe pence apeece to each of them in full of theire shares, partes & porcions due to them forth of my said estate. All the rest of my goods & chattells & other estate whatsoever whereof I shall dye possessed I give & bequeath the same & every part thereof unto my loveing wife Alice Milburne to bee by her disposed as she shall thinke fitt for the best advantage of herselfe dureing her life, and at her death to give & dispose the same amongst my three daughters Grace Milburne, Alice Milburne & Jane Milburne as she in her discretion shall thinke fitt. And lastly I doe hereby nomynate, make & appoint her the said Alice Milburne my wife the full & sole executrix of this my last will and testament. In witnesse whereof I have hereunto set my hand & seale the day & yeare first above written.
The marke of John Milburne [*sealed*][1]
Signed, sealed & declared as the last will & testament of the above named John Milburne thelder in presence of us, the marke of Christofer Stebben, James Lange [*signed*], Forster Pleasaunce [*signed*].

A true & perfect inventary of the goods, chattells and creditts late of John Milburne th'elder late of North Allerton in the county of Yorke, husbandman deceased, taken & appraized this twoe & twentieth day of July 1681 by us whose names are hereunder written, as followeth.

	£	s	d
Inprimis his purse & apparell	01	10	00
Item one old white maire with a leading carte with the geare & materialls thereunto belonging	05	00	00
Item one milch cowe	02	00	00
In the fore house			
Item one standing bedstead with old curtaines & vallans, one old fether bedd & boulster with twoe short codds, twoe coverlidds & one blankett	01	00	00
Item three pewter dublers with a salt seller and other smale lumber of pewter & tynne things	00	03	00
Item twoe iron potts, one little brasse pann with pott lipps & other lumber	00	05	00
Item one longe table, one forme, twoe wooden chaires, twoe little woodden stooles, twoe water skeeles & other woodden lumber	00	06	08
In the milkehouse			

One doosen of milke bowles with other wooden materialls belonging to the milknesse	00 02 06
In the parloure	
One old cubbord or almory, one little old table, one old bedstead & other lumber	00 04 00
Item one paire of lynne sheetes, twoe paires of course sheetes, twoe pillowebeares, one course table cloath & a doosen of napkins	00 13 04
Debts oweing to the deceased at his death	
Robert Greenesword oweing by bond	05 00 00
	16 04 06

Fo: Pleasaunce [*signed*], Chr: Hunton [*signed*], Thomas Thompson [*signed*], the marke of Christofer Grayson, appraisers.

Debts & rents oweing by the deceased at his death	05 00 00

[1] John Milburne was buried on 27 May 1681, four days after making his will.

54. ELLEN LEE, WIDOW, 1682

DPRI/6/B/1682/L1

A true and perfect inventary of all the goods & chattells of Ellen Lee widow late of North Allerton deceased.[1]

	£ s d
Inprimis her purse & apparrell	00 06 06
Item household goods	00 10 00
Item money in Mr Faucenberge hands & others	11 00 00
Summa totalis	11 16 06

[1] Ellen Lee was buried on 10 December 1682.

55. MICHAEL RYMER, CORDWAINER, 1683

DPRI/6/T/1683/R2

In the name of God, amen, the foureteenth day of January in the yeare of our Lord one thousand six hundred eighty two [*14 Jan. 1683*]. I, Michael Rymer of North Allerton in the county of Yorke, cordwainer, being sicke in body but of good & perfect memory (praised be God), doe make this my last will and testament in manner and forme following. First I committ my soule into the hands of almighty God my creator. And as for my temporall estate I doe dispose thereof as followeth. First I give & bequeath unto my daughter Margarett Porrett the summe of five pounds of lawfull money of England,

the bedd & bedding wherein I now lye and the cupboard standing betweene the forehouse & parlour in full of her filiall part or childes portion. All the rest of my goods and chattells, rights and credits (my debts, legacyes & funerall expences being satisfyed & discharged) I doe give and bequeath unto my wife & sonne William whom I make joynt executors of this my last will & testament. And I doe hereby revoke, annull & make voyd all former & other wills by mee heretofore made, published or declared. In witnesse whereof I have hereunto sett my hand & seale the day & yeare above written.
Michael Rymer his marke [*sealed*].[1]
Sealed, signed & published in the presence of Richard Surbert [*signed*] <iuratus>, Thomas Robinson [*signed*], James Adston [*signed*], John Wederlit his marke.

An aprasment made the 3 day of Febuary 1682 [*3 Feb. 1683*] of Michaell Rimer goods and chatell.

	£	s	d
Item imprimis his pourse and his parill	01	08	08
Item in his shope goods. Item showell & leder	16	00	00
Item one mare and hay. Item 3 cowes	13	10	00
Item in the fore house			
Item 2 kets, 2 chares, one tabill, a fourme, 20 pesis pouder with other empellments	03	10	00
Item in the buttery			
3 tubes, other empellments	00	10	00
Item in the parler			
one tabill with other empellments	00	02	06
Item in the chamber			
Item one tabill and a fourme, 3 beds and bedeing with other lineing & a chist, other empellments	10	00	00
[*total before expenses*	*45*	*01*	*02*]
Item oute of this pade for fu[n]erall expensis	03	01	06

John Skelton [*signed*], Richard Surbert [*signed*], Henarry Clife his marke, Timothie Baxter [*signed*].

[1] Michael Rymer was buried on 26 January 1683, 12 days after making his will.

56. GRACE LENGE, 1683

DPRI/6/B/1683/L1
March the 10th 1682 [*10 Mar. 1683*]

A perfect inventory of the goods of Grace Lenge of North Allerton late deseased, apprased by us.[1]

	£	s	d
Imprimis in the house			
one coubbart, one table	00	14	00
foure puder disses with other impelments	00	16	00
one chare with other impelments	00	15	00
In the parler			
tow beds with beding	01	02	06
one chist with other impelments	00	08	00
In the chamber impelments	00	10	00
Oweing to the deceased by Ralph Bell	20	00	00
And by William Sigsworth of Brompton	10	00	00
	33	05	06[2]

Thomas Bell, William Scales, Richard Bell, Ralph Bell.

[1] Grace Lenge was buried on 7 March 1683. She was the widow of Ralph Leng [52].
[2] Debts and total added in a different hand.

57. GEORGE HALL, 1683

DPRI/6/B/1683/H1

A true inventory of the goods of George Hall of North Allerton deceased.[1]

	£	s	d
Inprimis his purse & apparell	2	6	8
A pannell chest	0	5	0
A bedsted & a coffer	0	17	6
3 ewes & two lambs	1	2	6
	4	12	8
	[*recte* 4	*11*	*8*]

Appraisers: Thomas Flower [*signed*], James Coatsworth [*signed*], Robert Read [*signed*], F. Meriton [*signed*].

[1] George Hall was buried on 10 March 1683.

58. ANNE WYLEY, WIDOW, 1683

DPRI/6/T/1683/W2

In the name of God, amen, the tenth day of December in the yeare of our lord one thousand six hundred eighty one. I, Anne Wyley of Crosby Coate in the parish of North Allerton in the county of Yorke,

widow, being at present in health & perfect memory (praised be God), yet considering the mortality attending upon mankinde doe for the peace & quiet of friends & relations after my decease make this my last will & testament in manner following. First I commend my soul into the hands of almighty God my creator & my body to the earth whence it came. And for my temporall estate which it hath pleased God to bestow upon mee I doe dispose thereof as followeth. First I give & bequeath unto my daughter Jane Thompson three shillings six pence lawfull English money in full of all claymes & demaunds which shee or her husband in her right can or may have challenge or clayme of into or out of my estate. Alsoe I give & bequeath unto my daughter Margarett Robinson three shillings sixpence of like moneys in full of all claymes & demaunds which shee or her husband in her right can or may have challenge or clayme of, into or out of my estate. Alsoe I give & bequeath unto my sonne John Wyley & to my grandchilde Thomas his sonne each of them twelve pence. All the rest of my goods & chattells, rights & credits, terme of yeares & tenant right of my farme (my debts, legacyes & funerall expences being satisfyed & discharged) I doe give & bequeath unto my two sonnes Thomas Wyley & James Wyley equally betweene them, & I make & ordaine my said two sonnes Thomas Wyley & James Wyley joynt executors of this my last will and testament. In witnesse whereof I have hereunto sett my hand & seale the day & yeare first above written.
Anne Wyley her marke [*sealed*].[1]
Sealed, signed & published in the presence of John Robinson [*signed*] iuratus, George Robinson [*signed*], Thomas Wooller [*signed*].

An inveintorye of the goods an chattells moveable and unmoveable of Ann Wyle of Crossbe Coat in the countye of Yorke, widdow, which shee wass possesed upon at the time of her death, praised by us whose names are here under under written, Aprile 27 yeare 1683.

	£	s	d
Inprimis her purss and parrell	0	10	00
In the fore howse			
one cubbart, one table, one cheanee puder,[2] one cheese trough, one recken & pare of tonghes with other impliments	01	10	00
In the parlar			
three cafe bedes and three bede steads with cloaths belonging to them with one cheest	02	05	00
In the meilke howse			

one churne and bowles, three skeeles with other implyments	00	15	00
brass with one irion pott, one speete,	01	00	00
three peases of bakan	00	10	00
fower bee hives	01	10	00
three swine with pullan priced att	01	00	00
hard corne and barle	06	00	00
old hay prased att	02	00	00
eleven milke cowes	30	00	00
fower whys, one stoat	09	00	00
five yeare[l]ing sturkes	04	00	00
two old mears, one foale	04	00	00
nieten wesstran ews priced[3]	06	00	00
Totall summ	72	00	00
Funerall expences	05	00	00

John Foget his marke, John Arth [*signed*], Christopher Londer his marke, Oswald Harland [*signed*].

[1] Anne Wyley was buried on 16 April 1683, 14 months after making her will.
[2] The meaning is probably 'china and pewter'; perhaps 'one' has been written in error.
[3] Perhaps 'nineteen wethers and ewes' is meant.

59. GEORGE ROBINSON, LINEN WEAVER, 1683

DPRI/6/T/1683/R1

In the name of God, amen, Aprill the 25th in the yeare of our Lord God 1683. I, George Robinson of North Allerton in the county of Yorke, linnen weaver, beinge sick & weake in body but of sound & perfect memory (praised bee God), doe make this my last will and testament in manner & forme followinge. First I give my soule to almighty God my maker & my body to bee buryed in such decent manner as to my executrix hereafter named shall bee thought meete & convenient. Item I unto give my wife Susanna all that parte of the house north of the entry adjoyninge upon the house of Tymothy Hurst on the north with halfe of the garth thereunto belonginge dureinge her naturall life & after her decease I give the same unto my eldest sonn Percivall & his heires for ever. Item <after the death of my wife Susanna> I give unto my sonn George and his heires for ever that parte of my house south of the entry adjoyninge upon the house of Madam Talbott on the south with halfe of the garth & free egress & regress thereunto. Item I give unto my sonn Christopher for the terme of sixe yeares after my decease that house or backsettle

nowe in the possession of John Dent. And after the said terme of sixe yeares I give the said backsettle with the worke house thereunto adjoyninge unto my sonn George & his heires for ever. Item I give unto my sonn Percivall the summe of tenn pounds to bee paid him within twelve moneths after my decease. Item I give unto my sonn George the summe of tenn pounds to bee paid him within twelve moneths after my decease. Item I give unto my sonn Christopher the summe of tenn pounds to bee payd unto him within sixe moneths after my decease. Lastly I make my wife Susanna sole executrix of this my last will & testament. In witnesse whereof I have hereunto sett my hand & seale the day & yeare above written.
George Robinson his marke [*sealed*].[1]
Sealed, signed, published & declared <& after the death of my wife Susanna first interlined> in the presence of George Metcalfe [*signed*], Thomas Welbanck [*signed*], Thomas Meriton [*signed*].

A trewe inventarie of all the goods and chatteles, moveable and immoveable of George Robinson late of North Allerton deceased as they weere praised the eightteene day of May anno domini 1683 by us who are praisers.

	£	s	d
Item his purse and aparrell	03	06	08
Item 2 cubberts, 2 tables, 3 chaires. Item 1 firme, 2 buffett stooles, 1 glas chase and 1 chese trough all in the foer house	02	00	00
Item in the foer house			
13 flaggons, 17 dublers, 6 candlesticks, 4 puder chamber pots with severall other peices of puder, 1 warmeing pann	04	10	10
Item 3 paire of tongs, 1 fire shouvall, 1 pare of bellis, 2 spitts, 1 driping, 1 beife por, 1 shredding knife, 2 reckins	00	06	08
Item 1 flick of bacon, 2 of beife	00	08	00
In the parler joyning to the foer house			
2 beds with fedder beds belonging and all other bedding	04	00	00
belonging to 2 bedsteeds with 4 curttains & vallans	00	13	04[2]
Item 1 pannell chist	00	07	06
Item 2 little chists	00	04	00
Item 1 table, 2 chaires, 1 firme	00	10	00
Item in the milke houses 7 shelfs, 4 skeeles, 25 bowels	00	10	00
Item in the kichin			

1 table, 2 buffett stooles, 5 kettles, 1 pott, 2 pans, 1 frying pan	03	00	00
In the parler joyning to the kiching			
1 bedsteed & fedder bed & bedding belonging to itt	01	19	00
1 table leafe, 3 tubbs, 1 barrell, 2 kirns, 3 dozen of trenchers, 6 chesfats with 3 sinckers	01	00	00
In the chamber over the house			
2 bedsteeds, 1 trunell bed with bedding belonging to them	02	13	04
1 table, one firme, 4 stooles, 6 quisins	01	00	00
12 paire of sheets, 2 table cloths with 2 dozen of napkins	04	00	00
In the chamber over the parler			
3 bedsteeds with fedders beds and hainings belonging to them	09	00	00
1 table, one firme	00	05	00
In the chamber over the flower 2 chests	00	05	00
2 mares & on gelding with 3 cowes	15	00	00
1 swine	00	10	00
In the workehouse			
2 lomes, 2 geeres with other conveniences belonging to them	02	00	00
Item cloth in the house valewed lin and harden	05	00	00
Item 12 webs bleching	06	12	00
Item 10 scoer of yarne	00	16	00
2 behives with bees	00	13	04
Item 85 quarters of barly & malt	80	00	00
	140	01	08

Prised by us whose names are here subscribed. Timothy Hurist [*signed*], Thomas Welbank [*signed*], James Bowes [*signed*], Will: Wryght [*signed*].

[1] George Robinson was buried on 15 May 1683, three weeks after making his will.

[2] As two valuations are placed beside a single list of furnishings, it is not clear to which items each sum refers.

60. MATTHEW WALKER, SHOEMAKER, 1683

DPRI/6/T/1683/W1

In the name of God, amen, I, Matthew Walker now of North Allerton & late of Richmond in the county of York, shoemaker, sonne of Ralph Walker late of the parish of West Rounton in the said county, being somewhat infirme in body but of a very sound mind & memory, praised bee God, doe make & declare this my last will & testament in manner and forme following. That is to say, I give my body to the earth from whence itt came to bee buried in such decent manner as my executrix shall think fitt. And my soule to God whoe gave itt. And whereas I have by lease and release conveyed all my lands in West Rounton unto John Robinson of North Allerton & Hugh Robinson of the parish of North Allerton & their heires to the use of myselfe for life with remainder to the use of the heires of my body, & for want of such issue with remainder to the use of Mary Thompson of North Allerton widdow my aunt & her heires & assignes forever, subject neverthelesse & the said lands are by the said conveyance chargeable with the payment of twelve pounds apeice to my brothers & sisters as more att large thereby may appeare. And lest there bee any mistake or fault in the said conveyances or in the executing thereof I doe hereby declare my mind and will to bee and I doe hereby give and devise unto my said aunt Mary Thompson, widow, and her heires for ever all and singular my messuages, lands, closes, tenements and heraditaments within the parish of West Rounton & elsewhere within the county of York upon condition shee pay to every of my brothers & sisters mencioned in the said conveyances the summe of twelve pounds att their severall ages of one and twenty yeares and as they shall attaine to such age my said brothers & sisters severally upon receiving thereof first signing, sealing & delivering effectually a generall release & disclaime of all theire rights to the claime and demand of, in or to all my said lands unto the said Mary Thompson & her heires. And in case any of my said brothers or sisters dy before they shall attaine the age of one & twenty yeares then my mind & will is that my said lands shall not bee chargeable with the payment of the said summes mencioned to bee payable to such of my said brothers and sisters soe dying. And I doe alsoe give all my personall estate unto my said aunt Mary Thompson shee paying my debts & funerall expences out of my said reall & personall estate. And I doe hereby make my said aunt Mary Thompson <iuratus> sole executrix of this my last will & testament. Witness my hand & seale this foureteenth day of October in the yeare of our lord God one thousand six hundred eighty and three.

Mathew Walker [*signed and sealed*].[1]

Signed, sealed & delivered & published in the presence of us & our subscripcions made in the presence of Matthew Walker. George Meeke [*signed*], William Relper [*signed*], Ann Keddy [*signed*] iuratus.

[1] Matthew Walker was buried on 16 October 1683, two days after making his will.

61. WILLIAM RYMER, LABOURER, 1683

DPRI/6/B/1683/R1

A true inventory of all the goods & chattells of William Rymere labourer late of Allerton deceased, praysed the six and twentyeth day of December anno domini 1683 by us whose names are hereunto subscribed, videlicet:[1]

	£	s	d
Inprimis his purse and apparell	00	10	00
Item in moneys	04	00	00
Item one cupbord, two tables, one chair with other implements in fore house	01	00	00
Item one little kettle with some small pewter dishes	00	10	00
Item one <little> bed & chist with some implements in chamber	00	10	00
Item coales in colehole	00	05	00
Item three piggs	00	10	00
	07	05	00

Praisers: Volintine Raper [*signed*], Geo: Gamble [*signed*], Thomas Foster his mark, Thomas Swailes his marke.

[1] William Rymer was buried on 17 December 1683.

62. RICHARD FLOWER, GROCER, 1684

DPRI/6/T/1683/F1

In the name of God, amen, this sixth day of February in the sixe and thirtieth yeare of the reigne of our soveraigne lord Charles the second over England &c. kinge, annoque domini 1683 [*6 Feb. 1684*]. I, Richard Flower of North Allerton in the county of Yorke, grocer, being sicke & weake in body but of good & perfect remembrance, praised bee God, & callinge to mynd the fralety of this life & that all flesh must yeild to death & beinge desirous to sett things in order doe make this my last will and testament in manner and forme followeinge wherein is contayned my said last will & testament revoakinge all others by mee formerly made and this only to stand for my last will and testament. Inprimis I recommend my soule into the hands of almighty God my creator & my body to bee buried in such decent manner as shall seeme good to my executors hereafter named. And for my worldly

estate I dispose as followeth. First I give & devise unto my brother Christopher Flower of the city of Yorke, nowe apprentice to widdowe Salmon, tallow chandler, and to his heirs and asssignes for ever all my freehold estate scytuate, lyeinge & beinge in Brompton neare North Allerton aforesaid, he the said Christopher Flower his heires and assignes payeinge out of the same all such debt or debts as are nowe owinge by mee to the executors of George Dunn & Thomas Ward, my brother in lawe, and all such other debts as are oweing by mee to any other person whatsoever which my personall estate shall fall short in payment. And alsoe hee the said Christopher Flower his heires and assignes payinge out of my said reall estate unto Jane, the daughter of Henry Fulburne of Deighton in the county of Yorke, the summe of five pounds within sixe moneths after my decease and alsoe five pounds more unto the rest of the children of the said Henry Fulburne to bee equally devided amongst them within five yeares after my decease. And forty pounds unto the children of my sister Jane Ward to bee equally devided amongst them to bee payd unto them or theire father or mother if liveinge for theire use & if the father & mother bee dead then to the children's tutor att such tyme as the eldest child shall attayne the age of one & twenty yeares. And unto John Scarth my uncle the summe of forty shillings to bee payd att the end of twelve moneths after my decease. And unto each of William Coates fower children of Brompton aforesaid the summe of twenty shillings. And to the two children of James Coates my late master the summe alsoe of a twenty shillings to each of them to bee payd within twelve moneths after my decease. And to Thomas Dunn of North Allerton aforesaid the summe of five shillings & Judith Coates, servant to James Coates, the sume of two shillings & sixe pence. And lastly I make my said brother Christopher Flower & my sister Jane Ward sole & joynt executors of this my last will & testament. In wittness whereof I have hereunto sett my hand & seale the day & yeare first above written.
Richard Flower [*signed and sealed*].
Sealed, published & declared in the presents of us, John Coates [*signed*], John Richardson [*signed*] juratus, John Sigswicke [*signed*], G: Meriton [*signed*].[1]

A true and perfect inventory of all the goods and chattels of Richard Flower late of North-Allerton deceased as they were appraised by us whose names are underwritten. February the 7th 1683 [*7 Feb. 1684*]

	£	s	d
Inprimis. His purse and apparell	20	00	00

Goods in the shop	62 02 00
His horse & saddle	05 16 00
Linnen and other implements	04 01 11
Debts due to the deceased	30 00 00

William Coates [*signed*], Edward Richardson [*signed*], James Coates [*signed*], John Robinson [*signed*].

[1] Richard Flower was buried at Brompton on 8 February 1684, two days after making his will.

63. GEORGE TUKE THE ELDER, YEOMAN, 1684

DPRI/6/T/1684/T1

In the name of God, amen, the twenty nyneth day of December in the year of our Lord one thousand six hundred seventy & one. I, George Tuke the elder of North Allerton in the county of Yorke, yeoman, being of good and perfect memory (praised be God), doe make this my last will & testament in manner and forme following. First I commit my soul into the hands of allmighty God my creator and my body to be buryed in the churchyard of North Allerton. And for the temporall estate which it hath pleased God to bestow upon mee I do give & dispose the same as followeth. First I give to the poor of North Allerton aforesaid thirty five shillings & to the poor of Romanby five shillings to be distributed at my decease. Also I give & devise unto George Tuke, my onely sonne, his heirs & assignes for ever all that my messuage, burgage or tenement with th'appurtenances in North Allerton aforesaid wherein I now live (one roome called the kitchin part thereof with free ingresse, egresse and regresse to & from the same onely excepted) upon this condition neverthelesse that my said sonne George Tuke shall well & truely pay unto my daughters Isabell & Margarett twenty five pounds of lawfull money of England a piece to each of them within one yeare next after my decease and in case hee faile or refuse to pay & discharge the aforesaid severall summes of money unto my said daughters at the tyme herein before limitted, then it shall & may be lawfull to & for my said daughters Isabell & Margarett, or either of them, [to enter] into the said messuage or tenement herein before by mee devised and I doe hereby give them full power & authority to enter into the same & to have hold & enjoy the same untill the aforesaid severall summes of money be well and truely payd unto my said daughters. Also I give & devise unto my said sonne George halfe an oxegang of New Land with the appurtenances in North Allerton aforesaid which I hold for yeares of the

Bishop of Durham, but upon this condition alsoe that hee pay to my said daughters Isabell and Margarett the aforesaid summes of twenty five pounds a piece within the tyme aforesaid and in case of failure of payment it shall be lawfull for my said daughters to enter into the said halfe oxegang of land & hold the same untill the said summes of twenty five pounds a piece be respectively payd unto them. Also I give & devise unto my said daughters Isabell & Margarett for & during the terme of their naturall lives & the life of the longer of them the said roome called the kitchin, being part of my aforesaid messuage with free ingresse, egresse & regresse to & from the same. And after the decease of the survivor of them I give & devise the same unto my said sonne George his heirs and assignes for ever. Also I give & bequeath unto my said two daughters one of my kyne which they shall chuse and all my household goods equally betwixt them excepting one standing bed <with furniture> in the parlour joyneing on the street & two tables in the forehouse which I give to my sonne George. Also I give to my sonne George one pannell chest standing in the said parlour. Also I doe appoint William Harrison the younger of North Allerton aforesaid tutor of my said sonne George till hee come to the age of one and twenty yeares. Also I give to Anne Lee one shilling. All the rest of my goods and chattells, rights & credits, (my debts, legacyes & funerall expenses being payd & dishcarged), I doe give and bequeath unto my said sonne George <juratus> whom I make sole executor of this my last will and testament and I desire that the said William Harrison, soe farr as in hym lyes, doe see that all things in this my last will & testament be truely performed according to my true intent & meaning. In witness whereof I have hereunto sett my hand and seale in the presence of, the words (with furniture) being first enterlined.

George Tuke [*signed and sealed*][1]

John Robinson groser[2] [*signed*] juratus, George Thompson [*signed*].

[1] George Tuke was buried on 14 March 1684, more than 12 years after making his will.

[2] Reading uncertain.

64. JOHN STEPHENSON, 1684

DPRI/6/B/1684/S1

An inventory of the goods and chattells of John Stephenson late of North Allerton in the county of York deceased valued & apprised by us whose names are here under written.[1]

	£	s	d
A certaine debt owing to the intestate of foure poundes by bond whereby ~~the intestate~~ Robert Carter & Jane Thompson stand bond bound for payment, bond bearing date the 25th day of March 1675	04	00	00
the intestate's apparell	00	01	06
one bedstead & one covering	00	04	00
	04	05	06

Apprised by us this first day of May 1684. Cuthbert Surbert mark, Richard Surbert [*signed*], Samuell Wade [*signed*], William Dinsdale [*signed*]

[1] John Stephenson was buried on 30 March 1684.

65. ELIZABETH FOCONBRIDGE, 1684

DPRI/6/B/1684/F1

December 2th ([*16*]84)

An apprasement of the goods of the late deceased Mrs Elizabeth Foconbridge.[1]

	£	s	d
Imprimis her burse & apparell	1	10	00
Item for 1 table & 6 chares & pewther with other implements in the fore house	2	15	00
Item in the parlor 1 table with 6 chares	1	06	06
Item in the kiching 1 table, 2 potts, 1 ketle, 2 pans with other implements	1	02	08
Item in the chamber over the forehouse one bedstead with furniture & 1 litle table with other implements	2	14	06
Item in the chamber over the parlor one bedstead with furniture with one table & for 4 chares	3	14	10
Item 1 litle chamber over the entry 1 bed with furniture & 1 chist with lining with 2 stoles	2	08	03
Item 2 low parlors & 1 buttrie, 1 bed & 1 table with other implements	1	07	09
	16	19	06

Witnesse. Ma: Morlay [*signed*], James Whitton [*signed*], Richard Surbert [*signed*], Marke Nelson [*signed*].

[1] Elizabeth Foconbridge (or Fauconbridge) was buried on 21 September 1684.

66. HENRY FLOWER, PARISH CLERK, 1684

DPRI/6/T/1684/F1

In the name of God, amen, December the twenty second one thousand six hundred eighty & two. I, Henry Flower of North Allerton in the county of Yorke, parish clerke, being sick & weake but of perfect memorie, praised be God, I do here make this my last will & testament in manner & forme followeth. Imprimis I bequeath my soul to God that gave it & my body to be desently buried in the church yard of North Allerton at the discression of my executor. Item I give and bequeath to my son Thomas Flower all my goods moveable and immoveable and I do limitt my said son Thomas the terme of three moneths after my decease to carry away & remove all the said goods with all other utensills belonging or in any wise apperteining to my now dwelling house; and allsoe I give to my said sone Thomas tenn pounds to be paid within the terme of one yeare after my decease by my eldest sone & heire William Flower, & the said tenn pounds to be paid out of my house and land. Item I give to my son Stephen tenn pounds to be likewise paid out of my house and land by my aforesaid son and heire William Flower within the terme of one year after my decease. Item I give to my sone in law William Gamble one shilling. Item I give to my son in law John Wrightson one shilling. And last of all I constitute and make my sone Thomas <iuratus> Flower sole executor of this my last will and testament. In witness whereof I have hereunto sett my hand and seale this twenty second day of December 1682.

Henry Flower [*signed and sealed*][1]

Signed, sealed & delivered in the presence of us, Thomas Smelt [*signed*], Richard Stringer [*signed*] <juratus>, Hannah Lambe hir marke.

An appraisment maid by us whose naimes are heare subscribed of the goodes of Henry Flower parish clarke to the borrow of North Allerton deseased.

	£	s	d
Inprimis his purse and aparell	01	10	00
In the fore house			
1 long tabell, 1 littell tabell, 1 cubert, 10 small puter dishis, 2 flagons, 2 chares, 2 formes, 2 candellsticks, an severall other inplliments	01	10	06
In the parler			

2 standing beds and bedding, 1 panell chist, one tabell and one cofer	01	06	08
In the chamber over the fore house			
one trinell bed, 2 emtiy casks and one warming pan	00	05	06
In the chamer over the parellor			
2 borded chists and one cheese treugh, one spining whell to the valley	00	04	04
In the buttry			
1 iron pott, 2 littell pans, 1 pare of pott kilps to the vallue	00	04	00
	04	19	08
	[*recte* 05	*01*	*00*]

Simon Meeke [*signed*], William Jonson [*signed*], John Rimer [*signed*], Willam Scott <his marke>.

[1] Henry Flower was buried on 3 October 1684, nearly two years after making his will.

67. ELIZABETH ROPER, 1685

DPRI/6/B/1685/R1

An aprasment of Ellesabuth Roperes goodes latlle desesed.[1] First hir puers and aperell at [£]0 2[s] 6[d]. Two bedes and clloes be longein to them <at> 1 pound and six penes and wone chist and a tabell at [£]0 2[s] 6[d]. Whet fllouer and tubes at five shillins. Bras and puder at eight shellins. 2 teablles and a cobert and smol thinges at sixten shillines. Met and and yarne at 4 shellines and 6 penes; suger at nine shellines. Manchester waer at five shellines. Tobacko at 6 shillines and 8 penes. Sope and boxes at ten shillines. Wone maer at 2 pound and twelve penes. [*Total: £6 10s 8d*]

The prasers. William Hoge his marke, Thomas Swalles his marke, Cudbart Willabe his marke, George Porckter his marke.

[1] Elizabeth Roper was buried on 23 March 1685.

68. JOHN RYMER, CARPENTER, 1685

DPRI/6/T/1688/R1

In the name of God, amen, this first day of May anno domini 1685. I, John Rymer of North Allarton in the county of Yorke, carpenter, being very sick & weake but of perfect memory, praised bee God, doe make this my last will & testament in manner followeing. First and principally I committ my soule into the hands of almighty God my maker assuredly trusting in & through the meritts and mediation of Jesus Christ my redeemer to receive pardon of all my sinns and transgressions. My body I comitt to the earth to bee decently buryed in the churchyard of North Allarton, at the discretion of my executrix hereafter named. And for my reall and personall estate which God in mercye hath bestowed upon mee I give and bequeath the same as followeth. First I give and bequeath unto my eldest sonne George Rymer and to his heires forever all those twoe closes lyeing nere the towne of North Allarton called Lawsons Close & the Calfe Close together with the house in which Robert Read, whitesmith, nowe liveth in North Allarton, to bee entered upon by my said sonne ymediatly after the death and decease of Dorothy Rymer my wife & not before. Item I give & bequeath unto Richard Rymer, my second sonne, & to his heires for ever my nowe dwelling house in North Allarton aforesaid after the death & decease of my said wife & not before with all the houseing & other appurtenances thereunto belonging, and alsoe all that my close of ground called Dunnes Close, to bee entered upon by my said sonne Richard Rymer at his age of one & twenty yeares. Item I give and bequeath unto my youngest sonne John Rymer and to the child my wife is now goeing withall (if it proves a sonne) all that my close of arrable ground which I lately purchased of John Hall, clerke, to bee equally divided betwixt them, to have & to hold to them & to theire heires for ever. Item I give and bequeath unto my daughter Margarett Rymer the summe of fiftie pounds of currant English money to bee paid unto her when she shall come to the age of one & twenty yeares or shalbee married, which shall first happen, by my executrix hereafter named forth of my debts oweing to mee & my other personall estate. Item I give & bequeath unto the child my wife is nowe going withal (if it proves to bee a daughter) the summe of fortie pounds to bee alsoe paid by my executrix when the said daughter shall come to the age of one & twenty yeares or bee married, forth of my personall estate. All the rest of my reall & personall estate not herein before bequeathed together with my stock of goods & corne upon the ground, household goods, debts & other chattells & estate whatsoever whereof I shall dye possessed (together with the proffitts of all my lands dureing my children's mynorities) I give & bequeath unto my loveing wife Dorothy Rymer (with the tuturage of all my children during theire non ages). And I doe hereby make & ordaine her the said Dorothy <juratus> Rymer my wife full & sole executrix of this my last will & testament, hereby revoakeing & makeing null & voyd all former & other wills bee mee heretofore made, and this to stand & remaine

my last will & testament. In witnesse whereof I have hereunto set my hand & seale the day & yeare first within written.
John Rimar [*signed and sealed*][1]
Signed, sealed & declared as the last will & testament of the within named John Rymer in the presence of us, John Prest [*signed*], Robert Reede [*signed*], the marke of William Frankland, Forster Pleasaunce juratus [*signed*].

A true and perfect inventory of the goods and chattells, implements of household stuff, debts and other personal estate belonging to John Rymer late of North Allerton in the County of York joyner deceased, taken & appraised by Hugh Robinson, Thomas Coulson, John Prest & Thomas Taylor, the seaventh day of May anno domini 1685, as followeth:

	£	s	d
Inprimis his purse and apparrell	05	00	0
In the fore house			
Item two cupboards, one table, one fourme, one long settell, three chares one glass case & other small wooden lumber	01	15	0
Item eleaven pewder dishes with other smal pewder implements	00	10	0
Item one brass pott, three brass pans, one iron pott, two brass kettells, one iron reckon, one fire shovell & tonges & other iron lumber	01	00	0
In the parlor			
Item one standing bedstead, one pannell chest, three little coffers with other wooden lumber	00	15	0
Item one chaffe bed with three codes, one feather boulster & two pillows with blanketts and coverlitt	00	10	0
In the fore chamber			
Item two bedsteads, one pannell chest	00	15	0
Item two chaffe beds & chaffe boulster with blanketts and coverletts to them	01	05	0
In the back chamber			
Item one bedstead with curtaines & vallaines, one table and one fourme, one great kymnell, one coffer	01	00	0
Item one chaffe bed, one chaffe boulster, one codd with two blanckets and one coverlet	00	10	0
Item a boule of barley corne with one kneading trough	00	07	0
In the worke house			
Workeing tooles belonging to his trade	01	10	0

Phelkes in the worke house and cart dogges & fyrr powles, coope soales, firr trees, six firr deeles, two paire of carte wheeles, one ladder, one barrow with other lumber wood	05	19	0
In the back houses			
wayne speakes & phelkes, carte axle treese & lynmers, one cupboard, wayne axle trees & other peices of lumber wood	03	12	0
In the barne			
forty eller poules, one leape, one window cloath with other lumber	00	11	8
In the garth			
Item one cart boddy with other peices of wood	00	12	0
Item severall peices of wood lying in the streete before the doare	02	00	0
Item lining in the house			
two paire of lining sheets, four paire of harden sheets, two table cloaths and one dozen napkins	02	00	0
In the milk house			
Item two milke skeeles, one cherne & six milk boules	00	05	0
Goods upon the ground			
Two milke cowes, on whye & two calves	09	00	0
Six sheepe	01	10	0
One cart mare with the cart & all the materialls thereunto belonging	08	00	0
Item thirteene acres & halfe wheate upon the ground at forty shillings the acre	27	00	0
Item seaven acres & halfe of beanes & oates upon the ground at 20s. the acre	7	10	0
Debts oweing to the testator at the time of his death:			
Oweing by Elizabeth Lumley widdowe upon a morgage of a close of ground	20	00	0
Oweing by Elizabeth Metcalfe, widdow, upon bond	10	00	0
Oweing by Robert Welbanck, husbandman, upon bond	05	00	0
Oweing by William Allison by bond	05	00	0
Oweing more by him for sheepe	02	10	0
Oweing by Mr George Meriton for sheepe	06	13	4
Oweing by Richard Marshall, wheeleright, upon bond	10	00	0
Oweing by William Sigsworth of Brompton upon bond	10	00	0
Summ totall of the deceased personall estate	152	00	0

[1] John Rymer was buried on 7 May 1685, six days after making his will.

69. THOMAS WELBANK, YEOMAN, 1686

BIA [probate copy]

In the name of God amen, I, Thomas Welbanck the elder of North Allerton in the county of York, yeoman, being somewhat infirme in body, but of good and perfect memory, praised be God, doe make and publish this my last will and testament in manner and forme following. First I give my soule to God whoe gave it, and my body to the earth to be buryed in such decent manner as my executrix hereafter named shall thinke fitt. And as for my worldly estate God hath blessed me I dispose thereof as followeth. That is to say I give the back part of the messuage or tenement within North Allerton wherein Thomas Foster now liveth unto Jane my loveing wife for the terme of her naturall life with all convenient usage of the garth. And I doe alsoe give and devise the said back part of my said messuage after the decease of my said wife unto my sonne Thomas Welbanck, his heires and assignes for ever. And I doe alsoe give and devise the fore part and all the rest of my said messuage or tenement (being now in the possession of my sonne Thomas Welbanck) unto my said sonne Thomas Welbanck, his heires and assignes for ever, subject nevertheless and chargeable with the payment of a debt of tenne pounds lawfull English money which I owe unto Thomas Thompson of North Allerton aforesaid, and alsoe subject and chargeable nevertheless with the payment of seaven pounds lawfull English money unto my said loveing wife upon the five and twentyth day of March next following my death, and alsoe subject nevertheless with the yearly summe of thirty shillings lawfull English money unto my said loveing wife for & during her naturall life. And my minde and will is, and I doe hereby declare and order, that in case my said sonne Thomas faile to pay all and every or any of the said severall summes above mencioned as the same or any of them becomes due or payable, then it shall be lawfull for my said wife to enter into and upon the said premisses and every part thereof soe devised unto my said sonne Thomas, and hold the same <to her and her heires> untill all the said summes be paid and discharged by and with the profits thereof, together with all charges which shall be expended in about the same. And I doe alsoe give and bequeath unto my sonne in law Robert Smith the summe of tenne pounds lawfull English money to be paid by my executrix within foure monthes next after my decease, which I declare is to be in <full> discharge and satisfaction of the filiall part and porcion of Mary my daughter, wife of the said Robert. And I alsoe give and bequeath unto my sonne William the summe of

five shillings in full of his filiall part or child's portion, having before given him his share of my estate. And all the rest of my goods and chattels, my debts, legacies and funeral expences being first satisfied, I give and bequeath unto Jane my loveing wife whome I make sole executrix of this my last will and testament, hereby revoakeing and adnulling all former wills. In witnesse whereof I have hereunto sett my hand and seale the second day of January in the first yeare of the raigne of King James the Second anno domini 1685 [*2 Jan. 1686*].
Thomas Welbanck.[1]
Signed, sealed and published by the testator in our presence and our names subscribed in the testators presence and at his request, the words (to her and her heires) being interlined.
Witnesse Ma: Morlay; Robert Welbancks marke; R. Raikes.

[1] Thomas Welbank was buried on 13 January 1686, 11 days after making his will.

70. JOHN POWELL, 1686

DPRI/6/B/1686/P2

An inventory of the goods of John Powell late of North Allerton.[1]

	£	s	d
In the forhouse			
9 puder deish, 6 plaits, 4 flagins, 2 tankerds, 3 kindellsteicks, 4 podindishis, one positboulle, 1 chamerpot, one table, 2 chars, 2 pootts, 2 panns, one seler tumeler	1	10	0
In the parler			
2 fedder beeds, 2 rougs, 2 blankit, 2 boulsters, 4 pillers, 2 bedsteads with hangings tow them, one cheist of drawers, one panell cheist with 6 pare of shets, 2 tabellcloth and one dusin of napkins, 2 chars, one table, one larg seein glass	3	0	0
In the chamber			
2 bedsteids, one fedder beed, <one> flock beed, 2 rougs and hangings tow them, one table, tow boufeit stouls, one chare	1	2	0
In the bruhous			
2 mask fatts, 2 hogheads, 2 guillfatts	0	10	0
One hors, one swe with 6 pigs	2	0	0
[*Total*	*8*	*2*	*0*]

[1] John Powell was buried on 2 February 1686. The heading is in a different hand from the body of the inventory.

71. ALICE BRADLEY, WIDOW, 1686

DPRI/6/T/1686/B1

In the name of God amen this fower & twentieth day of February in the second yeare of the raigne of our soveraigne lord James the second over England etc king annoque domini 1685 [*24 Feb. 1686*]. I Alice Bradley of North Allerton in the county of Yorke, widdowe, being sick & weake in body but of sound & perfect memory (thankes bee to almighty God for the same) and callinge to mind the uncertaine state of this transitory life and that all flesh must yield unto death when[1] it shall please God to call, and beinge desireous to settle my worldly affaires to avoid disputes about the same afterwards doe make this my last will & testament wherein is contained my last will & testament in manner & forme followinge, revoakinge & absolutely annullinge all former & other testament & testaments, will & wills heretofore by mee made & declared either by word or by writeinge, notwithstandinge any promise or clause derogatory in the same, and this to bee taken for my only last will and testament & none other. First I give & bequeath my soul to almighty God my maker & to Jesus Christ my redeemer & to the Holy Ghost my sanctifier & my body to the earth from whence it came to bee buried in such decent & Christian manner as my executor hereafter named shall bee thought meete & convenient, there to rest untill my soul & body shall meete againe & bee joyned together att the joyfull resurrection & bee made partakers of the never fadeinge joyes of immortality which God in mercy, through the meritts of Jesus Christ alone, hath promised & prepared for all those that truely & unfeignedly repent & beleive in him. And touchinge such temporall estate of goods, chattels & debts as the Lord hath beene pleased, farr above my deserts, to bestowe uppon mee, I doe order, give, bequeath, devise & dispose of the same in manner & forme followinge. First I give & bequeath unto my sonn in lawe Christopher Robinson one shillinge of lawfull money of England. Item I give & bequeath unto my grand sonn, Thomas Bradley, the summe of forty shillings of lawfull money of England in full of his child's parte which hee may or can anywayes demand for or instead of Edward Bradley, his father late deceased, my eldest sonn, to bee paid by my executor hereafter named. And all the rest of my goods & chattels as well reall and personall, moveable and immoveable of what nature & kind or in whose hands soever the same bee, & other summe & summes of money oweing & due to mee (after my funerall expences defrayed & debts payd) I doe give & bequeath unto my sonn Thomas Bradley. And lastly I doe hereby nominate, make, constitute & appoint my said sonn, Thomas Bradley, sole executor of this my last will & testament. In witness whereof I have hereunto sett my hand & seale the day & yeare first above written.

Alice Bradley <her marke>[2]

Signed sealed published & delivered in the presence of us Elizabeth Procter her marke, Christopher Duckett his marke, juratus, Tho: Meriton [*signed*].

An inventory of the goods and chattels of Alice Bradley late of North-Allerton deceased as they appraised by us whose names are underwritten.

	£	s	d
Inprimis her purse & apparell	10	0	0
Item in the fore house one table, cupboard, pewter & other materials	02	0	0
Item in the cellar & kitchen brewing vessels and brass	03	10	0
Item in the back chamber two bedsteads, bedding & other furniture	05	0	0
Item in the entry chamber 2 beds, linen and other materials	07	0	0
Item in the chamber over the house one bed, bedding and other furniture	02	0	0
Item in the entry parlour one bed & other implements	01	10	0
Item in the middle parlour one bed, bedding, table & other materials	01	12	0
Item in the far chamber one bed & bedding	01	0	0
Item in the far parlour one table, cupboard and other necessaries	00	10	0
Item one sow & pigs	01	0	0
Item two tumblers	01	10	0
	[36	12	0]

James Bones [*signed*], Jo: Tomes [*signed*], Parcivall Robinson [*signed*]; John Calvert [*signed*].

1 'when' is repeated in the manuscript.

2 Alice Bradley was buried on 10 March 1686, 11 days after making her will.

72. MICHAEL PEMBERTON, GENTLEMAN, 1687

DPRI/6/B/1686/P1

A true and perfect inventary of all and singuler the goods and chattells, rights and creditts of Michaell Pemberton late of North Allerton in the county of York, gentleman, deceased, at the time of his death, taken and apprized this 28th day of February anno domini 1686 [*28 Feb. 1687*] by Thomas Meriton, George Drybrough, John Meriton & William Body.[1]

	£	s	d
Inprimis his purse & apparrell	05	00	00
In the fore house or hall			
Item 2 tables & one fourme	00	09	06
Item two wainescot chaires	00	05	00
Item two bussy leather chaires & six old chaires	00	09	04
Item one dresser cupboard, clock and case	02	00	00
Item fifteen pewter dishes, two dozen of pewter plates	02	10	00
Item three flagons, one chamber pot, nyne pottingers &c.	01	00	00
Item brass & iron warmeing pan, tonges, spitts &c.	01	00	00
Item one jack, racks and driping panns	00	10	00
Item one gunn	00	05	00
In the parlour			
Item 2 tables & one dozen of chaires	01	10	00
Item three carpitt cloathes	00	05	00
In the chamber over the seller stead			
Item one bed with the beding	02	10	00
Item one little table, one pannell chest & foure chaires &c.	00	12	00
In the chamber over the shopp			
Item one chest of drawers with lining	05	00	00
Item one seeing glass, six chaires & two stooles	01	03	00
Item one little table, 2 stands, one hanging shelfe	00	08	00
In the chamber over the hall			
Item one bedsteade with beding	02	10	00
Item one paire of gameing tables and one hanging shelfe &c.	00	05	00
Item one little table and five chaires &c.	00	06	00
In the chamber over the parlour			
Item three bedsteades with theire beding	06	00	00
Item one table, one chest of drawers &c.	00	13	04
Item one box, one chaire, two stooles &c.	00	06	00
In the scullery			
Item three potts, three kettles, one still	01	00	00
In the seller			
Item two hogsheads, one chirne &c.	00	06	00
Item one horse sadle and brydale &c.	05	00	00
	41	03	02

[1] Michael Pemberton was buried on 6 February 1687.

73. ISABEL FLOWER, WIDOW, 1688

DPRI/6/T/1688/F1

In the name of God, amen, I, Issabell Flower of North Allerton in the county of Yorke, widdow, being in good health and of good mind and memory, yet calling to mind my mortallity doe make this my last will and testament in manner and forme following. First I commend my soule to God who gave it, and give my body to the earth from whence it came to be buried in such decent manner as my executrix hereafter named shall think fit. And for the worldly estate with which God has blest me I give, devise and dispose of the same as followeth. And first I give and devise unto William Harrison of North Allerton in the county aforesaid gentleman and Richard Grimston, my sonne in law, of the same town and county gentleman, all those closes called or knowne by the name of Grayson Barughs, being part of my oxgang of land commonly called Old Land with one gate on Bullamoore thereunto belonging, in trust and to and for the only proper use and behoofe of my grandsonne George Meeke and to the heires of his body lawfuly to be begotten for and during all such terme & termes of lives as are or may be in being at the time of my decease. Alsoe I give all the remainder of the said oxgang of Old Land consisting of a new inclosure lying betwixt two highways in the field and adjoyning to the lands late in the possession of Francis Flint and of severall other lands & meadows lying in the open fields there, together with all & singuler other closes and the rights, members and appurtenannces to the said oxgang of Old Land belonging & apperteyning which I hold by lease from the Lord Bishopp of Durham unto my daughter Jane Grimston & the heires of her body lawfully to be begotten for & during all such terme & termes of life & lives as are or may be in being at the time of my decease. And my mind & will further is that if my said grandsonne George Meeke shall dye without issue of his body lawfully begotten during the continuance and being of any the life or lives in the said Bishopp's lease mentioned then I give and devise the said closes commonly called Graysonbarughs being part of my oxgang of land called Old Land with one gate on Bullamoore & the appurtenances to the same belonging unto my daughter Jane Grimston and the heires of her body lawfully to be begotten for and during the remainder of the said terme or termes of life or lives then to be in being. And in case my said daughter Jane shall alsoe dye without issue of her body my mind & will further is, and I doe hereby give and devise the further remainder of the Lord Bishopp's lease of the said oxgang of Old Land unto the children of my late sisters Cicily Bower, Anne Pye and Mary Pye, equally to be divided amongst them. Item I give and devise unto my daughter Jane Grimston and the heires of her body lawfully to be begotten all that my messuage and tenement wherein I now live. And alsoe I give and devise unto her all those my closes called & knowne by the name of North Rye Flatts upon condicion & subject neverthelesse with the provisoes & charges following, (that is to say), that my neice Dorothy Browne, the wife of James Browne, shall have paid unto her yearely out of the profitts of the said North Rye Flatts the sume of forty shillings for the terme & time of her naturall life, to be paid her halfe yearely by even porcions from the time of my death. And in case my said daughter Jane dye without issue of her body then I give the remainder thereof & of every part & parcell of the said lands & closes unto my said grandsonne George Meeke & the heires of his body lawfully to be begotten, and for want of such issue I give the further remainder unto my said sisters' children equally to be divided amongst them. Item I give unto William Harrison & Richard Grimston aforesaid the summ of ten pounds to be paid within halfe a yeare after my decease in trust & to & for the only proper use and behoofe of my said grandsonne George Meeke. Alsoe I give unto the said William Harrison and Richard Grimston ten shillings apiece. I give alsoe to every of my aforesaid sisters' children the summ of twenty shillings apiece. Item I give unto my cozen Elizabeth Lumley, widdow, the summ of twenty shillings. Item I give unto my sonne in law Symon Meeke the summ of five pounds as a token of my love. And alsoe to my sonne in lawe Richard Grimston I give five pounds as a token of my love. Item I give to my nephew William Flower & Ellinor his wife five shillings apiece. Item I give to my nephew Thomas Flower twenty shillings. Item I give unto my nephew Steven Flower five shillings. And alsoe I give unto the children of my said cosen William Flower the summ of five shillings apiece. And to the children of my neice Dorothy Browne the summ of five shillings apiece. I give unto Elizabeth Meeke, wife of my sonne in lawe Symon Meeke, the summ of twenty shillings to buy her a ring, and to her foure children five shillings apiece. Item it is my mind & will that my executrix hereafter named shall during the terme of her naturall life yearely and every yeare that day twelve month after my decease <give &> distribute the sum of twelve shillings to such of the needfullest poore of North Allerton aforesaid as she shall think fitt. And if my neice Dorothy Browne, the wife of James Browne, be living at the death of my said executrix then it is my mind & will that the summ of ten pounds shall be left unto her by my said

executrix. Item I will that forty shillings be given & distributed to the poore of North Allerton aforesaid at or on the day of my buriall, and fifteen shillings be then given to the poore of Brompton. And five shillings be then given to the poore of Romanby. All the rest of my goods and chattles (my debts, legacies and funerall expences being first discharged) I give & bequeath unto my loving daughter Jane Grimston whom I doe hereby make my sole executrix of this my last will & testament revoking hereby all former wills. Witnesse my hand and seale this twentieth day of November in the yeare of our Lord one thousand six hundred and eighty seven. 1687.
Issabell Flower her marke[1]
Signed, sealed, declared & published in our presence. And be it remembered that our names are subscribed as witnesses at the request & in the presence of the said Issabell Flower. Witnesse our hands, Thomas Bradley [*signed*], Thomas Flower [*signed*], Anne Hunton [*signed*].
May the 31th 1688. Received the originall of the last will & testament of the above named Issabell Flower from the hands of Mr Thomas Parker by me, Richard Grimston [*signed*].

[1] Isabel Flower was buried on 20 May 1688, six months after making her will.

74. SIMON PRIST, BLACKSMITH, 1688

DPRI/6/B/1689/P1

A true inventory of the goods & chattle of Simon Prist of Northallerton in the county of York, blacksmith, late deceased.[1]

	£	s	d
Imprimis his purse & apparell	01	00	00
The far chamber			
2 beds and bed steads and hangings, four cods, one rugg, one covering, one blankett, 2 tables, 3 formes, one trunck, one chest, one carpet	02	00	00
Item in the middle chamber			
3 bed steads, 2 chaff beds, 2 pair of hangings, 2 chests, 2 formes	00	15	00
Item in the fore chamber			
one livery cupboard, 3 chares, 2 truncks, 2 pannell chests, 2 formes, one desk, one dozen & a halfe of napkins, 4 pair of sheets, 3 table clothes	02	12	00
Item in the parlour			

one chaff bed & bed stead & hangings, one covering, one blanket, one table & forme, one pannell chest	01	3	00
one kettle, 3 pans, 2 brass candlesticks	01	5	00
In the celler brewing vessell with one kimling	0	14	00
In the forehouse			
12 pewter dishes, 3 flaggons, one posset bowle, 3 plates, 3 salts, 2 tankards, one chamber pott	01	12	00
one cupboard, 2 tables, one long settle, one dresser, one chaire, one dozen of trenchers, one forme	01	00	00
brass & other implements	00	06	06
2 paire of racks, 2 spits & dripping pans & one iron pott & kettle	01	00	00
For work gear in the shop	01	10	00
One cow & 2 sturks	04	10	00
5 sheep	01	13	04
2 horses	04	00	00
in all	25	00	10

John Calvert [*signed*].

[1] Simon Prist (or Prest) was buried on 27 May 1688.

75. JOHN SIMPSON, 1689

DPRI/6/B/1688/S1

A true inventory of the goods & chattells of John Simpson late of North Allerton deceased. Apprized the 8 day of January 1688 [*8 Jan.* 1689] by Hugh Finch, Francis Meriton, Cuthbert Hall, Percivall Robinson.[1]

	£	s	d
Chattells			
Inprimis his purse & apparrell	0	15	0
Item one cowe	2	0	0
Item one darke gray horse	3	0	0
Item one white gray horse	1	0	0
Item one cock of hay 5 fatham ½	4	0	0
Item 4 stack barrs	0	6	0
Item in the barne & woodhouse forty five peices of small wood	0	1	6[2]
Item 1 cart & furniture belonging to it	2	0	0
Item one parcell of coales	1	0	0
Item in the wood chambers 52 oake boards with other implement peices of wood	3	10	0

	£	s	d
Item 2 dozen chares & worke geare in the shop with other implements	2	15	0
Item in the litle parlour 1 bed & bedstead, 1 chist, 1 table frame, 1 half head bedstead and other implementts	2	0	0
In the buttery one iron pot, 2 barrills, 1 chirne, 1 bushell with other implements	0	6	0
Item in the parlour next the kichin 1 bed & bedstead and one cupboard	1	5	0
Item in the fore chamber 2 tables, 9 chares, 1 table frame, 1 litle stoole	1	1	6
Item in the kichin all the pewder there	1	5	0
Item in the kichin brass and iron and other implement things	1	0	0
Item one cupboard, 1 dresser, 1 table with some other implements	1	15	0
	29	11	0
Debts oweing to the deceased.			
By William Stephenson	1	1	6
By John Wilson	1	5	0
By James Rowth	1	7	0
By Mathew Pybus	0	2	6

In wittness where of we have hereunto sett our hands the day and yeare above written. Hugh Finch [*signed*], Francis Meiriton [*signed*], Cudbert Hall [*signed*], Parcivall Robinson [*signed*]. Praisers of the same.[3]

[1] John Simpson was buried on 19 December 1688.

[2] Reading of sum of shillings uncertain; could be 16s 6d.

[3] The authentication by the appraisers has been drawn from an original (fragmentary) inventory of John Simpson's goods, preserved as DPRI/6/B/1688/S1/3.

76. JAMES LOWERY, 1689

DPRI/6/B/1688/L1

An inventory of the goods and chattells of James Lowrey late of North Allerton deceased, apprized the 24th day of January 1688 [*24 Jan. 1689*] by William Harrison, James Conyers, Robert Nelson, John Tomes.[1]

	£	s	d
Inprimis his purse and apparrell	5	0	0
Item in the fore house			

two tables & one cupboard	1	0	0
Item six chares, one [..........][2]ments	0	10	0
Item seaven pewter dishes, 13 plates, one flaggon, one salt with a warmeing pan at	1	4	0
Item in the parlour			
one bedstead with bed & hangings and one forme	0	15	0
Item in the fore chamber			
one bedstead with bed and hangings	1	10	0
Item one chist of drawers, one table, six chares, 1 wanded chare with 2 cushons & 1 seeing glass	1	01	6
Item in the back chamber			
two bed steads	0	6	8
Item 3 pare of fine sheets	1	4	0
Item 3 paire of course sheets	0	10	0
Item in the butry			
six pewter dishes, 5 plates, 2 tankerds, 2 chamber pots with other implements	1	0	0
Item 2 potts, 3 panns	0	7	6
Item 2 dozen of napkins, 6 pillow beares & 3 towells	0	15	8
Item in the warehouse Holl[and] and cambrick with musling	21	3	0
Item lace	17	5	0
Item stockins & gloves	08	12	0
Item quilted petticoats & wast coates with quilts for a bed	7	13	0
Item ribonds	9	9	0
Item hoods & scarfes with head dresses & gauses	7	1	0
Item footings and fringes	3	9	0
Item scot[c]h cloth, call[ico] & blew linne	2	1	0
Item pinns and incle	0	10	0
Item caps & sciscers	0	12	6
Item lute string and allamode	9	9	0
Item dyper and damaske	4	7	6
Item rould silks & Indians	34	9	0
Item stuffe and searge	3	5	0
Item shockalees & painted callico	3	12	0
Item silke laces & soweing silke	2	2	0
Item 5 chares, 3 tables & one stool	1	0	0
Item 1 pare of hampers and six boxes	0	6	0
Item 3 glasses	0	4	0
Item a silver tankerd, 2 silver cups with 7 spoons	9	5	0
Item horses and hay	6	0	0
Item coales and manure	0	13	4

	171	12	8
In moneys	030	10	0
In booke debts	046	05	6
Sume total	248	08	02

[1] James Lowery was buried on 12 January 1689.
[2] At least three words illegible.

77. HELEN ADSTON, WIDOW, 1689

DPRI/6/T/1689/A1

In the name of God, amen, the fourth day of January in the yeare of our Lord one thousand six hundred eighty and eight [*4 Jan. 1689*]. I, Hellen Adston of North Allerton in the county of York, widdow, being sick in body but of good and perfect memory (praised be God), doe make this my last will and testament in manner following. First I commend my soul into the hands of almighty God my creator, and my body to be buried in the church yard of North Allerton. And for my temporall estate I doe dispose thereof as followeth. First I give and bequeath unto my grandchilde John Thompson five pounds of lawfull money of England and to my grandchilde Hellen Thompson tenn pounds of like moneys. Alsoe I doe give and bequeath unto my grandchildren Robert Smith and Mary Smith twenty shillings apiece. Also I doe will, give and devise unto my daughter Hellen Watson the back parlour and kitchinge thereunto adjoyning with the chambers over them, being parcell of the messuage, burgage or tenement in North Allerton aforesaid wherein I now live, with free and open way and passage into and from the said parlour, kitching and chambers, as well through[1] the entry passage of the said messuage as through the yard or backside thereof for and dureing the term of her naturall life. And after her decease I doe will, give and devise the same premisses unto Elizabeth Watson, her daughter, her heires and assignes for ever. Alsoe I doe give and devise unto my said sonn James Adston the shopp wherein hee now worketh with free and open way and passage to and from the same. Alsoe I doe give and bequeath unto my said sonn James Adston one standinge bedd, feather bedd, bedcloths and furniture standing in the mealchamber; to my sonn Mark Adston five shillings; to my sonn in lawe John Smith two shillings six pence. All which severall legacyes shall be payd out of my personall estate by my executrix hereafter named. Alsoe I give unto the aforesaid Hellen Thompson one cubboard in the back parlour. Alsoe I doe will, give and devise unto my daughter

Hellen Watson aforesaid the stable next adjoyning to the kitching, with the liberty and use of the well on the backside, and halfe of the garden for her naturall life, and after her decease, unto the said Elizabeth Watson, her heires and assignes for ever. All the remaining part of my said messuage, burgage or tenement with the appurtenances I doe will, give and devise unto the said Elizabeth Watson for her naturall life, (yeilding and paying yearly and every yeare unto my aforesaid sonn Mark Adston the full and totall summe of three pounds of lawfully money of England at four payments in the year by even and equall portions videlicet: fifteen shillings by the quarter to be duely paid for the full time and terme of his naturall life, and also to pay twelve shillings by the year unto my sonne James Adston abovesaid, six shillings every halfe yeare of like English mony, duely to be payd him for the terme of his naturall life), after her decease to the first sonn of the body of the said Elizabeth Watson lawfully begotten or to be begotten and the heires of the body of such first sonn for ever. And for default of such issue, to the use of all and every other sonn and sonnes of the said Elizabeth Watson and the heires of the body of such sonn and sonns, the elder and his hieres to be preferred before the younger and his heirs as they shall be in seniority of age and priority of birth. And for default of such issue to all and every daughter and daughters of the said Elizabeth Watson lawfully to be begotten and the heirs of the body of such daughter or daughters for ever. And for default of such issue to the said Helen Thompson and John Thompson and their respective heires by equall moyties. All the rest of my goods and chattells, rights and credits (my debts, legacyes and funerall expences beinge satisfyed and discharged) I doe give and bequeath unto the said Helen Watson whome I make sole executrix of this my last will and testament. Witness my hand and seale the day and yeare above written.
Ellen Adston her marke [*sealed*][2]
Sealed, signed and published in the presence of us. Robert Nelson [*signed*], James Whitton [*signed*], Christopher Hunton his marke.

An aprasement made of the goods and chatells of Ellen Adston widdow late deceased of Northallerton by us whose names are here under written: February the 9 1688 [*9 Feb. 1689*]

	£	s	d
Imprimis, her purse & aparrell	01	00	00
In the forehouse one table, one counter, two chaires with other impliments	00	05	00
Item in the forehouse puter & brase and iron	00	17	00

Item brase in the forehouse	00	15	00
Item in the fore parler one table, one chest, one standing bed & one running <bed>	00	13	04
Item in the back parler one bed & bedding	01	06	08
Puter in the back parler	00	10	00
Item one cubbert, one table with other impliments	00	13	04
Item in the kiching brase & iron with other implyments	01	10	00
Item in the buttre brueing vessell	00	07	00
Item in the fore chamber one standing bed with bedding	01	06	08
Item one cubbert, one table, one fourm, one chest, one chaire with other implyments	01	00	00
Item in the meale chamber one bed & bedding with other implyments	00	15	00
Item in the back chamber two beds & beding with other implyments	02	10	00
Item coales	00	16	00
Totall	14	05	00

Witness our hands, Robert Nelson [*signed*], Parcivall Robinson [*signed*], Thomas Butcher [*signed*], Henry Danby his marke.

1 'through' repeated in MS.

2 Helen Adston was buried on 19 January 1689, fifteen days after making her will.

78. RICHARD GRIMSTON, GENTLEMAN, 1689

DPRI/6/T/1689/G1

In the name of God, amen, I, Richard Grimston of Northallerton in the county of Yorke, gentleman, calling to minde the frailty and incertainty of man's life and being of a good and sound minde and memory doe make this my last will and testament in manner following. As to my wordly estate I dispose thereof as followth. Imprimis, I give to my uncle Thomas Grimston's children sonnes and daughters living twenty shillings apeece severally as a token of my love. Item I give to my cozen Margarett Grymes five pounds as a token of my love. Item I give to my servant Thomas Thompson twenty shillings and to my servant Mary Kirby twenty shillings and to my servant Emme tenn shillings and to my servant Elizabeth ten shillings. Item I give to my kinsmen and friends Richard Staines esquire and William Kitchingman gentleman the summe or value of a guinea to each of them to by a ring for each of them in remembeance of me. And for the clearing of all doubts that may arise touching the lands, tenements and hereditaments I enjoy and possesse in right of my wife and which were or did belong to my wive's mother or

brothers, I doe hereby declare I did not[1] make, doe or suffer any act, matter or thing whereby to aliene or incumber the same, yett nevertheless as much as in mee lyes I do by this my last will give, devise and bequeath all and singuler other my said lands, tenements & hereditaments and alsoe all and singuler other my lands, tenements & hereditaments whatsoever as well freehold and leasehold in fee simple and fee tayle for terme of lives and yeares unto my loving wife Jane Grimston her heires and assignes for ever. And I doe also give all the residue of my goods and chattells and personal estate unto my said loving wife. And I doe make and appoint my said loving wife Jane Grimston sole executrix of this my last will and testament. And I doe hereby expressly fully and utterly revoke all former wills by me made and hereby declare this to bee my last will and testament. In witness whereof I have hereunto sett my hand and seale this two and twentieth day of Aprill in the yeare of our Lord God one thousand six hundred eighty and nine.
Richard Grimston seale [*not sealed*][2]
Signed, sealed & delivered by the said Richard Grimston in our presence and our names subscribed in his presence and by his direcions, the word (not) being first interlined, witnes, Joan Neile [*signed*], Dorothy Brownes marke, R. Raikes [*signed*].

The above written is a true copy of the last will and testament of Richard Grimston late of North Allerton gentleman deceased, the originall whereof was drawn by mee & published in my presence and my name subscribed as a witness to the signing thereof. And this copy has been carefully examined with the originall & it agrees there with, witnes my hand this twentieth day of December anno domini 1689. R. Raikes.

1 Emphasis as in MS.
2 Richard Grimston was buried on 11 May 1689, three weeks after making his will.

79. JANE PYBUS, SPINSTER, 1689

DPRI/6/B/1689/P2

An inventory of the goods of Jaine Pybus late of North Allerton in the county of Yorke spinster deceased.[1]

	£	s	d
Her purse & apparrell	1	0	0
Due to the deceased for wages	0	16	0
	1	16	0

Allerton 30mo Septembris 1689

[1] Jane Pybus was buried on 8 August 1689.

80. PERCIVAL ROBINSON, 1691

DPRI/6/B/1691/R1

A true and perfect inventory of the goods of Percivall Robinson late of North Allerton deceased, apprized the 5th day of March (91) by William Harrison, James Coats, Percival Robinson.[1]

	£	s	d
Inprimis his purse and apparrell	01	06	08
In the forehouse			
2 table, 3 chares, 3 stooles, one jack, 1 chafing dish, 1 spitt, one pair of bellows, grid irons, one iron grub, chopping knife, one brass ladle, two candlesticks, one pair of tongs, one fire shovell, six pictures	00	15	00
In the buttery			
one tin driping pan, one tin flagon, one dish cover, one skeele, four stone platers, 4 pewter spoons, 12 trenchers, one iron pot, two prass pans, thirty 8 pound and ½ of pewter at 7d per pound, 3 dishes or pigons	01	06	08
In the parlour			
one bedstead, one feather bed with curtains and bedcloths, one old table, one firme, one fir cupboard, one wanded chare, one buffet stoole, two cushon covers, four pictures, 1 runlet, one meale basket	00	13	04
Two bedsteads, one flock bed, 2 rugs, a sute of old darnick curtains	01	04	04
Two wood boxes, one ridle, one pye board, 3 pair of ordinary linnen sheets, two table cloths, 12 napkins, 2 pillowbears, one old leaven cloth	00	15	00
In the work house			
1 candle case, 1 chopping trough, 1 beating trough, six tubbs, one brass kettle in a frame, 4 stays of firr, 6 dozen of candle broaches, 2 chopping knives, one ladle, two wood mells, 1 parcell of tallow computed to 8 stone 3 pound and a halfe	02	09	00
In the shop			
one shop chest, one weighing balk, one pair of skales wood, severall lead weights amounting 7 stone,			

2 pair of brass skales, one old lanthhorn, 2 dozen pound of candles, 9 boxes in & case	01 05 06
	10 05 06
	[*recte* 09 15 06]
Debts oweing to the intestate	20 00 00

[1] Percival Robinson was buried on 22 January 1691. An administration bond was issued on 16 April 1691, confirming that the date of the inventory (5 March 1691) is given according to modern usage.

81. CHRISTOPHER APPLETON, 1691

DPRI/6/T/1691/A1

In the name of God, amen, I, Cristofer Applton of Northallerton, elder, being in perfect memery, blesed be God. I make my last will and testiment as followeth. Item I leave to my sone George my house and garth, back housing and the tantubs ~~when he comes~~, my wife haveing the south roumested for her life when itt folles to me. Item I leave to my son Cristofer Hicklay Close and my son George to pay ten pounds out of the house to him. Item I leave to my sone Samwell Galicar Close. My debts and funerall charges to be pad out of my stock, and <the rest of> my goods and chatels for my wife to bring up the children withall. I make John Calvert and Robert Wellbanck my exsecketers.

In wittnes here of I have sett my hand and seall.

Cristofer Applton his mark [*sealed*][1]

Mary Shemeld [*signed*], Mary Callvert her mark, George Shemeld [*signed*].

Aprasment of all Christopher Apelton goods being lattly deseased.

	£	s	d
His purs and appareall att	2	10	0
In the low parlear			
one cobert with puter belonging to witt, one table and 10 chars att	2	0	0
In the fore hous			
one table, one forme, one longsetle, one dreser table, 6 puter dishes with other small things att	1	10	0
In the buttry			
one catle, one pot, 2 pans, 2 dozen of bowles att	2	0	0
In the chamber			
1 bedd and beding, 2 chests, one table att	0	15	0

7 pare of shets, 7 pillowbers, one table cloth, 1 dozen of napkins	1	10	0
One hay stack, one swine att	2	10	0
Tow cows att	5	0	0
Thre horses att	10	0	0
Thre sheep att	1	0	0
Carts and cart geer att	2	10	0
4 ackers of peas att	1	6	8
Maner att	1	0	0
9 dack of ledder att	43	0	0
11 backs att	6	12	0
13 peces att	2	12	0
9 dozen of calfe skins att	7	10	0
42 bends green att	6	10	0
8 streight bends	3	4	0
8 fore bends at	1	12	0
7 small bends att	0	4	0
4 peces, 4 belies att	0	18	0
22 heads	1	0	0
6 hors skins att	0	15	0
Un chopt bark att	4	10	0
15 quarters of chopt bark	6	0	0
[*Total*	*117*	*18*	*08*]

George Shemeld [*signed*], John Awmars [*signed*], Christopher Hunton <his marke>.

[1] Christopher Appleton was buried on 5 May 1691.

82. GEORGE DRYBROUGH, 1691

DPRI/6/B/1691/D1

September the 26 1691. A true & perfect inventory made of all the goods and chattles moveable & unmoveable of George Drybrough of North Allerton in the county of Yorke late deceased. Appraized by us whose names are underwritten &c.[1]

	£	s	d
Inprimis his purss and apparell	10	00	00
Item in the fore house one table, one drusser, one long settle, a warmeing pan & other implements	01	12	00
In the parler 2 little tables, 2 standers, 6 chaires, one silver tumbler, one seeing glass	03	02	00
In the buttery in pewder, brass & other implements	02	02	00

In the chamber over the parler two beds & bed steades with furniture, one chist drawers, two chaires, 1 pannle cheste, one nest boxes	04	10	00
In the chamber over the fore house two little beds with furniture, 2 little tables, one pannle cheste, 11 chares, 9 stoales & other implements	05	18	04
Lining			
4 paire lin sheets, 8 paire course sheetes, 2 paire course pillivers, 1 dosen napkins, 2 linn table cloths, 2 linn webs	04	14	08
In the milke house			
20 boales, 10 shelves, 2 skeeles, 1 firme & other implements	00	08	00
In the fore shopp 4 bedd steeds & 1 coffer	02	01	03
In back shopp & worke house			
20 routh bedd steades unmade upp, 56 ½ inch oake boardes, 30 oake plankes & other peices of wood, 3 coffins, 2 styes, 1 grunstone with all the worke toales	15	02	06
In the pasture			
4 kine & 1 stirke, one mare & one rooke hay	13	10	00
A swine	00	09	09
	63	10	06
Depts owne to the deceased	02	05	00
Dept owne by the deceased for ½ yeare rent	04	00	00

John Coates [*signed*], James Coates [*signed*], Geo: Dunn [*signed*], William Harrison [*signed*].

[1] George Drybrough was buried on 14 May 1691.

83. JANE BRADLEY, SPINSTER, 1692

DPRI/6/T/1692/B1

In the name of God, amen, the fourthteine day of Aprill in the yeare of our Lord one thousand six hondered & ninty. I, Jane Bradley of Northallerton in the county of York, spinster, being sicke in body but of good and perfect memory praised be God do make this my last will and testament in manner and forme following. First I give my soul into the hands of allmighty God my creator and my body to be buryed in the church yard of North Allerton. And for the temporall estate which it hath pleased God to be stow upon me I do dispose there of in manner following. First I give to Thomas Bradley, fellmounger, sonne to Edmond Bradley, a bedstead, tow bowsters,

tow kods, a chafbed & a fetherbed, tow samron sheets, tow blankitts, tow coverlids & a roug and twenty shilings in money. Secondly I give to Thomas Bradley, alle keeper, sonn of Thomas Bradley, one shiling and twelfe pence apeice for his tow childer as there partes. Thirdly I give to Margret Duning all my close, both lining and woolling & twenty shilings in money. Fourthly I give unto Thomas Bradley, the housband of Margrey Bradley, five shilings & to Jane his daughter five shilings. Fifthly I give to the thre childer of Edward Bradley, the bellman, five shilings apeece, which is fifteen shilings. Sixtly I give to Thomas Bradley, sonne of Richard Bradley, and to his eldist daughter either of them five shilings, which is tenn shiling. Sevently I give Edward Bradley, the barber, five shilings for his wife. And eightly I give Richard Smith, fellmonger, five shilings & to Mary his wife tenn shillings. Ninthly I give to Peter Burdan a yallow coverin. And lastly I do make George Smith my sole executer of this my last will & testement. And it is my will & pleasuer that George Smith, excecuter, shall se this my will accomplished, first discharging my buriall expences & then give to them above named there parts as abov<e> written. I give to John Tison one shiling & to his wife my spining wheele. In witnes hereof I have here unto set my hand & seale the day and yeare above nameed.
Jane Bradley hir mark [*sealed*][1]
Sealed and delivered in the presence of John Ballmer [*signed*], George Smith [*signed*], John Stockdale [*signed*], Richard Smith [*signed*].

The inventary of Jane Bradley who decesed the 7th of February 1691 [*7 Feb. 1692*], by us whose names are subscribed as followeth.

	£	s	d
Imprimis hir purrs & aparrill	06	00	00
Item one bed & what belonged to it	01	04	00
Item puder & brasse	00	04	00
Item 3 stowels, a table with other things	00	08	00
Item wheat, a swill with implements	00	02	00
Item lining with a covering more	00	11	00
9 kokes	00	04	00
	08	13	00
The debtes of the deceased[2]			
Imprimis Margret Duning	01	00	00
Item Thomas Bradley, fellmonger	01	00	00
Item Edward Bradley's 3 childer, bellman	00	15	00
Item Thomas Bradley & his daughter	00	10	00
Item Richard Smith & his wife	00	15	00

Item Thomas Bradley, alle kepar, <&> childer	00	03	00
Item Edward Wells rere of rent	00	08	06
Item John Thomas for rent	00	06	08
Item Edward Bradley, barber	00	05	00
Item Jane Bradley	00	05	00
Item John Tison	00	01	00
Item hir feunerall expences	03	00	00
	08	09	02

John Gibsone [*signed*], Robert Stringer [*signed*].

[*On a separate sheet:*]

Know all men by these presents that I, George Smith of North Allerton in the county of York, yeoman, executor of the last will and testament of Jane Bradley late of North Allerton aforesaid, deceased, doe renounce all my right, title and intrest in and to the said will and doe desire that administracion of the goods and chattells of the said deceased may be granted to Richard Smith, my father. Witness my hand this 12th day of May anno domini 1692.

George Smith [*signed*]

Witness Christopher Watkin [*signed*].

1 Jane Bradley died on 7 February 1692 and was buried the following day, almost two years after making her will.

2 The majority of these debts are the legacies to individuals mentioned in Jane Bradley's will.

84. RICHARD ATKINSON, 1692

DPRI/6/B/1692/A1

Maii the 12th 1692.

An appraisement made of the goods and chattles of Richard Atkinson late deseaced by us whose names are under written.[1]

	£	s	d
Imprimis his purss and apparell	01	00	00
In the fore house a cubbertt, 4 dublers, one flaggon, one candlestick, one table, tow stooles, 2 chares, one chist	01	06	08
In the parler one <chafe> bed and 2 pair of sheets, on coverlett, on blankett, tow pillevers	00	14	00
In the parler one loome with geeres	00	15	00
[*Total*	*03*	*15*	*08*]

Timothy Hurst [*signed*], George Tuke [*signed*], Edward Johnson [*signed*], Parce[val] Robinson [*signed*].

1 Richard Atkinson was buried on 16 April 1692.

85. ROBERT LAMB, ROUGH MASON, 1693

DPRI/6/B/1692/L1

A true and perfect inventory of all & singuler the goods and chattells of Robert Lamb late of North Allerton in the county of York rough mason deceased, valued and apprized by us whose names are here under written the seaventh day of January in the yeare of our Lord God one thousand six hundred ninety and two [*7 Jan. 1693*].[1]

	£	s	d
Imprimis his purse and apparell	00	05	00
Item one bedstead, bedd & bedding all very worn	00	10	00
Item one cupboard & two pewther dishes	00	05	00
Item a paire of thongs & an iron pott	00	02	06
Item one table	00	01	00
Item one stone ax, one hammer & one troughill	00	03	00
Item one cow	02	00	00
	03	06	06

the marke of Adam Tessimond, the marke of Thomas Thompson.

[1] Robert Lamb was buried on 4 January 1693.

86. JOHN SIMPSON, 1693

DPRI/6/B/1693/S1

May 8th [16]93

An aprasement made of the goods and chattills of John Simsons of Northallerton late deceased by us whose names are here under written.[1]

	£	s	d
Imprimis his purse and his aparrell	01	00	00
Item in the low parler one tabill, one chest, one coffer, one trunk, two boxeses with other inplyments	00	13	04
Item in the backe parler two beds at	01	10	00
Item in the fore house one cubbertt, one tabill	00	10	00
Item puter & brase with other small implyments	00	10	00
Item one cheese pres at	00	01	00
Item two geild cows at	05	10	00
Item two cows att	07	00	00
Item one stirke	01	00	00
the totall sume	16	14	04

Robert Nellson [*signed*], John Lafield [*signed*], John Jhinson [*signed*], Simon Tod [*signed*].

Direct it to Henry Sayer iuratus, coram Samuel Martin.[2]

[1] John Simpson was buried on 5 May 1693.
[2] This line added in a different hand.

87. ANTHONY WATSON, MERCHANT, 1693

DPRI/6/B/1693/W1

Houshold stuff belonging to Anthony Watson merchant in North Allerton late deceased. Apprized & valewed the first day of June [*1693*] by Mathew Pybus, Robert Nelson, John Gillinge and William Smelt.

	£	s	d
Inprimis his purse and apparrell	05	00	00
Item in the fore house two tables, one longsettle, 9 chaires & one jack with other implements	01	15	00
Item in the butterey 9 pewter dishes, 13 plaites with a chirne, a paile and a flasket and other implements	01	10	00
Item two brass potts, one pann and a warming pann, two candlesticks of peuter, one chamber pott and a tankerd, a flaggon & other implements, one dresser table in the butterey	01	00	00
Item in the best chamber one bedstead with hangings, one feather bed & other furniture; one dozen of chaires, one chest of drawers with a table, one looking glass and a little glass case	06	00	00
Item in the second chamber one bedstead with hangings and one feather bed and such as belongs it, one truckle bed with bed cloathes, another truckle bed and two feather beds belonging to them, one pannell chist, one creddle and one chaire	02	00	00
Item in the little chamber one cubbert, 2 trunkes with other implements	00	10	00
Item in lining, three dozen of napkins, fower table cloathes, 5 paire of linn sheetes, six paire of course sheetes, six paire of pilloveares	03	08	00
Item in plaite, one tankerd, 1 tumbler, 4 silver spoones	05	00	00
The total	26	03	00
One galloway	02	00	00
Item one cow	03	05	00
Item one peice of old hay	01	00	00
In all	06	05	00
Shopp goods belonging the deceased.			
Inprimis fustions and dimothyes and other such remnants	03	10	00

Item buttons	04	00	00
Item fine threds, caddices, ribbins, gallownes, ferrits, cards, silke fringes, moehaire fringes & braide	13	15	08
Item gloves and silk edging	02	05	00
Item hatts	15	00	00
Item stockings, silke threds, inkle and white paper	15	00	00
Item black and mixt searges	12	13	04
Item careseys	03	10	00
Item broad cloath	08	03	06
Item gold and silver lace and gold and silver thred, alamode, whale bone, flanill, mild searge & callicoes	13	00	00
Item stuffes, callimankers, camletts, parragons and tobacco	08	07	04
Sugar loafes and other grosseryes	02	10	00
The totall	101	04	10
[*Inventory total*	*134*	*02*	*10*]

88. GEORGE TUKE, YEOMAN, 1694

DPRI/6/T/1694/T1

In the name of God, amen, I, George Tuke of North Allerton in the county of York, yeoman, being weake in body but of perfect memory doe make this my last will & testament. I doe give unto my two sisters Isabell Tuke and Margret Tuke my whole personall estate. Item I doe give unto my two sisters Isabell Tuke and Margret Tuke one close or parcell of land containeing the estimation of two acres or upwards called by the name of Whorner Maupis and to be in the said Isabell Tuke and Margret Tuke's disposeing to whome they please. Item I doe give unto the said Isabell Tuke and Margret Tuke one ox gang of land called by the name of Old Land with its rights. Item I doe give unto the said Isabell Tuke and Margret Tuke one house with the backhouseing, barne and common right dureing their naturall lives. Item I doe give unto Robert Thearsby the younger of Morton after the decease of Isabell Tuke and Margarett Tuke one oxgang of land with the house, backhousing, barne and common right, the said Robert Thearsby the younger paying to Avarill Haukeswill five pounds, to Thomas Thearsby five pounds, to Ann Thearsby five pounds, to George Thearsby five pounds, that the said Robert Thearsby the younger shall pay before entrance. Item I doe give unto Robert Thearsby the elder and Ann his wife five shillings. Item I doe give unto the poore of North Allerton the use of five pounds to enter after my decease to be paid at the next Christmas after that the said Isabell Tuke and Margaret Tuke & Robert Thearsby the younger

and his heires shall forever hereafter pay the said six shillings once a yeare without fraud or let. In witness I have hereunto set my hand and seal the twenty first day of August in the year of our Lord 1693. George Tuke.[1]
Sealed and delivered in the presence of Marke Calvert his mark, Ralph Humphrey his mark, Thomas Foster.

May the 23 anno domini 1694. Received the originall last will and testament of the said George Tuke deceased where of this is a true copy.
Witness. Isabell Tuke <her mark>, Margret Tuke <her mark>, William Harrison [*signed*].

[1] George Tuke was buried on 29 October 1693, two months after making his will.

89. ROBERT JACKSON, HUSBANDMAN, 1694

DPRI/6/B/1694/J1

A true and perfect inventorie of the goods and chattells and other personall estate of Robert Jackson late of North Allerton in the county of Yorke, husbandman, deceased, taken and apprized this nineteenth day of March by Symon Taylor, Thomas Flower his marke, Blaze Driver, Robert Stringer as followeth.[1]

	£	s	d
Imprimis his purse and apparell	01	00	00
In the forehouse			
one long table, one forme, one large cupboard, one woodden chaire and one woodden stoole with other implements	00	15	00
Item seaven pewter dishes, two pewter flaggons, two pewter plaites, one pewter <tankerd, 2 pewter> candlestick, one brass candlestick with other implements of iron	01	00	00
In the butterey			
Item fower pewter dishes, one brass bason, one press, one milke skeele, one dozen of trenshers and other small implements	00	10	00
In the chamber over the parlour			
one pannell chest, one little table, one trunck, 6 milk boules	00	06	08
In the chamber over the forehouse			

one bedstead with the beding upon it, three bushells of wheat, one old chaire	01	00	00
In the fould yard			
Item two draught oxen	10	00	00
In the feild			
Two new calven kine	07	10	00
Two draught horses	05	00	00
Ten sheep	03	00	00
One carte, one pair of old wheiles, one plough	02	00	00
One pyke of barley	04	00	00
Wheat sowne upon the ground three acres	06	00	00
Four acres of beanes sowne	04	00	00
One pyke of hay	01	10	00
In all	47	11	08
Debts oweing to the deceased at his death			
Oweing by Thomas Flower husbandman by bond	20	00	00
Debts oweing by the deceased at his death			
Oweing to Mr Grymston and Blaze Dryver	10	00	00
Oweing to Mary Drybrough	01	10	00

[1] Robert Jackson was buried on 15 March 1694.

90. JOHN HARPER, VICAR OF NORTHALLERTON, 1694

DPRI/1/1700/H5

In the Name of God, amen, the 17 day of March anno domini 1693/4. I, John Harper <vicar of North Allerton in the county of York> being sick in body but of good and perfect memory, thanks be to almighty God, and calling to remembrance the uncertain estate of this transitory life, and that all flesh must yield unto death when it shall please God to call, do make, constitute, ordain and declare this my last will & testament in manner and form following, revoking and adnulling by these presents all and every testament and testaments, will and wills heretofore by me made and declared either by word or writing. And this is to be taken onely for my last will and testament, and none other. And first being penitent and sorry from the bottome of my heart for my sins past, most humbly desiring pardon and forgiveness for the same, I give and commit my soul unto almighty God my saviour and redeemer in whom, and by the merits of Christ Jesus, I trust and believe assuredly to be saved, and to have full remission and forgivenesse of all my sins; and that my soul with my body at the general day of resurrection, shall rise

again with joy and through the merits of Christ's death and passion possesse and inherit the kingdome of Heaven, prepared for his elect, and chosen, and my body to be buried in such a place, as it shall please my executor or executrix hereafter named to appoint. And now for the setling of my temporal estate, and such goods, chattels and debts, as it hath pleased God, far above my deserts to bestow upon me; I do order, give and dispose the same in manner and form following, (that is to say). First, I will that all those debts and duties as I owe in right or conscience to any manner of person or persons whatsoever, shall be well and truly contented and paid, or ordained to be paid within convenient time after my decease, by my executor or executrix hereafter named. Item I give and bequeath to my brother Nicholas Bryan five shillings, and to each of his children as much; to my neice Elizabeth Harper (if she will accept of it) one shilling. Item to my neice Mary Harper sixty pound to be paid over to William Miller of Ford for her use; my meaning is that it should remain in his hands, he paying for the use of it, till she be married, and if she dye unmarried, then it shall be divided among my brother Brian's children by equal portions. Item I bequeath unto my nephew Robert Davidson the summe of ten pounds to be paid to him either when he goes to an apprenticeship or the university. And of this my last will and testament, I constitute and appoint Elizabeth Harper my beloved wife sole executrix. Witness my hand and seal this seventeenth day of March anno domini 1693/4
John Harper [*signed and sealed*][1]
Signed and sealed in the presence of us Samuel Martin [*signed*], James Whitton [*signed*].

[1] John Harper, vicar of Northallerton from 1686 to 1694, was buried on 29 June 1694. The son of Edward Harper, yeoman, of Bishop Wearmouth, Co. Durham, he was born *c.*1636–67 and educated at Sedbergh School, in the West Riding of Yorkshire, before being admitted sizar at St John's College, Cambridge in 1654. He was awarded an MA in 1662. He was vicar of Berwick upon Tweed before moving to Northallerton: J. and J. A. Venn, *Alumni Cantabrigienses* (Cambridge, 1922–54).

91. ROBERT NELSON, 1695

DPRI/6/B/1695/N1
Aprill the 7th 1695. An apprizement made of the goods & chattells of Robert Nelson of North Allerton lately deceased by us William Harrison, James Whitton, Henry Sayer, Marke Nelson.[1]

	£	s	d
Imprimis his purse and apparell	05	05	00
Item in the house			
2 tables, 5 chares, one long settle, one jack, one wanded chare, one warming pann, 3 stooles, 2 pare of tongs, one fire shovell, one speet, 4 cushions, one reckon with other implements	02	16	04
Item in the entrey parlour			
one bedstead, one chaff bed, one bolster, one rugg with curtaines, one blankett, 2 tables, 7 chares, one voyder, one paire of window curtaines, one chest, one white table cloth	02	02	06
Item in the little parlour			
one bedstead, one feather bed, one bolster, one rugg, one paire of blankets with curtaine, 2 chares & one coffer	01	03	04
Item in the chamber over the entry			
one bedstead, one feather bed, one bolster, 2 feather cods, one rugg, one coverlett with hangings, one blankett, one chest of drawers, one seeing glass, one case of knives & tenn chares, one voyder, 4 paire of linn sheets & three paire of course sheets & 8 pillowbeers, one dozen and a half of linn napkinns & one little table	06	09	06
Item in the chamber over the house			
two little truckle bedds, 3 coverletts, one pannell chest, 3 shelves, 10 bowles, 2 skeeles, 2 cheesefatts & 2 sinkers	00	17	10
Item in the pantry			
7 pewter dishes, 4 plates, one posset bowle, 3 brass candlesticks, one flaggon, one tankard, one dish cover, one plate, one dozen of trenshers, one little cupboard, 2 salts, one mustard pott	01	04	06
Item in the kitching			
one iron pott, 3 panns, one plank table, one swill, one paire of racks	00	09	00
Item in the milk house			
one hogshead, two tearces, one chirne, one cheese trough, one meall tubb, one milk paile, one brass kettle, 6 shelves, one cheese press	01	01	04
Item in the malt chamber 16 quarters of malt	10	14	00
Item in the kilne one bushell, 3 sacks, one shovell	00	04	06

Item in the stable one old chest, one rack, one mainger,			
10 sheep heck, one peck, one ladder			
Item one silver tumbler	00	10	00
Item in the barne one cart and cart geeres & 8 stack barrs	01	11	04
Item 2 mares	05	10	00
Item 60 sheep and 3 kine	47	00	00
Item 3 horses	18	00	00
Item 2 whyes	06	00	00
Item 2 oxen	07	00	00
Item 2 stotts	06	00	00
Item 2 calves	02	00	00
Item 2 scotch kine	04	00	00
	130	07	02
Debts oweing by the deceased as followeth			
To Matthew Morley of Stoaksley	100	00	00
To Nicholas Stephenson	30	00	00
	130	00	00

[1] Robert Nelson was buried on 6 April 1695.

92. WILFRID SADLER, 1695

DPRI/6/B/1697/S1

December the 21st 1695.

A true and perfect inventory of all the goods and chattells of Willfrid Sadler of Thornborrow in the parish of North Allerton late deceased. Apprised by us whose names are underwritten.[1]

	£	s	d
Inprimis his purse and apparrell	02	10	00
Item in the fore house			
two tables, three chaires with stooles and other necessaryes	01	05	00
Item in the parlour			
two bedsteades with bedding and two chests, one cupboard to the value of	01	15	00
Item in the larder			
two kettles, eight pieces of pewter with other wooden utensills	03	00	00
Item in the milk house			
one churne, one stand with bowles & such like necessaries	01	00	00
Item in the chamber			
one bedd, one tubb with bedding & other things	01	00	00

Item in the shopp, wright worke tooles with wood and other implements	02 00 00
Item corne in the barne & in stacks	12 00 00
with winter corne sowne on the ground	15 00 00
Item nine kine within calfe	30 00 00
Item foure young beasts	07 10 00
Item one maire to the value of	02 00 00
Item sheepe to the value of	05 00 00
Item hay to the value of	10 00 00
The whole summe	94 00 00

William Sadler, Thomas Brittaine, James Sadler, Robert Fleetom.

[1] Wilfred Sadler was buried on 15 December 1695.

93. JOHN KAYE, GENTLEMAN, 1697

DPRI/6/T/1697/K1

In the name of God, amen, I, John Kaye of Wisk Moore[1] in the county of York, gentleman, being weak in body but of good sound & perfect mind and memory, praised bee God, doe make and publish this my last will & testament in manner and forme following. And first I commend my soule into the hands of almighty God who gave it and my body to the ground from whence it came to bee buried in such decent & comely manner as my executrix hereafter named shall think fitt. And for the worldly goods wherewith God hath blessed mee I give, devise and dispose thereof in manner and forme following. Imprimis, I give & devise unto my well-beloved wife Elizabeth and heires & assignes all that close or parcell of ground called and known by the name of Turkitt Flatt conteining by estimacion twenty acres or thereabouts bee the same more or lesse; all those two closes or parcells of ground called by the name of Fold Closes conteining together by estimacion thirteen acres bee they more or lesse; all that other close or parcell of ground called the Stripe adjoyning upon the lands of Edward Foxton on the north conteining by estimacion six acres bee the same more or lesse; all that other close or parcell of ground called Midle Close conteining by estimacion seaven acres bee the same more or lesse; all that one other close or parcell of ground called Far Winter Close conteining by estimacion twelve acres bee the same more or lesse; all those other two closes or parcells of ground called and known by the name of Dynnis Closes conteining together by estimacion fifteen acres bee the same more or lesse; and all that my reversion expectant upon the death and decease of Francis Kay, my father, & Ursula Kay, my mother of all that messuage, tenement or dwelling house called Wiske Moor House wherein I now live; of all that one close of pasture ground called by the name of Wisk Moor conteining by estimacion fourescore acres or thereabouts bee the same more or lesse; of all that one other close or parcell of ground called by the name of Wiske Ings and a paddock thereunto adjoyning conteining by estimacion twenty one acres bee the same more or lesse; all such share and part as I have to the revercion of one close called the Rigg adjoyning on Allerton Street on the east conteining by estimacion seaven acres bee the same more or lesse; all which said messuage, tenement, lands, closes or parcells of ground and premises are scytuate, lying or being within the precints & territories of Brompton in the county of York (except the said two closes called Dinnis Closes and the said close called the Rigg which are lying and being within the precincts & territories of North Allerton[)] & all in the occupacion of mee or my assignes upon the speciall trust and confidence in the said Elizabeth my wife reposed; to have and to hold the same and every part thereof with their & every of their rights, members and appurtenances unto the said Elizabeth my wife, her heires & assignes to and for the use and behoofe of my eldest sonn John untill hee doe attaine unto his full age of one & twenty yeares & then to his heires & assignes forever, subject nevertheles and chargeable with and lyable to the payment of the severall porcions to my younger children herein after named, that is to say, Imprimis I give & bequeath unto my daughter Ursula, my daughter Elizabeth, my sonne William, my sonne Francis and my daughter Grace to each of them the summe of one hundred poundes of lawfull English money to bee paid unto them severally & respectively when they & every of them shall attaine to their severall & respective ages of one & twenty yeares. But if it shall soe happen that if any of my above named sonnes or daughters shall happen to dye and depart this life before they or such of them soe dying attaine to their or such of their full age of one & twenty yeares, then my mind and will is that my said sonne John and all and singuler my lands & premisses shall be discharged from the payment of such porcion or porcions unto my younger children or such of them as shall bee then living or any part thereof. And my mind and will is that if it shall soe fall out that my <said> wife Elizabeth bee with child, then that such sonn or daughter soe to bee born of [the][2] body of my said wife shall have paid unto him or her the summe of one hundred pounds of like lawfull English money when hee or she shall attaine to the full age of one and twenty yeares. But if it shall happen that such child bee born and brought

forth and happen to dye & depart this life before itt attaine to the full age of one & twenty yeares then my mind & will is that my said sonne John & my lands & premisses shall be discharged from the payment thereof unto any of my abovenamed children now living or any of the survivor or survivors of them. And alsoe that all and every my above named sonnes & daughters shall out of the rents, issues and proffitts of my said lands, closes and premisses bee mainteined, educated and brought upp untill they attaine unto their severall and respective ages of one & twenty yeares & alsoe such sonn or daughter as may bee born or brought forth after my decease. But if it shall soe fall out and happen that my said sonne John neglect and faile to pay (unto my other children above named or to such child as hereafter may bee born) the aforesaid severall summes of one hundred poundes a peice when they shall severally attaine unto their respective ages of one & twenty yeares, then my mind and will is and I doe hereby declare that it shall & may bee lawfull to and for such child or children soe wanting his or her porcion severally and respectively as the same shall become due & payable into my said lands, closes and premisses, to enter and hold the same & every part thereof till hee or shee bee fully paid and satisfied. And as a further token of my love unto Elizabeth my wife I give and devise unto her one of the said closes called Dynnis Closes, that is to say the lesser of them, to hold to her for and dureing the term of her naturall life, but as noe satisfaccion nor noway in discharge of her thirds. Item after my debts and funerall expences bee paid and discharged I doe give and bequeath unto my said loving wife Elizabeth all and singuler my goods and chattells, rights and creddits & tuicion of my said children <and I doe make my said wife Elizabeth executrix of my last will & testament> and doe publish and declare this my last will and testament, and I doe hereby revoke, disannull and make voyd all other wills and testaments by me heretofore formerly made. In witnes whereof I have hereunto sett my hand & seall this foure & twentieth day of May in the yeare of our Lord God one thousand six hundred ninety & six.
John Kaye [*signed and sealed*][3]
Signed, sealed, published & declared by the within named John Kay to bee his last will & testament in our presence. Cuthbart Fletem [*signed*], Thomas Brass [*signed*], Francis Kaye [*signed*].

A true and perfect inventory of the goods & chattells of John Kaye of Wiskmoore gentleman lately deceased, apprised by us whose names are under written this twenty 7th day of May anno domini 1696 as followeth.

	£	s	d
Inprimis his purse and apparrell & household stuffes att	10	00	00
In the New Ground			
two oxen & three stirks att	14	00	00
one dunn colt att	11	00	00
one bay colt and a foale att	06	10	00
sixteene ewes & fourteene lambs att	11	04	00
fifteene acres of hard corne att	30	00	00
six stirks att	7	16	00
In Wisk Moore Ground			
one paire of three yeare old steers att	07	00	00
four two yeare old stotts and one why att	10	00	00
thirty hogg sheep and five lambs att	13	10	00
twenty ewes & twenty eight lambs att	14	00	00
three acres of wheat att	06	00	00
twelve acres of oates att	12	00	00
thirty stookes of old wheat att	02	00	00
two cowes and two quyes att	10	00	00
nine milk cowes & two bulls att	37	10	00
four young calves att	01	00	00
two working horses att	03	00	00
one swyne att	00	13	00
one waine att	01	10	00
	206	13	00

Apprised by us: Roger Hillson, John Wade, Cuthbert Fleeteham, John Wilson his marke.

[1] Wiske Moor (SE 352 972), two miles north of Northallerton.
[2] MS reads 'my' but 'the' is presumably intended.
[3] John Kaye was buried at Brompton on 26 May 1696, two days after making his will.

94. ALICE RAPER, WIDOW, 1697

DPRI/6/T/1697/R1

In the name of God, amen, I, Alice Raper of North Allerton in the county of York, widdow, being infirme in body but of sound & perfect mind & memory, praised bee God for the same, do make & publish this my last will & testament in manner and forme following. Imprimis, I commend my soule to God who gave it & my body to the earth from whence it came to bee buried in such decent & comely manner as by my executor hereafter named shall bee thought fitt and convenient. And as for the worldly goods wherewith God hath

blessed me I give, devise and dispose thereof in manner and forme following. Imprimis, I give & bequeath unto Christopher Robinson of North Allerton skinner and to his executors, administrators and assignes all my household goods, house hold stuffe and all and singuler other my goods and chattells, rights and creditts, hee the said Christopher Robinson paying <& giving> unto such person or persons as shall bee hereafter named such legacyes as shall bee mencioned (that is to say) to Valentine Raper one great cupboard & two pewter dishes & two candlesticks. Item I give & bequeath unto Valentine Rymer one bedd, bedd stead & bedding <now being in the hands of Anne Raper at Romanby> if hee the said Valentine Rymer come to North Allerton or Romanby within twelve yeares & alsoe one pewter dish & two candlesticks, but if it soe fall out that the said Valentine Rymer do not come or appeare within the said terme then my mind & will is that the said bedd, bedstead & bedding shall be given & delivered unto the said Valentine Raper. Item I give & bequeath unto Anne Raper the summe of twenty shillings & all my cloaths (except one coate & one petticoate which I give & bequeath unto Elizabeth Hollin[)]. Item I give & bequeath unto Jane Kanetty two pewter dishes. Item I give & bequeath unto Anne Abbott one long settle, one flaggon & one dozen of trenchers. And I do hereby make the said Christopher Robinson executor of this my last will & testament & do hereby appoint and direct the said Christopher Robinson to pay and discharge my funeral expences, debts & legacyes & I do declare this to bee my last will & testament. In witnes whereof I have hereunto sett my hand & seale this seaven & twentieth day of Aprill in the yeare of our Lord one thousand six hundred ninety & seaven.
The marke & seale of Alice Raper.[1]
Signed, sealed & published by the testatrix at her request & by her direcions in our presence. The marke of Dameras Gamble, The marke of Easter Peacock, Francis Kaye [*signed*].

A true appraisement and inventory of the goods & chattells of Alice Rayper lately deceased in the town of North-Allerton in this present year 1697 and praised by us whose names are under written.

	£	s	d
Imprimis her purse & apparrel	02	00	00
Item six chests	00	08	00
Item three tables	00	05	00
Item two old bedsteads	00	04	00
Item 2 beds, 2 boulsters, 2 pillows, 4 coverlitts	01	00	00

Item 4 pair of sheets	00	10	00
Item one silver tumbler	00	06	08
Item 6 smal pewter dishes with other smal peices	00	06	00
Item some inckle, laces & pins	00	02	06
Item some Duch bread	00	15	00
Item some treakle	00	02	00
Item one horse	01	15	00
	07	14	02

James Rowth, George Shemeld, Thomas Rayper.

[1] Alice Raper was buried on 2 May 1697, five days after making her will.

95. HENRY CLIFFE, CURRIER, 1697

DPRI/6/T/1697/C1

In the name of God, amen, I, Henry Cliffe of North Allerton in the county of Yorke, currier, being infirme & sick of body but of good & perfect memory, praised bee God, doe make & publish this to bee and conteine my last will and testament as to my worldly estate. Imprimis I give and devise unto Mary Cliffe, my daughter by my first wife, and to her heirs for ever all that my burgage, mesuage or tenement in North Allerton aforesaid wherein I now dwell upon condition that shee my said daughter doe pay all my just debts and that shee my said daughter or her heires shall doe also pay unto Mary Cliffe, my grand daughter, the summe of ten pounds of lawful English money when my said grand daughter shall attaine to her age of one & twenty yeares and shall & doe alsoe in the meane while pay unto my said grand daughter foure shillings yearly by foure equall quarterly payments from & after my decease for & towards her maintenance, which said ten pounds I give as a legacy and porcion to & for my said grand daughter, and doe subject & charge my said burgage, mesuage or dwelling house with the paymentt thereof. And I doe direct that my said grand daughter shall upon her receipt thereof seale & execute a generall release & disclaim of all her estate, right & title of, in & to the said burgage, mesuage or dwelling house unto my said daughter Mary Cliffe & her heires else the said legacy not to bee paid. But I declare my mind & will further to bee that if my said grand daughter shall dye and depart this life before shee attaine to her full age of one & twenty yeares then my said guift & legacy of ten pounds not to bee paid or payeable nor my said house to bee charged therewith. But then I declare my mind & will be to bee that in such case of my said grand child's death that my daughter

Mary Cliffe & her heirs shall pay out of the profitts of my said house the summe of fourty shillings of lawfull English money unto my daughter Elizabeth Cliffe & the further summe of fourty shillings like money unto my daughter in law Mary Cliffe, the widow of my late sonne Henry Cliffe. And if it happen that my own daughter Mary Cliffe neglect or faile to pay the said several sumes of money soe charged & payeable out of my said house or any of them, then that it shall & may bee lawfull to & for my said grand daughter & other daughters to enter into & upon my said house & hold the same until due payment bee made with reasonable charges. Item I give unto my loving wife and unto Elizabeth, my daughter, all my household goods, household stuffe & implements of household, bedding, linnen, pewther, brasse, iron & other household utensills except the bedd & bedstead whereon I usually lodge, two pewther dishes & two plates which I give unto Mary Cliffe, my eldest daughter, but noe bedding belonging to the bedd, only the feather bedd and bedstead. Item I give unto my nephew & servant Christopher Cliffe all my shopp geer & work tooles, hee paying to my daughter Elizabeth ten shillings. Item all the rest of my goods and chattells, rights & creditts (my debts & funerall expenses being first discharged & satisfied[)] I give & bequeath unto my own daughter Mary Cliffe whome I make sole executrix of this my last will & testament, hereby first declaring my mind & will to bee that my wife shall enjoy her third part of my house for her life quietly. And I doe hereby revoke all former wills by mee made. In witness whereof I have hereunto sett my hand & seale this sixth day of December in the year of our Lord God one thousand six hundred ninety and seaven.
The marke & seale of Henry Cliff.[1]
Signed, sealed & published by Henry Cliffe in our presence & our names hereto subscribed in his presence & by his direcions, witnes our hands. R. Raikes [*signed*], William Harrison [*signed*], John Bayne [*signed*], Thomas Tempest [*signed*].

A true inventory of the goods of Henry Cliff, currier, late of North-Allerton deceased apprazed the thirteenth of December 1697 by James Bowes, John Tones, Robert Welbanck and John Jhinson as followeth.

	£	s	d
Inprimis his purse and apparrell	00	05	00
Item in the fore house			
two tables, one cupboard, two buffetts formes, one long settle, 8 pewther dishes, two plates, three			

flaggons and candlesticks, one large kettle, one iron pott & pann, one chaire, two tankreds, one pewther cup, one glass case, two paire of tongs, one brass ladle & one skeele	00	15	00
Item in the parlour			
two bedsteads with bedding, one table, one chest, one buffett forme, one press, two cushions, one pewther dish, one buffett stoole, two little barrells & one chaire	00	15	00
Item in the chamber one old bedstead	00	01	06
Item in the shopp			
five knives, two working boards, two old hogsheads, one runlett of oyle, two graineing boards & one steele	00	14	06
Summa	02	11	00

[1] Henry Cliffe was buried on 13 December 1697, seven days after making his will.

96. WILLIAM COOPER, 1698

DPRI/6/B/1698/C1

The apprizement of the inventory of Mr William Cooper deceased, duely made and estimated by us whose names are underwritten.[1]

	£	s	d
Imprimis Mr Cooper his purse and apparrell thirty shillings	1	10	0
Item bookes estimated to the value of two pounds tenn shillings	2	10	0
Item an old clock and old desk eighteen shillings and sixpence	0	18	6
Total	4	18	6

Apprized by us: John Todd, George Shemeld.

[1] William Cooper, clerk, was buried on 1 October 1697: Ingledew, *History and Antiquities*, p. 198.

97. JOHN ROBINSON, PARISH CLERK, 1700

DPRI/6/T/1700/R1

In the name of God, amen, I, John Robinson of North Allerton in the county of York, parish clark, being in weak estate of body but of a sound and perfect mind and memory, (praise be therefore given to almighty God), do make and ordain this my last will and testament in manner and form following (that is to say); first and principally I commend my soul into the hands of almighty God, hoping through[1] the meritts, death and passion of my saviour Jesus Christ to have full and free pardon and forgiveness of all my sinns and to inheritt everlasting life, and my body I commit to the earth to be decently buried at the discretion of my executrix here after named. And as touchin the disposure of all such temporal estate as it hath pleased almighty God to bestow upon me I give and dispose thereof as here followeth. Imprimis I will that all my debts and funeral expences be discharged and paid by my executrix here after nominated. Item I give and bequeath unto George Robinson, my only son, and to his heirs all that house, burgage or tenement scituate, standing and being in North Allerton in the county of York aforesaid on the West Row thereof abutted and bounded on the south with the burgage or messuage of Henry Whitton and on the north with the burgage or tenement now in the tenure of George Jackson, together with all its appurtenances, shops, cellars, buildings, back house, stables, backsides, garth, gardens, orchards or whatever heretofore did or now doth appertain unto the same house, burgage or tenement for ever, to enter upon the same so soon as he shall come unto the age of one and twenty years of age. Item I give and bequeath thirty pounds of lawfull monyes of England to be payed by my said son George Robinson unto my only daughter Mary Robinson so soon as shee shall attain unto the full age of one and twenty years of age. And then, upon the non payment of the said summ of thirty pounds, to enter upon, have, hold & possess the two fore shops, the one whereof is now in the possession of John Coulson, plummer, and the other now in the tenure of Anthony Metcalfe, dier. And all the rents, issues and profitts to take to and for her own propper use and behoofe till the payment of the said summ. Item I will and ordaine Elizabeth Robinson, my now dear wife, sole tutor and guardian of George Robinson, my said son, and Mary Robinson, my daughter aforesaid, untill they or either of them respectively shall attain unto the full age of one and twenty years of age. And shee to have, receive and take all the rents, issues and proffitts of the above bequeathed burgage and premisses untill the full expiracion of the time of her guardianship above limmitted tow<ards> the maintenance and support of my said son and daughter above named. But in case my said wife should depart this life before the end of the time above limmitted then I nominate and appoint my brother in law Andrew Ewbank and Mary Kirby feoffees in trust to see, order and take care and guardianship of my said son and daughter untill they attain unto the age and years aforesaid. Item I constitute and appoint Elizabeth Robinson, my said dear and welbeloved wife, sole executrix of this my last will and

testament. And I do hereby dissanull and make void all other wills and testaments heretofore made or done. In wittness whereof I have here unto sett my hand and seale this 14th day of November anno domini 1698.
John Robinson [*signed and sealed*][2]
Signed, sealed and delivered in the presence of us, Francis Meriton [*signed*], Cuthbert Sudbert's mark, Andrew Ewbanke [*signed*], John Todd [*signed*].

December 9th anno domini 1698.
An apprizment of the inventory goods & chattells of John Robinson of North Allerton parish clark late deceased by us whose names are under written.

	£	s	d
Inprimis purse & apparrell	02	00	00
Item pewther & other furniture in the fore house	02	00	00
Item furniture & other implements in the kitching	01	10	00
Item in the kitching chamber, furniture to the value of	01	15	00
Item in the chamber over the fore house, furniture to the value of	01	00	00
Item in one other litle chamber, furniture to the value of	00	10	00
Item in the chamber over the fore shopp, furniture to the value off	01	05	00
Item linnen to the value of	02	10	00
	12	10	00
Debts own by the deceased John Robinson	20	00	00

Francis Merriton, Andrew Ewbanke, James Ewbanke, John Todd.

1 'through' repeated in ms.
2 John Robinson was buried on 15 November 1698, the day after making his will.

98. CHRISTOPHER HUTTON, HUSBANDMAN, 1699

DPRI/6/B/1699/H1
A true inventory of all & singuler the goods & chattells of Christopher Hutton late of North Allerton deceased, husbandman, praized this first day of Aprill by Thomas Flower, Henry Jienson, Cuthbert Surbert & Ralph Humphrey as followeth, (videlicet)

	£	s	d
Imprimis his purse and apparrell	05	00	00
Item two cowes	06	00	00
Two heifers & one calfe & hay	04	00	00

Eighteen sheep	06 06 00
One pare of oxen	07 05 00
Two mares & a fole & an old horse	09 00 00
Two carts with other implements belonging to husbandry	03 10 00
Nine acres and a halfe of wheat	14 05 00
Fiveteen acres of ware corne	15 00 00
The corne belonging to Codey field	03 02 06
The corne in the barne & the manure	04 05 00
The corne in the garner & a table & some other small implements	01 10 00
In the entry parlour one standing bed & bedding thereunto belonging with some other implements	01 00 00
In the fore parlour one bedstead & bedding thereto belonging with severall other implements of household stuff	01 05 00
In the fore house one dresser, 2 chares with pewter & brass & other small implements	02 01 06
In the milk house some shelves & implements belonging	00 05 00
	87 15 00
	[*recte* 83 *15 00*]
Debts owing to the intestate	
By Simon Taylor	04 00 00
By Wiltshire Brown	02 02 06
By Elias Robinson	
By John Wayd[1]	
By John Tayler	00 16 02
Debts owing by the intestate to his mother Brown & other persons & for funerall charges, charges of administration etc.	25 04 02

Ralph Humphrey, Thomas Flower, Cuthbert Surbert, Henry Jienson.

[1] No sums are recorded against the names of Elias Robinson and John Wayd.

99. ANTHONY BLAKELOCK, INNHOLDER, 1700

DPRI/6/T/1700/B1

In the name of God, amen, I, Anthony Blakelock of North Allerton in the county of York, inholder, being some what infirme in body but of good and perfect mind and memory (praised bee God), do for the setling and disposall of my temporall estate both reall and personall make and publish this my last will and testament in manner and forme following (that is to say), Imprimis I give and devise unto my loving wife Jane Blakelock all that messuage, burgage or tenement wherein I now live, one shopp in the occupacion of my daughter in law Anne Blakelock together with the malt kilne, out houses and garth to the said messuage and premisses belonging and alsoe now in my occupacion (always excepted one work house & chamber over itt and one peice of the garth now or late in my sonne Anthonye's occupacion and which I have granted and devised unto my said sonne Anthony for a terme of yeares determinable upon his life) for and dureing the terme of the natureall life of my said loving wife. And from and after the death and decease of my said wife my mind and will is, and I do hereby give and devise all my said messuage, burgage or tenement, shopp, malt kilne, garth and appurtenances thereunto belonging and all my estate therein unto my grandsonne Richard Blakelock and the heires of his body lawfully to bee begotten, and for want of such issue I give and devise the same and every part thereof unto the right heires and assignes of my said grandsonne Richard Blakelock for ever. Item I give and bequeath unto my daughter Jane Blakelock all that parcell of land lying and being in North Allerton aforesaid called the Butts, adjoining upon Turker field, and all my estate, tennant right & terme of yeares or lives therein or thereto unto her, her heires and assignes for ever. Item I give and bequeath unto every of my other children the summe of one shilling haveing heretofore provided for them. Item I declare my mind and will to bee and I do hereby will and direct that all my just debts (except such as are upon mortgage) which I owe unto any person or persons whosoever shall bee paid and satisfied out of my personall estate, and I do hereby give and bequeath all the rest and residue of my personall estate, goods and chattells, debts, rights and creditts unto my said loving wife Jane Blakelock and my said daughter Jane Blakelock equally to bee divided and shared among them, share and share like. And I do hereby make and appoint my said loving wife and my said daughter Jane joynt executrixes of this my last will and testament. And I do hereby revoke, disannull and make voyd all former wills by mee formerly made. And I do declare this to bee and contein my last will and testament. In witness whereof I have hereunto sett my hand and seale this thirteenth day of March in the yeare of our Lord God one thousand six hundred ninety eight [*13 Mar. 1699*].

Anthonye Blakelocke [*signed and sealed*][1]

Signed, sealed & published by the testator Anthony Blakelock by his direccions and att his request in our presence, <the marke of> Robert Thornton, Matthew Bowes [*signed*], Francis Kaye [*signed*].

A true & perfect inventory of the goods & chattells of Anthony Blackelock of Northallerton deceased, appraized by us whose names and under written Aprill 4th 1700.

	£	s	d
Inprimis his purse and apparrell	01	00	00
Item in the fore house 2 tables, 1 furm, 1 long setle, 4 chares, 2 stooles with other implements	00	12	00
Item in the litle parlour 1 bedstead & beding	00	05	00
Item in the great parlour 3 bedsteads and beding	01	06	08
1 cupboard, 1 table, 1 furm and 3 chares	00	12	00
In the kitchin, 2 ketles, 1 pott & one pann	00	16	00
In pewther in the buttery	00	07	00
In the fore chamber 2 bedsteads & beding, 1 table, 2 furms, 4 chares & 2 stooles	03	00	00
In lining	00	12	00
In the litle chamber 1 bedstead, 1 table & 3 chists	00	12	00
One hand mill, 1 cistern, 1 pump	02	10	00
In the cellar 1 team, 1 anker, 2 tubs	00	04	06
One cow	03	00	00
3 ews & lambs	01	00	00
Hay & 3 bores	00	03	04
1 sow & 3 piggs	00	10	00
Malt in the kill	03	00	00
	19	10	00
Money owing by the testator	25	00	00

Robert Stringer, James Bowes, John Tomes, William Robinson.

[1] Anthony Blakelock was buried on 15 March 1700, a year after making his will.

100. ANTHONY BLAKELOCK JUNIOR, 1700

DPRI/6/B/1700/B1

A true and perfect inventory of the goods and chattells of Anthony Blakelock junior deceased November 10th by us whose names is underwritten 1700.[1]

	£	s	d
Inprimis his purse & apparrell	00	05	00
Item in his worke house 3 tubbs	00	10	00
In spetches in the chambers	00	01	06
Total	00	16	06

John Tomes, James Wetherill, James Bowes, Robert Stringer.

[1] Anthony Blakelock junior was buried on 5 November 1700. He was the son of Anthony Blakelock above [99].

101. CUTHBERT SURBUTT, YEOMAN, 1702

DPRI/6/T/1702/S1

In the name of God, amen, I, Cuthbert Surbutt of North Allerton in the county of York, yeoman, being infirme in body but of good and perfect mind & memory, praised bee God for the same, but being mindefull of my mortality do make and publish this my last will and testament in manner and forme following (that is to say): Imprimis, I commit my soule to God who gave it & my body to earth from whence it came to bee buryed in such decent and comely manner as my executrix hereafter named shall think fit. And as for the worldly estate wherewith God hath blessed mee I give, bequeath and dispose thereof in manner and forme following. Imprimis, I give and devise all that my messuage, burgage or tenement scytuate lying and being in North Allerton aforesaid on the East Row there wherein I now dwell, with the kilne, barne, stables, gardens, backsides, rights, members and appurtenances whatsoever to the same belonging unto Mary Surbutt my loving wife for and dureing the terme of her natureall life, and from and after the decease of my said wife I give and bequeath my said messuage, burgage or tenement with the appurtenances thereunto belonging unto John Surbutt, my sonne, for and dureing his natureall life only and then to the heires of the boddy of the said John Surbutt lawfully begotten or to bee begotten <for ever> and for want of such issue then I give and bequeath the same to the use and behoofe of Mary, the wife of John Sadler, Anne Layfeild, the wife of Allan Layfeild, and Margrett Wilkinson, the wife of William Wilkinson, my three daughters, and to their heires and assignes for ever chargeable nevertheles. And my mind and will is that if it shall so happen that either my said sonne, John Surbutt, or his heires or my said three daughters or their heires shall hold and enjoy my said messuage, burgage or tenement and premisses, the party or partyes so holding and enjoyeing the same shall well and truely pay or cause to bee paid unto William Willoughby, if then living, the summe of sixteen poundes of lawfull English money. And if it shall so happen that the said William Willoughby shall dye and depart this life before the enjoyment of my said messuage and premisses as aforesaid, then my mind & will is that such party or partyes so holdeing and enjoyeing the same premisses shall well and truly pay or cause to bee paid unto Margarett Sadler, my grand

daughter, the abovesaid summe of sixteen poundes immediately after the entring upon my said messuage and premisses with which I do hereby charge my said messuage, burgage and premisses. Item I give & bequeath unto Mary, my loving wife, all the rest of my goods and chattells, rights and creditts (my debts & funerall expences being first paid and discharged). And I do hereby make the said Mary Surbutt, my loving wife, sole executrix of this my last will and testament & doe hereby revoke, disannull and make voyd all former and other will or wills by mee formerly made, and doe hereby declare this to bee and contein my last will and testament. In witnes whereof I have hereunto sett my hand & seale this nineteenth day of June in the yeare of our Lord God one thousand seaven hundred and two.
the marke & seale of Cuthbert Surbutt.[1]
Signed, sealed delivered & published by the testator at his request and by his direccions in our presence, James Conyers [*signed*], Marmaduke Sidgswick [*signed*], Fr: Kaye [*signed*].

A true and perfect inventory of the goods and chattels of Cuthbert Surbutt of Northallerton late deceased – valued and appraised by us whose names are underwritten. August the 4th 1702.

	£	s	d
Imprimis, his purse and apparell	01	00	00
In the fore house.			
Item one table, one form, 6 chaires, one long settle, one iron pan, one reckon, one pair of tongs and a fire-shovell with other implements	01	00	00
Item in the back parler, 2 bedsteads with beding, one table, one form & one chair	02	00	00
Item in the passage parler, one little table & 4 chairs	00	05	00
Item in the entry parler, one bedstead with beding, one table and a little cupboard	01	00	00
Item in the fore chamber, one bedstead with beding, one table, nine chairs, one form & 2 stooles	01	11	08
Item in Scott chamber, 4 bedsteads & beding, one table, one form, one chair & 2 stooles	00	19	04
Item in the seller, 3 tearses & 2 tubs	00	03	03
Item in the brewing house, one kettle, one cooller and one masking tubb	00	13	04
Item in the kill in malt	01	13	07
Item one cow, 2 horses, 2 young beasts & ten sheep	04	02	06
Item one cart, one plough & a pair of harrows	00	14	06

Item pewter	01	00	00
Item in linning	01	00	00
Item one sow & pigs	00	10	02
	17	13	04

John Tomes, Simon Arnett, Henery Wood, Allan Layfield.

[1] Cuthbert Surbutt was buried on 30 July 1702, six weeks after making his will.

102. ALICE MILBURNE, 1703

DPRI/6/B/1703/M1

A true and perfect inventory of all the goods and chattells of Alice Milburne late of North-Allerton deceased apprized this last day of December 1703 by us whose names are subscribed as followeth.[1]

	£	s	d
Inprimis her purse and apparrell	00	06	08
Item one bedstead & a table and a coverlett & an old chaire	01	00	00
Item a debt due to the deceased	09	00	00
	10	06	08

Francis Merrington, Joseph Fawdington.

[1] Alice Milburne was buried on 31 December 1703.

103. JOHN COULSON, 1704

DPRI/6/B/1704/C1

A true & perfect inventory of the goods & chattells of John Coulson of North-Allerton deceased taken & appraised by us whose names are under written the 9th of May 1704.

	£	s	d
Inprimis his purse & apparrell	04	00	00
Item 2 pair of vise for glasien work	01	05	00
Item 12 stone 9^{lb} ½ of lead	00	12	08
Item 1 firkin of glass	00	12	00
Item 1 pair of great bellass	00	05	00
Item 1 iron kettle	00	05	00
Item 1 frame for casting lead with & other odd implements	00	10	00
Item 1 pair of large smith vise	00	04	00
	07	13	08

George Jackson, Henry Whitton, John Bayne, Jacob Harrison.

104. FORSTER PLEASAUNCE, GENTLEMAN, 1704

DPRI/6/T/1704/P1

In the name of God, amen, I, Forster Pleasaunce of North Allerton in the countie of Yorke, gentleman, being at this present (praise to almighty God for it) in reasonable good health of bodie & of perfect memory, calling to mind the uncertainty of this mortall life and that all flesh must yeild to death when God is pleased to call, doe therefore this present eight day of Aprill one thousand seaven hundred make, constitute, appoint & declare this my last will and testament in manner followeing, by these presents revoakeing and makeing voyd all former wills and testaments heretofore by mee made & declared either by word or writeing, and this and noe other to bee taken for my last will and testament unrevocable at any time dureing my life. And first being hartily greived & penetent for all my sinnes past most humbly beseeching God almighty to forgive mee them all, I committ my soule into the hand of almighty God, hoping & assuredly trusting in & by the merritts & mediation of Jesus Christ my deare redeemer to have full & free forgiveness of all my sinns, and that both my soule & boddy at the generall resurreccion shall rise againe with joye, & through his merritts, death & passion shall inherite the kingdome of heaven; my bodie I committ to the earth to bee decently buried where my executrix hereafter named shall thinke fitt, and for settleing my temporall & personall estate, and such chattells, goods & debts oweing unto mee as it hath pleased God of his goodness (farr above my defects) to bestowe upon mee, I doe hereby order & dispose of the same as followeth. First I will & order that the summe of thirty pounds which I ame oweing & indebted to my neece Mary White (daughter of my sister Anne White, late of Branspeth in the countie of Durham deceased), and alsoe the summe of tenn pounds which I likewise owe & ame indebted unto my neece Elizabeth Hackworth, another of the daughters of my said sister Anne White deceased, and for which they have my bond severally for the payment thereof, bee punctually & severally paid unto them within three moneths next after my decease by my executrix hereafter named, in case the same moneys happen to bee unpaid att my decease. Item I give & bequeath unto my daughter Jane Watson, wife of George Watson of Old Malton, gentleman, five guynneys in full of all her parte & share of my reall & personall estate whatsoever, to bee paid unto her within one moneth next after my decease by my executrix hereafter named. Item I give & bequeath unto my deare wife Elizabeth Pleasaunce my dwelling house in North Allarton

nowe in my owne possession with all appurtenances thereunto belonging, to have & to hold my said house with thappurtenances unto my said wife & her assignes for ever from the time of my death & not before, to bee disposed of as she shall thinke fitt & convenient. All the rest of my goods & chattells, readie money, debts oweing unto mee, silver plate, and all other my reall & personall estate whatsoever whereof I shall dye possest, I doe give & bequeath unto my said wife Elizabeth Pleasaunce to bee by her disposed of after my death as she shall thinke fitt & convenient, my debts & funerall expences being first discharged & paid. And lastly I doe hereby nomynate, appoint & declare my said wife Elizabeth Pleasance to bee my sole executrix of this my last will & testament. In witness whereof I have hereunto sett my hand & seale the day & yeare above written.
Fo[rster] Pleasaunce [*signed and sealed*][1]
Signed, sealed & declared as the last will & testament of the above named Forster Pleasaunce (the King's double stampe first affixt) in the presence of us, John Todd [*signed*], Henry Whitton [*signed*], Ritchard Rimer [*signed*].

A true & perfect inventory of the goods & chattells of Foster Pleasance gentleman deceased. Appraised by us whose names are underwritten as followeth, this twelfth day of May anno domini 1704.

	£	s	d
Inprimis. In the hall			
one dozen of leather chaires and two tables	03	00	00
In the dineing room			
half a dozen of cayne chairs & two tables & some small pictures	04	00	00
In four little lodging roome			
four beds, bedsteads & beding & chares, two pair of chests of drawers with two or three looking glasses	06	00	00
In the kitching			
one dozen of pewter dishes, two dozen of plates & other implements	02	00	00
	15	00	00

Apprized by us, Robert Danby, Thomas Cust, Thomas Wood, James Cust.

[1] Forster Pleasance was buried on 26 April 1704, four years after making his will.

105. EUSTACE SLINGER, SPINSTER, 1704

DPRI/6/T/1704/S1

In the name of God. Amen. I, Ewstace Slinger of North Allerton in the county of Yorke, spinster, being sick and weake butt of good and perfect memory (praised bee God), doe make and publish this my last will and testament in manner following, (that is to say). First I recomend my sole to almighty God my maker and redeamer. And as for the personall estate which God almighty has been pleased to bestow upon me I dispose thereof as followeth, videlicet I give and bequeath unto my neise Anne Mitchell the summe of two pounds and tenn shillings. Item I give and bequeath unto Syth, sister of the said Anne Mitchell, being my neise, the summe of two poundes and tenn shillings and an enamelled gould ring. Item I give and bequeath unto my brother's servant Margarett Bowman the summe of five shillings and I doe alsoe give and bequeath unto my neighbour Sarah Rowth the summe of one shilling and six pence. And as for the rest of my estate reall or personall of what kinde or nature soever I doe hereby give and bequeath (my funerall expences first discharged) unto my loving brother in law William Allanson who I doe hereby constitute and appoint sole executor of this my last will and testament. It is alsoe my will and pleasure that Thomas Slinger, my nephew, shall have and receive of said executeors the summe of five shillings in full of all claimes under me. I witness whereof I doe hereby publish this my last will and testament the second day of June anno domini 1704.
Eustace Slinger [*signed and sealed*][1]
Signed, sealed and published in our presents and our names subscribed in her presence and by and with her consent, William Drybrough [*signed*], John Stringer [*signed*], Geo: Pemberton [*signed*].

A true inventory of the goods & chattells of Utis Slinger late of North-Allerton in the county of Yorke spinster deceased, appraised by us as followeth.

	£	s	d
Inprimis, one bedstead with a bed & beding to the same belonging	00	13	00
Item one cupboard	00	03	00
Item two pewter dublers	00	02	06
Item 3 plates	00	01	06
Item one pott & severall small implements	00	03	00
	01	03	00

Appraised by us whose names are under written, John Stringer, William Scott his marke, George Pemberton [*signed*].

[1] Eustace Slinger was buried on 7 June 1704, five days after making her will.

106. ISABEL TUKE, SPINSTER, 1704

DPRI/6/T/1705/T2

In the name of God, amen, I, Isabel Tuke of North Allerton in the county of York, spinster, being weak in body but of perfect mind & memory (praises to almighty God), do make this my last will and testament in manner and form following. Imprimis I do give unto Robert Thearsby my whole personal estate. Item I give unto George Thearsby five shillings. Item I give unto Ann Craike five shillings. Item I give unto Thomas Thearsby five shillings. Item I give unto Averill Hawkswell five shillings. Item I do give forty shillings to be distributed among the poor of North Allerton at or before my funeral solemnity. Item twenty shillings to the poor of Brompton & Romanby in like manner to be distributed at or before my said funeral. Item I do give & bequeath unto the poor of North Allerton the entire use, interest or amount of five pounds to enter and become payable immediat<ly> after my decease, to be paid at the next Christmass after (to witt six shillings) by the said Robert Thearsby over and above the six shillings formerly charged by my brother's will & that he and his heires shall for ever hereafter annually pay or cause to be paid the said annual summ of six shillings at the time above specified without any fraud, evasion or lett. In witness whereof I have hereunto sett my hand & seal this first day of May in the year of our Lord one thousand seven hundred & three.

Issabel Tuke <her mark> [*sealed*][1]

Memorandum. I do constitute and appoint the said Robert Thearsby sole executor of this my last will & testament in witness of us.

Sealed, signed & delivered in the presence of us, William Harrison [*signed*], John Rimer [*signed*], John Todd [*signed*], John Todd junior [*signed*].

An appraisement made the eight day of June [*1704*] of the goods & chattells of Isabell Tuke late deceased.

	£	s	d
Inprimis her purse & apparrell	02	10	00
In the fore house			
two tables, one long settle, 1 reckon, one paire of			

bellows, 2 plank firms, 2 chaires, another plank firme, 2 clogg firms	00	10	00
In the fore parlour			
one bedstead, one feather bed, 3 pair of sheets, four pillowbears, 2 coverlids, 1 blanckett, 1 stooll & one chair	01	02	00
In the back parlour			
2 bedsteads, 1 feather bed & 1 chaff bed with hangings, 2 coverlids, 1 blankett, 1 cubart, 1 pannall chist, 1 table, 1 wanded chair, 1 wood chair, 1 little cubart, 1 little firm, one cushing	01	00	00
In the chambers			
2 chists & 1 coffinn	00	02	00
In the buttery			
4 pewter dishes, 1 plate, 1 chamber pott, 2 poding dishes, 1 tanckard, 3 spoones, 1 salt, 1 tumbler, 2 brass candlesticks, 2 wire candlesticks, 1 lantron, 1 laddle, 6 trenshers, 2 brass panns	00	10	00
In all	05	14	00

Wee whose names are here underwritten was then praisors of the said goods. William Harrison, Thomas Whitehead, Robert Younge, James Wetherill.

[1] Isabel Tuke was buried on 7 June 1704, 13 months after making her will.

107. WILLIAM ROBINSON, LINEN WEAVER, 1705

DPRI/6/T/1705/R1

In the name of God, amen, I, William Robinson of North Allerton in the county of Yorke, linnen weaver, being somewhat infirme in body but of very sound and good mind and memory, praised bee God, doe make and publish this to bee and conteine my last will and testament as to the disposall of my estate reall & personall. First I give and devise unto my eldest sonne John Robinson for the terme of his naturall life only all that one chamber comonly called by the name of the cloth chamber wherein hee and I have our bedds and doe usually <lodge> being part of my dwelling house in North Allerton with full and free ingresse, egresse & regresse thereto and free way & passage <at all times> to & from the same in, by & through the low roome, fore house and chamber over the fore house or kitchin now in possession of my sonne Samuel Robinson. And immediately from & after the decease or death of my said sonne John Robinson I doe give & devise all the said chamber only (discharged & excluded from all such ingresse, egresse, regresse, way & passage in, by & through low roome & kitchin & chamber over the same now in my sonne Samuel's occupacion), unto my sonne Samuel Robinson & his heires for ever. Item I give and devise unto my said sonne Samuel Robinson and to his heirs and assigns for ever all that part of my burgage mesuage or tenement in North Allerton being reckoned the fore part thereof conteining one forehouse, one buttery, one parlor, one milkhouse and all the chambers over them now in the occupacion of Mathew Story. And alsoe I give unto my said sonne Samuel and to his heirs all the long garner and the shopp or workhouse and the stable next to the said shopp and the colehouse, which said last mencioned premisses are alsoe part and parcell of my burgage or tenement in North Allerton & are now in the occupacion of my said sonne Samuel. And I doe alsoe give & devise unto my said sonne Samuel & his heirs forever one moyety or halfe part of the garth & the orchard <& garden> on the backside of the said burgage and a moyety or halfe part of the well, subject to and chargeable with the payment of the annuall and cleare yearely summe of foure pounds of lawfull money of England unto my eldest sonne John Robinson yearely and every yeare for and during the terme & time of the naturall life of my said sonne John, the same to bee paid (without any deduccion, defalcacion or abatement for or in lieu of any taxes, imposicions or assessments imposed or charged or to bee imposed or charged by any Act or Acts of Parliament made or to bee made) unto my said sonne John att foure dayes or times in the yeare, that is to say upon the first day of May, the first day of August, the eleaventh day of November & the second day of February in every yeare during my said sonne John's naturall life, and the first payment thereof to begin & bee made upon the first of the said dayes which shall first happen next after my decease. And if it shall happen that my said sonne Samuel, his heirs or assignes, doe neglect & faile to pay the said annuall or yearely payment of foure pounds unto my said sonne John for his life att the aforsaid severall daies & times & in manner as aforesaid, then my mind & will is, and I doe hereby give full power & authority & direct that it shall & may bee lawfull to & for my said sonne John upon every such default or neglect or failer of payment into all & every the aforesaid premisses by mee given & devised to my said sonne Samuel to enter & the same to have, hold & enjoy untill due payment thereof & all arrerages of the same (if any bee) bee fully paid & satisfied together with all my said sonn John's reasonable charges of suit & otherwise. And I doe hereby give & devise unto my daughter Jane, the wife of Robert Sheilds,

and to the heirs & assigns of my said daughter for ever all that low roome or kitchin and the chamber over it now in the occupacion of my said sonne Samuel Robinson, and alsoe all that one low room & the chamber over itt now in the occupacion of John Foster, and alsoe the colehole farmed by John Foster, and alsoe my new stable next to the well being now in the occupacion of Mathew Story, and alsoe the other moyety or halfe part of the garth, garden & orchard and well on the back of my said burgage or tenement. And I declare my mind & will to bee that all the rest & other part of my burgage & tenement in North Allerton not before given to my sonne John for his life & to my daughter Jane & her heirs shall goe & bee held & enjoyed by my sonne Samuel & his heirs. Item I give to John Jackson, servant to my sonne Samuel, my every day wearing suit of cloaths. Item I give unto my said sonne John all other my wearing cloathes and apparell and the bedstead, bedd, bedding & bed cloathes whereon hee usually lyes or lodges, and alsoe one peice of new kersey or cloth which I gott lately made with intent therewith to cloath my selfe. And I give all the rest of my goods & chattells & personal estate unto my said sonne Samuel & daughter Jane, (except the bedd whereon I ly and lodge), which said bed & bedding thereto belonging my will is and I doe give the same to my said daughter Jane and all the rest of my said goods between Samuel & Jane. And I doe make & appoint my said sonne Samuel & daughter Jane joynt executors of this my last will & testament. And I doe hereby revoke all former wills by mee made and declare & publish this to bee & conteine my last will & testament. In witnesse whereof I have hereunto sett my hand & seale the third day of March in the third yeare of the raigne of our sovereigne lady Queen Anne over England &c. annoque domini 1704 [*3 Mar. 1705*]
William Robinson [*signed and sealed*][1]
Signed, sealed & published by William Robinson in our presence & our names subscribed as witnesses in the presence of the said William Robinson and at his request & by his direccions, witnesse our hands, John Simpson [*signed*], Robert Robinson [*signed*], R. Raikes [*signed*].

A true & perfect inventory of the goods & chattells of William Robinson of North-Allerton deceased, Aprill the 20th 1705, valued & appraised by us whose names are under written.

	£	s	d
Inprimis his purse & apparrell	02	00	00
Item in the cloth chamber 1 little cupboard, 2 old chaires, one long chest & one <little> table	00	10	00

Item in the kitchen one table, 1 forme & one warmeing pann	00	06	08
Item in the fore house, one long settle & 1 fleak	00	03	04
Item in the fore chamber, one little forme	00	10	06
Item the stable racks & mangery & one corne chist	00	05	00
Item the barne, 2 old winder cloths, 1 bushell, 1 peck, one pair of harrows, 4 forks, & one seck	00	03	04
Item two ews & three lambs	00	10	00
	04	08	10

William Harrison, A. Tomes, John Foster his marke.

[1] William Robinson was buried on 21 April 1705, six weeks after making his will.

108. WILLIAM SCOTT, YEOMAN, 1705

DPRI/6/T/1705/S1

In the name of God, amen, the eighttenth day of May one thousand seaven hondered & foure 1704. I, William Scott of Northallerton in the county of Yorke, yeman, being weeke of body but of good & parfeck memory, blessed be the Lord for it, do make this my last will and testement in forme and manner as followeth. First I bequeth my sowell unto the Lord my maker and my body to be buryed in the church yeard of North Allerton, and as for the temprall estate the which it hath pleased God to bestow one me I do dispose thereof as followeth. Imprimis I make John Scott, my onely sonn, my sole excequter of what I have and if he shall die without issue or hares then it shall returne a part to my wife relations & other part to my owne as followeth. I give John Scott, Elizabeth Falle, Ralfe Scott & Richard Scott, John Ollever & Thomas Ollever for the none ares of John Scott my sonn affter his decease to fall to these and they to share equall what may be left more or less without any gille or frood one of them to another. And it is my will and pleasuer that Thomas Thompson juner and John Stringer to be tuteress of my sonn John Scott & he to be under there tuishon for the turme of six yeare affter my decease and they to discharge my debts & funerall expences and the said Thomas Thomson and John Stringer I do impower to let to any parson my whole estate or any part or parsell thereof to the good in tent thatt it may returne to the benifitt of John Scott my son. And this I hope they will youse the best meines they can to forther the same & in witness whereof I have here unto sett my hand and seall the day and yeare as a bove written.
William Scott <his marke>[1]

In the presence of Robert Stringer [*signed*], John Pibuss <his marke>, George Smith [*signed*].

June the 6th 1705. An apraisement then of the goods & chattells of William Scott lately deceased & praised by us whose names are underwritten – James Rowth, William Boddye, John Dent.

	£	s	d
Inprimis one cubert	00	04	00
one bedstead	00	04	00
three litle chists	00	02	00
one caff bed & beding	00	04	00
two chaires	00	01	00
puther & brass	00	05	00
other implements	00	02	00
corne growing	01	00	00
horse & cart	02	00	00
Total	04	02	00

[1] William Scott was buried on 29 May 1705, a year after making his will.

109. FRANCIS FLINT, YEOMAN, 1705

DPRI/6/T/1705/F1

In the name of God, amen, I, Francis Flint of North Allerton in the county of Yorke, yeoman, being somewhat infirme of body but of sound and a disposing mind and memory but being mindfull of my mortality doe make & publish this to bee & conteine my last will & testament in manner & forme following. First I commend my soule to God who made it and my body to the earth from wheare it came to bee interred as my executrix hereafter named shall think fitt. And as for my temporall estate wherewith God hath blessed mee I give and bequeath the same as followeth. Imprimis I give to my sonne Francis Flint five shillings [with][1] the estate & interest of my house which I lately setled by deed I declare to bee in full of his porcion and what else hee can or may claime out of my estate reall & personall. Item I give unto my daughter Anne Ingram, the wife of Thomas Ingram, the summe of five shillings. Item I give to my daughter Dorothy Harrison, wife of Christopher Harrison, the summe of five shillings and I declare the said guifts & legacies to my said daughters to bee in full discharge of theire respective & several porcions & filial parts & shares of and out of my estate reall & personall because I have

formerly provided for them & given them porcions according to my ability & what I intended for them. And I give all the rest, residue & remainder of my personall estate, goods & chattels (my debts, lagacies & funerall expences being thereout first deducted) unto my deare & loving wife Ellen Flint whome I make sole executrix of this my last will and testament. And I doe hereby revoke, disadnull and make voyd all & every will & wills by mee formerly made & published. And I doe declare this present writing to bee & conteine my last will and testament. In witness whereof I have hereunto sett my hand and seale this second day of September in the yeare of our Lord God one thousand seaven hundred & foure.
Francis Flint <his mark & seale>[2]
Signed, sealed & published by the said Francis Flint to bee his last will & testament in our presence & our names subscribed as witnesses thereto in his presence & at his request & by his direcions in the presence of us, Richard Johnson <his marke>, Jane Jackson [*signed*], James Conyers [*signed*].

A true & perfect inventory of the goods & chattells of Francis Flint late of North-Allerton deceased. Apprized by us whose names are under written, June 25th 1705.

	£	s	d
Inprimis his purse & apparrell	01	10	00
Item in the fore house one table, one dresser with pewter & other implements	01	00	00
Item in the fore <chamber> one bed with beding, one table & chaires	01	10	00
Item in the back chamber, 2 bedds, table & chairs	01	15	00
Item in the fore parlour, one bed, one table	01	00	00
Item in the back parlour, 1 bed, 1 pannell chist, 2 cha[i]rs	01	15	00
Item in the brew house, one copper, brass & wood vessell	02	10	00
In lining	01	[...	...]
One old horse, one cow & one pigg	03	00	[...]
	14	10	[...][3]

James Conyers, William Harrison, George Dunn, J. Tomes.

1 MS reads 'which' but 'with' is presumably intended.
2 Francis Flint was buried on 8 June 1705, nine months after making his will.
3 The final three sums are defective as the page is torn. The sum total appears to be incorrect, as the figures amount to at least £15.

110. TIMOTHY BAXTER, WEAVER, 1705

DPRI/6/T/1705/B1

The sixt day of September one thousand seven hundred and two. I, Timothy Baxter of Northallerton in the county of York, weaver, being now healthfull in body and in good & perfect remembrance, praised be God, doe make and ordain this my last will and testament in manner and form following that is to say: First I give & bequeath my soule into the hands of allmighty God my maker & creator & my body to the earth from whence it came. And as touching my outward & temporall estate: Imprimis I give & bequeath unto my daughter, Jane Baxter, her heirs & assignes for ever, all my land and state of inheritance withall and singular their appurtenances whatsoever, lying and being within the town & feilds of Skelton in Cleavland provided they must not enter of the said lands & premisses till after the decease of me & my daughter Mary Rogers, late wife of my sonn Francis Baxter. And if it shall happen my daughterr Jane Baxter to die unmarid & have no issue than I give all the aforesaid lands and premisses in Skelton aforesaid unto the children of my daughter Ann Hunter equally to be devided amongst them, and likewise I give unto my said daughter, Jane Baxter, the tennancy <right> of my ground in Gisbrough which I now farm <&> hold by lease under William Chaloner esquire, provided that <she> shall pay out of the profits of my ground in Gisbrough unto Frances my wife the sum of tenn shillings in the yeare during her naturall life if shee happen to survive me, and likewise I give out of the profits of my ground in Gisbrough unto my sister Jane Duck & her foure children each of them five shillings, and the tenn shillings in the year above given unto my wife I give it in full consideracion of her thirds or widdow right out of my personall estate. And I doe hereby make & ordaine my daughter Jane Baxter my sole and absolute executrix of this my last will & testament. In witness whereof I have hereunto set my hand & seale the day & yeare first above written.

Timothie Baxter [*signed*][1]

Sealled published and declared in the presence of us, John Duck his mark, Ann Rogers her mark, R[ichar]d Rogers [*signed*].

Memorandum that the within named Timothy Baxter upon further consideration soon after the confirmation of this will within written dothe give unto the four children of his sonn, Raiph Hunter, each of them two shillings & six pence as witness his hand the 12th day of September anno domini 1702

Timothie Baxter [*signed*]

Testees R[ichar]d Rogers [*signed*], Ann Rogers her mark, John Duck his mark.

A true & perfect inventory of the goods & chattells of Timothy Baxter of North-Allerton deceased November 2nd 1705. Valued & apprized by us whose names are underwrittern.

	£	s	d
Imprimis his purse & apparrell	00	06	08
Item in the house 1 table, 1 chair & other implements	00	06	08
Item in the chamber his loome & geers	00	10	00
Summa	01	03	04

C. Tomes, Ed. Flunders, Smll. Robinson, John Pibus.

[1] Timothy Baxter, a Quaker, was interred on 1 July 1705, nearly three years after making his will: Ingledew, *History and Antiquities*, p. 199.

111. THOMAS THOMPSON, HOSTELER, 1705

DPRI/6/T/1705/T1

In the name of God, amen. I, Thomas Thompson of North Allerton in the county of York, hosteler, being some what infirme in body but of a good sound & disposing mind and memory doe make & publish this to bee & conteine my last will and testament as to my reall & personall estate wherewith God hath blessed mee. Imprimis I give & devise unto my friend Mary Kirby, spinster, for the terme of her naturall life all that my close or parcell of ground in North Allerton which I purchased of George Jackson & others. And after her decease I give & devise the same close lands & grounds unto my nephew John Thompson, the sonne of my brother John Thompson, & his heirs & assignes for ever. Item I give unto my uncle Thomas Thompson five pounds. Item I give unto my aunt Frances Walker five pounds. Item I give unto my nephew Thomas Clark <twenty> pounds. Item I give unto my neice Elizabeth Thompson twenty pounds. Item I give unto my sister Anne Harreson twenty pounds and give unto her children to each & every of them five pounds. Item I give unto my brother John Thompson twenty pounds. Item I give unto Jane Moon, John Scruton, Robert Smythe & Thomas Tyson to each & every of them five shillings. Item I give unto Alice Hunt, Susannah Haw & Rose or Rosamund Shaw to each & every of them two shillings and six pence. Item I give unto Dorothy Sweeting five shillings. Item I give unto Jane Lamb, my aunt in law, the summe of five pounds. Item I give unto my cozen Elizabeth Thompson & to her

children five pounds to bee equally divided among them. Item I give all the residue of my personall estate (my funeralls first deducted) unto my brother John Thompson, my sister Anne Harrison and to my friend Mary Kirby, equally to bee divided among them. And I doe make and appoint my said brother John Thompson, sister Anne Harrison and Mary Kirby joynt executors of this my last will and testament. And I doe hereby revoke and disadnull all former wills by mee made. In witnes whereof I have hereunto sett my hand & seale the three & twentieth day of October in the yeare of our Lord God one thousand seaven hundred and five.
Thomas Thompson [*signed and sealed*][1]
Signed, sealed & published by the said [*Thomas*][2] Thompson in our presence & our names subscribed as witnesses thereto in his presence & att his request & by his direcions the word (twenty) in the bequest to Thomas Clark being interlined over the razure before sealing & publishing, witnesse our hands, R. Raikes [*signed*], George Meeke [*signed*], John Todd [*signed*].
Mr John Todd was sworn to this will by Charles Neile.[3]

1 Thomas Thompson was buried on 28 October 1705, five days after making his will.
2 Thompson's forename was omitted.
3 For Charles Neile, vicar of Northallerton, see below [150].

112. WILLIAM HARRISON, YEOMAN, 1706

DPRI/6/T/1703/H1
In the name of God, amen, I, William Harrison of North Allerton in the county of Yorke, yeoman, being in good health and of sound mind and memory (praised bee God for the same) and knowing the incertainty of this mortall life and being desireous & minded to dispose of my worldly estate I doe make and publish this writing to bee and conteine my last will and testament in manner and forme following. And first whereas <there is setled> upon or to the use of Joane, my loving wife, for and as her joynture the south part of my dwelling house in North Allerton aforesaid from the entry thereof southwards and the low stable and the low malt kilne with ingresse, egresse & regresse thereto & therefrom, and one close or parcell of ground called Hail Stone Moore Close, alias House Close, in North Allerton, <my will is> that it shall bee in my said wive's choice either to hold her said joynture lands and tenements or in lieu thereof (if shee wave and give up her joynture deed within three months next after my decease or next after request to her in that behalfe to bee made unto

my sonne in law Francis Dobson of Easingwould, his heires or assignes) that then she the said Joane my wife shall have, take and receive and that there shall then bee issueing and goeing out of all and singular and every of my mesuages, closes, lands, tenements & hereditaments as well freehold and leasehold for terme and termes of life or lives held under the Bishop of Durham as copyhold lands and tenenments scituate, lying and beinge in North Allerton aforesaid and in Romanby in the said county of Yorke the clear annual or yearely rent or summe of twelve poundes of lawfull English money, tax free and over and above all manner of taxes, assessments, aides, rates or imposicions laid or charged or which shall or may bee laid or charged thereon by any Act or Acts of Parliament or otherwise howsoever, and without any deduccion, allowance, defalcation or abatement or reprisall for or in lieu of taxes, rates, impositions or assessments charged or chargeable upon the said lands and tenements, rent or annual payment or any part thereof. The said yearely rent or annual payment to bee soe had, taken and received by and to bee paid and payable unto my said wife yearely and every yeare during her natural life quarterly and by foure equall quarterly payments in every yeare from and after my decease, and the first quarterly payment thereof to begin and bee payable to her at the end of three calendar months next ensueing or coming after the day of my decease. And in such case, and if it shall soe happen that the said yearely rent or annual payment or summe of twelve pounds shall bee behind or unpaid, in part or in all, att any of the said daies or times above limited or mencioned or appointed for the payment thereof or whereon the same ought to bee paid according to the purport and true meaning of this my will, then my mind and will is that it shall and may bee lawfull to and for my said wife and her assigns into all and every or any of my said mesuages, lands and tenements to enter, and the same and every part thereof to hold and enjoy untill due payment thereof bee made with all her reasonable costs and charges. And I doe hereby charge and subject all and every of my said lands and tenements with the payment of the said annual summe or yearely rent of twelve pounds unto my said wife in manner aforesaid. Item I doe hereby give and devise unto my sonne in law Francis Dobson and to his heires and assignes forever all and every of my mesuages, houses, barnes, malt kilns, malt milnes, closes, lands, tenements, leases and hereditaments whatsoever, freehold, leasehold and copyhold, lying and being in North Allerton and Romanby aforesaid, and the revercion and revercion[s], remainder & remainders, terme and terms of lives and tennant rights thereof, and all my estate, right, title & interest, use, trust, possession, claime and demand of, in and to the same and every part thereof, nevertheless subject and lyeable to and charged & chargeable with the payment of all my just debts and with the payment of all the legacies, guifts, bequests, yearely rents & annual payments in and by this my last will mentioned and expressed. And I doe will that all my just debts and legacies shall bee paid and satisfied out of my said mesuages, lands, tenements and hereditaments, but nevertheless soe and in such manner as not to obstruct, incumber, impede, lessen or hinder or bee a charge upon the said yearely rent or annual payment of twelve pounds by mee given to my wife for and during her life. Item my mind is and I doe by this my will direct, order and appoint that Margaret Staines, widow, my daughter and the heirs and assigns of my said daughter Staines shall upon the request and at the costs and charges of my said sonne Francis Dobson his heirs or assigns grant, release & convey unto and to the use of my said sonne Dobson and his heirs all and every of the said mesuages, lands, tenements, hereditaments by mee devised unto my said sonne Dobson, and all the estate, right, title, interest, use, trust, revertion, remainder, terme of lives and expectancy whatsoever of my said daughter Margaret Staines and of the heirs of my said daughter Staines of, in and to all and every of the said mesuages, lands, tenements and leases and which should, shall, may, might or ought to come and discend unto her or her heirs by vertue of my setlement or joynture made to or for the use of my wife or otherwise might discend or come to the said Margaret, my daughter, as coheire of mee. The same to bee granted, released and conveyed pursuant to certaine articles and covenants of agreement made between Thomas Staines (late husband of my said daughter) & mee upon or relating to and concerning the mariage between the said Thomas Staines and Margarett which said articles beare date the fourth day of June which was in the yeare of our Lord God one thousand six hundred eighty and eight. And I doe direct that such conveyance, grant or release or other assurance shall bee made in & by such proper wayes and meanes as by councell learned in the lawes of this realme shall or may bee reasonably devised or advised pursuant to & conformable with the said articles and covenants. Item I doe give and bequeath unto my five grand children, William, Anne, Johannah, Margaret & Elizabeth, the sonne & daughters of the said Thomas Staines by my said daughter Margarett, the summe of fifty pounds equally to bee divided amongst them and to bee paid to them, theire guardians or tutors for theire use before or att the end of seaven yeares next after my decease. And in case any of my said grandchildren happen to dye

before such payment bee made then the part, share or proporcion of him or of them soe dying shall goe & bee paid to the survivors of them. And I doe direct that all such moneyes as I did owe to my sonne Staines at the time of his death, or such part thereof as shall bee unpaid at the time of my decease, shall bee duely paid & satisfied by my sonne Dobson his heirs or assignes unto the executors or administrators of my said sonne Staines before or at the time that my said daughter Margaret shall or doe make & execute such grant, release, conveyance and assurance as above directed. And whereas one Thomas Barker, deceased, did in his life time depositt into my hands five pounds for the use of the poore of North Allerton, I will and direct that my sonne Francis Dobson shall pay the said summe of five pounds unto the church wardens and overseers of the poore of North Allerton for the time being within three yeares next after my decease and shall alsoe pay to them interest for the same yearely in the meane time to bee by them disposed, paid, laid out & given pursuant to the last will, order and directions of the said Thomas Barker. Item I doe further give and bequeath unto my said loving wife my best bedd in the white chamber with the bedstead, curtains, coverings, bedding & furniture thereunto belonging at best times used, and alsoe one paire of my best sheetes and my best pillowbeares, pillowes, bolsters and coverings fitt for the same bedd. And I doe give all the rest of my goods and chattells and personal estate whatsoever & wheresoever unto my said sonne Francis Dobson the better to inable him to pay my just debts and legacies. And I doe desire that my body may be interred within the parish church of North Allerton amongst my ancestors there. And I doe hereby revoke, disadnull & make voyd all former wills by mee made. And I doe constitute, make and appoint my said sonne Francis Dobson sole executor of this my last will and testament. In witnes whereof I have hereunto sett my hand and seale the twelfth day of January in the second yeare of the reigne of our soveraigne Lady Queen Anne, annoque domini 1703 [*12 Jan. 1704*].
William Harrison [*signed and sealed*][1]
Signed, sealed & published by the said William Harrison to bee his last will and testament in our presence and our names subscribed as witnesses thereto in the presence and at the request & directions of the said William Harrison, witnes our hands (the words (there is setled) and the other words (my will is) being interlined before sealing[)], witnes, R. Raikes [*signed*], Ann Raikes [*signed*], George Blanshard [*signed*].

[1] William Harrison was buried on 24 January 1706, two years after making his will.

113. SUSAN ROBINSON, 1706

DPRI/6/T/1706/R2
April 28 1706.
Old Susan Robinson disposed of her goods before us as followeth. To Susan, the daughter of George Robinson, the newer & larger cupboard with all things upon it & in it & the glass case adjoining. To Dorothy, the other daughter of George Robinson, the other cupboard with four dishes, one red bed in the fore chamber. To Christopher Robinson, her son, three dishes & three flagons upon the older cupboard & a howle dish. To him also a bed in the innermore chamber with yellow curtains next the chamber door. To Susan, the daughter of George Robinson, four setwork chairs, & a table in the chamber where they stood. To George Robinson, her son, the other two beds in the innermore chamber. To Susan, the daughter of George Robinson, two beds in the fore chamber, the one next the window & the next to it. To Thomas, the son of Christopher Robinson, the bed in the parlor next the buttery door. To Percival, the son of George Robinson, the other bed in the parler. The long table in the fore house to go with the house. To Susan, also the daughter of George Robinson, half a dozen buffit stooles & a pannel chest in the parlor. Two pair of the best linnen sheets, one pair to one son & one pair to the other. The remaining linnen to George Robinson's two daughters. The four going dublers[1] to George Robinson.
Witness our hands, C. Neile [*signed*], Jane Wooller [*signed*].[2]

August the 19th 1706. A true inventory of the goods & chattells of Susannah Robinson late of North-Allerton deceased.

	£	s	d
Her purse & apparrell	00	05	00
the furniture in the fore house	00	16	06
the furniture in the parlour	00	10	00
the furniture in the fore chamber	00	14	06
furniture in the back chamber	00	08	04
	02	14	04

Edward Wooller, Robert Welbank, Edward Ludlow marke, Jacob Harrison.

1 Reading uncertain.

2 Susan Robinson was buried on 1 May 1706, three days after making her nuncupative will. She was the widow of George Robinson [59]. The will appears to be in the hand of Charles Neile.

114. WILLIAM DENNIS, YEOMAN, 1706

DPRI/6/T/1706/D1

In the name of God, amen, I, William Dennis of North Allerton in the county of York, yeoman, being infirme in boddy but of a sound and perfect mind and memory, praise bee God for the same, doe make and publish this my last will and testament in manner and forme following, that is to say: Imprimis I committ my soule God who gave it & my body to the earth from whence it came to bee buryed as my executrix hereafter named shall think fitt. And as to the worldly goods wherewith God hath blessed mee I give, devise and dispose thereof in manner and forme following. Imprimis I give and bequeath unto Phillip Unthank all that my pew seate or place in the parish church of North Allerton aforesaid to hold the same with all the rights, members and appurtenances thereunto belonging unto the said Phillip Unthank his heires and assigns for ever. Item I give and bequeath unto the wife of George White of Pickall one shilling, and to his two daughters to each of them the summe of five shillings to bee paid unto them and every of them within one month next after my decease. All the rest of my goods and chattells, rights and creditts & personall estate of what kind or nature soever I give and bequeath unto my trusty and well beloved friend and kinswoman Mary Anderson of North Allerton aforesaid, widdow, and I do hereby make the said Mary Anderson sole executrix of this my last will and testament. And I do alsoe hereby revoke, disannull and make voyd all other will and wills by mee formerly made. And I do hereby declare this to bee and conteine my last will and testament. In witnes whereof I have hereunto sett my hand and seale this sixteenth day of February in the yeare of our Lord God one thousand seaven hundred and five [*16 Feb. 1706*].

the marke & seale of William Dennis.[1]

Sealed & delivered & published by the testator to bee his last will and at his request wee subscribed our names as witnesses hereto.

The within written will was sealed & delivered by the testator & published to bee his last will and testament and at his request wee were desired to sett our hands as witnesses thereto, witnes our hands, William Smelt [*signed*], Lawrence Lowcock [*signed*], Francis Kaye [*signed*].

August 15° 1706. Apraisement then made of the goods & chattells of William Dennis lately deceased & praised by us whose names are underwritten.

	£	s	d
Imprimis, his purse & his apparrell	00	01	06
Item one trunell bedstead	00	01	00
one canvis bed	00	01	00
two coverings	00	01	06
one pair of sheets	00	01	00
2 shifts	00	00	06
one litle pann	00	01	00
	00	07	06

John Prest, James Rowes, William Boddye, James Rowth.

1 Following a service in Northallerton, William Dennis was buried at Kilvington, near Thirsk, on 13 August 1706, six months after making his will.

115. PERCIVAL ROBINSON, MALTMAN, 1706

DPRI/6/T/1706/R1

February the 10th [*1694/5*]

In the name of God, amen, I, Percival Robinson of North Allerton in the county of York, maltman, being in good health of body and of sound and perfect mind and memory, praise be therefore given to almighty God, do make and ordaine this my present last will and testament in manner and form following (that is to say), first and principally I commend my soul into the hands of almighty God hoping through the meritts, death and passion of my saviour Jesus Christ to have full and free pardon and forgiveness of all my sins and to inherit everlasting life; and my body I commit to the earth to be decently buried at the discretion of my executor hereafter named. And as touching the disposure of all such temporall estate as it hath pleased almighty God to bestow upon me I give and dispose thereof as followeth. First I will that my debts and funeral charges shall be paid and discharged. Item I give unto my loveing brother George Robinson and his heires all that one half of the house or tenement wherein I now live which is given and bequeathed to me by my father's last will and testament and in as full and ample manner as is perticularly there exprest with all the right, title, interest, property, claime or demand which I either now have and enjoy or may hereafter have, claime or enjoy with all immunitys, priviledges and appurtenances whatsoever thereunto belonging, clear and free of and from all and all manner of right, title, interest, property, claime & demand which any one shall or may have or claime by, from or under me for ever. Item I give and bequeath unto my loving brother Christopher

Robinson the sum of five shillings. Item I give and bequeath <five shillings> unto my brother Christopher's wife, and five shillings apiece to either of his children. All the rest & residue of my personal estate, goods and chattells whatsever I do give and bequeath unto my loving brother George Robinson whom I constitute and make full and sole executor of this my last will and testament. And I do hereby revoke, dissanull and make void all former wills and testaments. In witness where of I the said Percival Robinson to this my last will and testament being contained in one sheet of paper set my hand and seal anno domini 1694/5.
Parceval Robinson [*signed and sealed*]
Sealed & delivered in the presence of Henry Danby [*signed*], William Harrison [*signed*], Jacob Harrison [*signed*], Elizabeth Steward <hir marke>.

September the 11th 1706. A true inventory of the goods & chattells of Parcivall Robinson late of North-Allerton deceased.[1]

	£	s	d
His purse & apparrell with other necessarys	02	00	00

[1] Percival Robinson's will was not proved until 1706, more than 11 years after it had been drawn up. The date of his death has not been established.

116. HENRY WHITTON, GROCER, 1707

DPRI/6/T/1707/W1

In the name of God, amen, I, Henry Whitton of North-Allerton in the county of Yorke, grocer, being of sound and disposing mind and memory, praised be God for the same, doe make, publish and declare this my last will and testament in manner following, that is to say, I will and direct that as soon as conveniently may be after my decease an appraisment or valuation shall be made of all the plate, linnen, household goods, shop goods, wares, merchandizes and all other the personall estate which I shall leave att the time of my decease. And that so much of the said plate, linnen and household goods as shall in the judgement of my executors hereinafter named amount to a third part in value of all my plate, linnen and household goods shall goe and be unto my dear wife Elizabeth Whitton, her executors and administrators. And as to the remainder of the said plate, linnen and household goods and also as to all my wares, merchandizes, shop goods and other goods and chattells whatsoever, my will is that my said executors shall after my death sell and dispose of the same or such part thereof onely as they shall think fitt, and out of the money arising by such sale doe and shall raise and pay the summe of fifty pounds of lawfull money of England to and for my said wife upon her giving security to the satisfaccion of my said executors to repay the same to my said executors upon her marrying again with any person after my decease, or att the day of her death which shall first happen. And the residue of the money arising by such sale and also the said goods, chattells and personall estate that shall remain unsold or undisposed of, and also the said fifty pounds from and after the decease of my said wife, I will and appoint shall goe unto and be equally divided amongst all and every the children that I shall have att the time of my decease to be paid and delivered to them respectively att their respective ages of one and twenty yeares or marriage, which shall first happen, share and share alike. And in case any of them shall happen to dy before his, her or their part or share thereof shall become due and payable as aforesaid, the part or share of him or her dying to goe unto and be equally divided amongst the survivors or survivor of them as and when the original part or share of such survivors or survivor shall become payable by vertue of these presents. And in the mean time, untill the same respective parts or porcions shall become payable such money as shall ~~be putt~~ arise out of the said personall estate shall be putt forth att interest and the interest and proceed thereof from time to time as the same shall be received shall goe and be applyed as the said executors shall think fitt for or towards the educacion or maintenance of the same children or such of them and in such manner as to my said executors shall seem meet. And in case my said executors shall think itt proper to raise or pay any summe of money for the putting or placing out James Whitton my son as an apprentice or otherwise in order to the gaining him an employment or way of living, the same shall or may be deducted or allowed out of the principall money or share hereby intended for the said James. And my will and mind is that whatsoever my said executors shall doe either in the dividing or disposing of any part of my said personall estate or in the selling, ordering or management therof or in the disposing or employing the interest of my said children's porcions, shall be binding and concluding to all my said children and wife and to all other persons concerned therein, my mind and will being that my said executors shall not receive any the least vexations, trouble or disturbance for undertaking so troublesome a trust in which I am satisfyed they will demean themselves with great faithfulnesse and integrity. And the selling, disposing, dividing or keeping any part of the said personall

estate I leave solely to their judgment and discrecion and also the disposing the interest of the porcions of such of my children as shall be and while they are under the age of one and twenty yeares. And my will is that if any losse shall happen by putting out att interest any money that shall arise out of my personall estate my said executors shall not be accountable for the same. And I doe hereby nominate, constitute and appoint my trusty freinds John Wells of Stockton in the county of Durham merchant my father in law and James Whitton of Bedall my brother joynt executors of this my will, hereby revoking all former wills by me att any time heretofore made. In witnesse whereof I have hereunto sett my hand and seale this twelfth day of February in the fourth yeare of the reign of Queen Anne of England &c. annoque domini 1705 [*12 Feb. 1706*].
Henry Whitton [*signed and sealed*][1]
Signed, sealed, published and declared by the above named Henry Whitton as and for his last will and testament in the presence of us who have subscribed our names as witnesses thereunto in his presence, Mark Jackson [*signed*], John Rudd [*signed*], Farrow Eden [*signed*].

A value of the goods of Mr Henry Whitton deceased.

	£	s	d
Imprimis to purse and apparrell	25	00	00
Item to severall goods in the shop &c.	187	07	00
Item to household goods &c.	52	05	04
In all	264	12	04

[1] Henry Whitton was buried on 30 October 1707, 18 months after making his will.

117. GEORGE MEEKE, GROCER, 1707

DPRI/6/B/1708/M1
An appraisement of the goods & chattells of George Meeke late of North-Allerton, grocer, deceased appraised by us whose names are underwritten as followeth.[1]

	£	s	d
Imprimis in the fore chamber			
one bed & bedding & appurtenances thereto belonging	02	10	00
twelve chaires	01	01	04
a large looking glass	00	09	07
Item in the back chamber, 2 bedsteads & beding	03	14	05
Six chaires	00	07	03

Grocerys in the shop & sellar	08 16 10
	16 19 05

Appraisors: George Pemberton, Jacob Harrison, Robert Loftas, Richard Rymer.

[1] George Meeke was buried on 11 November 1707.

118. JOHN RYMER, YEOMAN WEAVER, 1708

DPRI/6/T/1708/R1

In the name of God, amen, the third day of December in the yeare of our Lord God one thousand seaven hundred and eight. I, John Rymer [of] Gronston Crook in the parish of North Allerton in the county of Yorke, yeoman, being of whole minde and in good and perfect rememberance, laud and praise be given to almighty God, make and ordain this my present testament concerning herein my last will and testament in maner and form following, that is to say, first I commend my soule unto almighty God my maker and redeemer and my body to be buryed in the parish church yard of North Allerton. Item I will that all such debts and duties as I owe of righte or of conscence to any person or persons be well and truly contented and paid by my wife Ellin Rymer, whom I make my executor, and after my debts and funerall expenes be paid I will that my wife Elling have my house and land at Grunston Crook tell my son John Rymer accomplish the ages of one and twentie yeares. And my wife to have all my personall estate. And after my son John accomplish the ages of one and twentie yeares I will that my son John, his heirs, executors, administrators or assignes pay to my wife Elling Rymer during her naturall life the summ of two pounds and ten shillings yearely and every yeare during her said naturall life, that is <to say> if the childe that my wife Elling Rymer is soposed to be with accomplish the ages of one and twenty yeares, I will that my son John Rymer, his heirs, executors, administrators or assigns pay to the childe (my wife is soposed to be with) the full and just summ of forty pounds when the childe shall or may accomplish the ages of one and twenty yeares. If my two childer live to accomplish the ages of one and twenty yeares then I will that my son John Rymer pay to his mother my wife Elling Rymer her thirds out of the said lands above writ, but if one of my childer should dy before they accomplish the ages of one and twenty yeares then I will that the other shall pay my wife Elling two pounds and ten shillings yearely and every yeare during her naturall life, but if it pleas God both my childer should dy before my wife Elling Rymer

I will that she my wife have and injoy my lands and house during her naturall life and fifteen pounds to dispose of at her death to be truly and justly paid to the said Elling Rymer <or her> assignes by those who may fall lawfull heir or heirs to the said land and house. And I do utterly revoke and adnull all other former testaments, wils whatsoever by me anywase before this time made, named, willed and bequeathed, whereunto I have set my hand and seale after these words writ which is enterlined – to say, or her.
John Rymer [*signed and sealed*][1]
Testes Jacob Duffielld [*signed*], Thomas Davisone [*signed*], Will: Heuthwait [*signed*].

The inventory of all the goods & chattells of John Rymer of Gronstone Crook in the parish of North Allerton in the county of York weaver deceased, appraised by us whose names are hereunder written. 11° December in the year of our Lord God 1708°.

	£	s	d
Imprimis, his purse & apparrell	01	00	00
Item in the forehouse one bed and bedding belonging to itt, one table & chairs, one dresser with pewder & all other implements belonging the forehouse	04	02	06
Item in the chamber one ordinary bed and one kettle in the milkhouse with other milk vessell	00	12	06
Item two loomes with sleares & geares and one prentis and all other things belonging to the trade	02	12	06
Item two cowes and hay	04	02	06
Item about three stookes of corne	00	07	06
Item one acre and a rood of stuble corne sowne downe	01	05	06
Item a few coales, a litle manuer & two hens	00	07	06
	14	10	06

John Jhinson, Francis Bolton marke, William Allcock marke, Henry Jhinson junior.

Debts owne by the deceased	10	00	00
[*remaining*	*04*	*10*	*06*]

[1] John Rymer was buried on 4 December 1708, the day after making his will.

119. WILLIAM GAILES, 1709

DPRI/6/B/1709/G1
May the 2^{d} 1709.

A true and perfect inventory of the goods & chattells late of William Gailes of North-Allerton deceased.[1]

	£	s	d
Imprimis his purse and apparrell	00	12	06
The household goods	01	03	06
One cowe	02	11	06
One sheepe	00	08	00
	04	15	06

Appraised by us whose names are underwritten. Jacob Harrison, Robert Straker, Thomas Gamble, Christopher Welbanke.

[1] William Gailes was buried on 14 June 1708. His inventory, however, was not drawn up until 11 months later.

120. MARY HUNTON AND MERRIAL NELSON, 1709[1]

DPRI/6/B/1709/H1

A true & perfect invintory of the goods & chattills of Mary Hunton & Meriell Nelson lately deceased.

	£	s	d
Imprimis a bed & bedstead, a cupboard & drawers & 6 pewter dishes	1	0	0
2 chairs, 2 stands & some small picturs	0	5	0
A little silver tumbler	0	7	6
A bible & other bookes	0	5	0
Her clothes & purse & apparell & a table & other implements	0	10	0
	2	7	6

Valued by us, Will: Alonson [*signed*], John Bayne [*signed*], Henry Sayer [*signed*], Will: Drybrough [*signed*].

[1] Mary Hunton and Merrial Nelson were sisters; for the latter's will, see below [122].

121. WILLIAM STOCKDALE, YEOMAN, 1709

DPRI/6/T/1709/S1

In the name of God, amen, I, William Stockdale of the parish of North Allerton in the county of Yorke, yeoman, being sick and weak in body but of sound & disposing mind & memory (praised be almighty God for the same), doe make and ordaine this my last will and testament in manner and forme following (that is to say) first and principally I commend my soul into the hands of almighty

God hopeing through the merits, death and passion of my saviour Jesus Christ to have full and free pardon and forgivenesse of sinns and to inherit everlasting life. And as touching the disposition of such temporal estate wherewith it hath pleased almighty God to blesse me, I give and dispose thereof as followeth. Imprimis my will and mind is that my debts and funerall expences shall be paid and discharged. Item whereas I am now lawfully seized and possessed of and in certain <closes>, lands and tenements lying and being within the parish of North Allerton aforesaid which are as follow (that is to say), one close or parcell of ground called and known by the name of Hailstone Moor Close being formerly three common rights & conteining six acres or thereabouts adjoyning upon certain lands late belonging to Mr Rymer on the south and lands late belonging to the Lady Fretchvell on the north. One other close or parcel of ground called Hailestone Moor Close lying and being upon a flatt or parcell of ground called Hailstone Moor adjoyning upon certain lands late belonging to Ralph Humphrey on the south and lands late belonging to one Thomas Flower on the north and conteining by estimacion two acres or thereabouts, which said two closes or parcells of ground with all their rights, members and appurtenances I give, devise and bequeath in manner & forme following (that is to say), I give, devise and bequeath one full halfe part thereof unto my dear and loveing kinsman John Newsam of Bromton in the parish of North Allerton aforesaid, yeoman, his heires and assignes for ever to have and to hold one full halfe part of the above mencioned closes or parcells of ground with one full halfe part of all and singular their appurtenances unto the only proper use and behoofe of the said John Newsam, his heires and assignes for ever. Item I give, devise and bequeathe the other halfe part of the above mencioned closes or parcells of ground with the other halfe part of all and singular theire rights, members & appurtenances unto James Wilkinson of Deighton in the parish of North Allerton aforesaid, yeoman, and Jane his wife theire heires and assignes for ever, to have and to hold the same unto the only proper use and behoofe of them the said James Wilkinson and Jane his wife their heires and assignes for ever. Provided alwayes neverthelesse and my will & mind is that my dear and loveing wife Allice Stockdale shall hold and enjoy the above mencioned close or parcell of ground called Hailstone Moor Close and which is above mencioned to contain only two acres or thereabouts, and shall and may have, take and receive the rents, issues and profitts thereof for her own proper use & behoofe for & during the terme of her naturall life. Item I give and bequeath unto my brother-in-law

Ralph Humphrey and unto my sister Anne, wife of the said Ralph Humphrey, to each of them two shillings and six pence of lawfull money of Great Britain in full of what they or either of them shall or may claime or demand out of my reall and personall estate. Item I give, devise and bequeath all the rest, residue and remainder of my personall estate, goods & chattells whatsoever unto my said loveing kinsmen John Newsam and James Wilkinson equally to be devided between them share and share alike. And I doe nominate and appoint them the said John Newsam and James Wilkinson joynt executors of this my last will and testament. And lastly I commit my body to the earth to be decently buried at the discretion of my said executors. And I doe heeby revoke, disanull and make voyd all former wills and testaments by me heretofore made. In witnesse whereof I have this my last will and testament set my hand and seale this eight and twentieth day of December in the yeare of our Lord God one thousand seaven hundred and seaven.
the mark of William Stockdale [*sealed*][1]
Signed, sealed and declared and published by the said William Stockdale to be his last will & testament & our names subscribed hereunto as witnesses in his presence and at his request (the word closes being first interlined[)], Thomas Crosfield [*signed*], Thomas Duning [*signed*], Thomas Newsam [*signed*].

[1] William Stockdale was buried at Brompton on 4 January 1709, more than a year after making his will.

122. MERRIAL NELSON, SPINSTER, 1709

DPRI/6/T/1709/N1
In the name of God, amen, I, Merrial Nelson of North Allerton in the county of York, spinster, being infirme in body but of sound & perfect mind & memory, praised bee God for the same, but being mindfull of my mortality do make and publish this my last will & testament in manner and forme following. Imprimis I commend my soule to God who gave it & my body to the earth from whence it came to bee buryed in such decent & comely manner as my executors hereafter named shall think fitt at an equall charge between them share and share like. And as for the wordly goods wherewith God hath blessed mee I give and dispose thereof in manner and forme following (that is to say). Imprimis I give & bequeath unto William Nelson, George Nelson & Jane Nelson, sonnes and daughter of Robert Nelson late of North Allerton, yeoman, deceased to each of them the summe of six pence to

bee paid to them or such of them as shall bee then living within one month after my decease. Item I give & bequeath unto Mary Watson, Alice Watson and William Watson, sonne & daughters of Anthony Watson late of North Allerton aforesaid, silk weaver deceased, to each of them the summe of sixpence of lawfull English money to bee paid unto them or such of them as shall bee then living alsoe within one month next after my decease. Item all and singular the rest of my goods and chattells, rights and creditts and personall estate whatsoever (my debts, legacyes and funerall expences being first thereout paid and discharged[)] I give & bequeath unto my loving brother Mark Nelson and my loving sister Mary Hunton both of North Allerton aforesaid or to theire executors or assignes to bee shared, parted & devided between them, their executors of assignes proporcionably share and share like. And I do hereby make my said brother Mark Nelson & my sister Mary Hunton joynt executors of this my last will and testament and I do hereby revoke, disannull and make voyd all former & other will or wills by mee formerly made. And do alsoe hereby declare this to bee and contein my last will and testament. In witnes whereof I have hereunto sett my hand & seale this tenth day of November in the yeare of our Lord God one thousand seaven hundred and two.
the marke & seall of Merrial Nelson.[1]
Sealed, published & delivered by the testatrix & at her request & by her direccions in our presence, Henry Whitton [*signed*], Elizabeth Robinson [*signed*], Francis Kaye [*signed*] juratus.

[1] Merrial Nelson was buried on 14 June 1709, more than six and half years after her will was made. A joint inventory of her possessions and those of her sister Mary Hunton is filed separately (above [120]).

123. ROBERT RAIKES, GENTLEMAN, 1710

BIA/68/157 [probate copy]
Will of Robert Raikes late of Northallerton esquire deceased proved by Robert Raikes esquire son sole executor 11th September 1712.
In the name of God, amen, I, Robert Raikes of Northallerton in the county of York, gentleman, being in good health of body (tho afflicted with a sore & lame leg) & being of a good, sound & disposing mind & memory (praised be God for the same[)] & being mindfull of my mortality & desirous to settle & dispose off the reall & personal estate wherewith it hath pleased almighty God to bless me, I do for that purpose make & publish this to be & containe my last will & testament concerning my said estate. Imprimis I give & devise unto

my only son Robert Raikes & to his heires for ever all that my manor of Aislaby in the county of Durham and all my farms, messuages, cottages, closes, lands, tenements, fishings, fisheries & heraditaments in Aislaby aforesaid. And also all my other farms, messuages, cottages, closes, lands tenements & heraditaments whatsover, as well freehold & copyhold as also leasehold, lying & being within the several parishes, townships & territorys of North Allerton, Brompton, West Rounton, Drypool, Finghall, Carperby, Scruton, Mawnby upon Swaile & Kirby upon Wisk & elsewhere in the county of York, subject & chargeable to & with the several charges, gifts, bequests, portions, legacys & payments in & by this my last will, charged & appointed to be paid according to the purport, true intent, legal & equitable meaning of this my last will. And in the first place do give & devise unto my loving wife, Ann Raikes, one annuity or yearly rent, summe or payment of fourscore pounds of lawfull money of England, clear & over & above all reprisalls, to be paid to her by two equal payments half year from immediately next after my decease for & during the natural life of my said wife, without any deductions, defalcation or abatement for or in lieu of my taxes, assessments, aids or impositions to be laid or charged or imposed by any Act or Acts of Parliament made or to be made or otherwise, however, upon condition nevertheless & so as my said wife shall & do take & accept thereof in full recompense, satisfaction & discharge aswell of all the covenants & agreements on my part to be performed by vertue of certain articles of agreement made some little time before or near about the time of our marriage between her father, Mr William Darcy (since deceased[)] & me. As also in full satisfaction & discharge & recompense of all her dower & thirds & right & title of dower & thirds & whatever else my said wife can or may or ought or could have claime or demand forth out of my estate real & personal by any law, custome or usage whatsoever. And if my wife be pleased & content & agree so to accept of this my devise & gift to her (as I doubt not but she will, this my will being made with her privity & approbation) then my will is & I do hereby charge all my said manors, farms, lands, tenements & hereditaments with the payment of the said annuity, yearly rent & summe of fourscore pounds to my said wife in such manner & at such days & times as aforesaid. And that then & in such case of my said wive's acceptance thereof & agreement thereto, I do declare my mind & will further to be, and I do hereby charge all my said manors & all my farms, lands, tenements & hereditaments aswell freehold, leasehold as copyhold with the payment of all & every of the yearly & other summ & summes of money as are in & by this my will given

& appointed to be paid to my two daughters, Mary Raikes & Ann Raikes, aswell for their respective maintenances & supports untill their several marriages as also for their several & respective portions to be paid upon the terms & contingencys in this my will mentioned & according to the true meaning of this my last will & not otherwise, that is to say, my mind & will is & I do hereby subject & charge all my said manors, farms, lands & hereditaments with the yearly payment of threescore pounds of lawfull money of England, clear & without any deduction for taxes or any other matter or thing, unto my daughter Mary Raikes, to be paid to her by two equal payments halfe yearly from the time of my decease untill my said daughter Mary shall marry or take husband, for & as her maintenance or livelyhood. And in like manner my will is, & I do give unto my daughter Ann Raikes the yearly summe of sixty pounds of like money to be paid to her without any deduction whatsoever by two equal payments from and immediately next after my decease for & as her maintenance & livelyhood. And I do charge & subject all my said manors, farms, lands & hereditaments with the payment thereof untill such time only as my said daughter Ann shall marry & take husband & no longer. And my mind & will is that such payment of the said yearly summe of sixty pounds to my said daughters respectively shall cease upon their several & respective marriages. And if it shall happen that my said daughters or either of them shall happen to dye unmarryed & not having benn marryed, my will is & I do hereby give to my said daughter, or such of them as shall dye unmarryed, severally & respectively the respective summe of two hundred pounds with full power to give & dispose /thereof/[1] as to them or either of them respectively shall be thought meet & fit. And I do charge my said lands with the due payment thereof in such manner as to my said daughters or either of them respectively shall direct & appoint. And my will is further that when my said daughters or either of them shall marry & take husband, that then & in such case & cases I give unto my said daughters severally & respectively, portions suitable to such settlements as their said husbands respectively shall make to them respectively of freehold lands & tenenments in fee simple, at the rate of ten pounds per annum for every hundred pounds in money without fraud in the yearly value of such lands so to be settled. And the yearly rents to be computed as they have been for the greater part of one & twenty yeares last past before the making of this my will & so that no dwelling houses, barns, mills, kilnes be to be reckoned of any value in such settlement or settlements. And so & provided as the whole portion to each of my said daughters respectively do not surmount the summe of one thousand pounds of like money, and so & provided that such lands & tenements so to be setled on my daughters or either of them be setled by such ways & means as shall or may be reasonably devised or advised by councell learned in the laws of this land to the end & purpose that they shall be as a joynture or joyntures respectively for my said daughters, that their respective husbands shall be only tenants or tenant for the life of the lands to be setled, and that the same lands shall descend & come to the first & every other son & sons respectively & successively as they shall be in priority of birth of the husband or husbands begotten on the body or bodys of my said daughters respectively. And the heirs males of such son & sons respectively & successively as they shall be in priority of birth & seniority of age, the elder son & sons & the heirs of his body always to be preferred & preferrable before the younger son & sons & the heirs of his or their bodys, & for want of such issue then to discend & come to the issue female of such husband & husbands respectively to be begotten on the body or bodys of my said daughters respectively. And if more than one daughter then such daughters to take as tenants in common & not as joynt tenants with remainder or remainders over, faleing such issue to the heirs & assignes of such husband or husbands respectively. And so & provided that such settlement or settlements be made & executed before the marriage or marriages of my daughters respectively, or at least that before such their said respective marriages, the party or parties with whom my said daughters shall or either of them shall respectively marry, shall article & agree to & with my said son, his heirs or assignes, within six months next after the solemnization of such marriage to make proper settlement or settlements accordingly & of such yearly value as shall be agreed on pursuant to this my will for which one hundred pounds is to be paid for every ten pounds per annum in land to be setled according to the true meaning hereof. But so neverthelesse that my said son, his heires or assignes, do pay the money for such settlement or settlements of lands accordingly & of such yearly value as shall be agreed on pursuant to this my will at the time of the making & executing thereof, or at least give good & sufficient security to such person or persons who shall so marry my daughter or daughters, well & truly to pay the same with interest at the rate of five pounds per centum by the year within six moneths next after the making & executing of such settlement or settlements, provided always further, & my will nevertheless is, that if such person or persons with whom my said daughter or daughters shall respectively marry have not lands & tenements of freehold in fee simple sufficient to settle upon such marriage or marriages to require the payment of one thousand pounds at the rate of one hundred pounds for lands of ten pounds per annum discharged from all incumbrances but covenants & articles before marriage to make good such settlement or settlements within the time before limited, then & in such case or cases, if it shall appear that such person or persons cannot make good such purchase of lands so to be setled by moneys of his or their owne but shall become indebted for the same or any thereof, my will is that my said son Robert Raikes & his heires shall only pay one hundred pounds for lands of every ten pounds per annum which such person or persons who marrys my said daughters or either of them shall have of their owne or bona fide purchase with their own moneys without contracting any debt or debts for such purchase & which shall be freed & discharged of & from all charges prior estates & incumbrances. And as a further encouragement & inducement for my said daughters not to marry with necessitous persons, my will further is, and I do hereby direct that if it shall so happen that my said daughters or either of them shall marry & shall have two or three children respectively, one which is to inherit such lands as are to be setled on the marriage or marriages of my said daughters, then in such case my will is and I do hereby charge all my said lands with the payment of one hundred pounds apiece severally & respectively to the two younger children which my said daughters shall respectively have next &, other than such child as shall then in probility take by the settlement on such respective marriages, the same to be paid to such child or children respectively when they shall severally attaine to their several & respective age & ages of one & twenty yeares or be marryed whether shall first happen, provided nevertheless, & my will is that if such person or persons who shall marry my said daughters shall & will (when such younger child or children (if they happen to have any such) shall attaine to the age of one year) lay out & expend one hundred pounds in the purchase of lands to be setled on such younger children not exceeding two by either of my daughters & on the heires of such /younger/ child or children. Then & in such case & cases I will that my son Raikes shall pay, lay out & expend the like summe of one hundred pounds in the purchase of such or other lands, such purchases to be made by the father of such child or children & the lands to be setled on such child or children, his & their heires, not exceeding two, by each of my said daughters. And that then such payment by my said son towards such purchase or purchases for such children shall be in full payment & discharge of the like summe & summes above directed to be paid to such child or children at their respective age or ages of one & twenty years or at their respective marriages, whether should first happen. But in case my said wife shall not or do not think fit or shall or do refuse to accept & take the aforesaid annuity of fourscore pounds per annum for her life upon the terms & conditions aforesaid, then my mind & will is, and I do hereby appoint & give to my said daughters respectively, only five hundred pounds apiece for their portions to be paid to them when they shall severally attaine to their respective full ages of one & twenty years or be married, whether shall first happen & interest for the same half yearly in the meanwhile, at & after the rate of six pounds per centum by the year for their respective maintenances. And that then & in such case of my said wife's refusall to accept off the said annuity on the terms aforesaid, all my former bequests & gifts to my said daughters of threescore pounds per annum untill their respective marriages & of the several summes of money to be paid to their intended husbands on making such settlements as aforesaid, & of the gifts of one hundred pounds apiece to their younger children & all matters, conditions & contingencys relating thereto in this my will, heretofore given & appointed to be paid & charged on my said lands, shall cease & be utterly null & voyd. And in such case my will is that my said lands shall not be charged or subject to or with the payment thereof or any part thereof or with any other summe or summes of money, gifts or portions to my said daughters or to either of them save only with the payment of five hundred pounds apiece to them with interest at the rate of six pounds per centum by the year as above directed in that behalfe. Item I give to my sister, Mary Deighton (though she has very often highly disobliged me) one annuity, yearly rent or summe of five pounds of lawfull English money & appoint & charge the same to be paid out of my lands to her tax free & without any abatement or deduction whatsoever by equal payments half yearly from the time of my decease. And my will is that her husband shall not intermeddle with the receipt thereof. And I will & appoint that my son & his heirs shall pay the same as it becomes due and payable to her own hands or to her special order to any other person (save her husband), the same being intended for my sister's maintenance & subsistence, yet as upon no pretense or colour whatsoever that my said sister or her husband shall have any power or authority to grant, sell or assign the said annuity or yearly summe /or any part thereof/ to any person or persons whomsoever. And my will is that if my sister or her husband do at any time sell or assigne or grant the said annuity or yearly summe to any other person or persons that then & from the time of such grant, sale or assignment thereof, the further payment thereof to cease & determine. And that my said lands shall not then be charged with the payment thereof. And my will is that my sister's note or receipt testifying the payment of such annuity or yearly summe shall be a sufficient discharge to & for my said son Raikes, without any act or concurrance of her husband. And my will further is that in case my said son, Robert Raikes, his heirs or assignes, shall or do happen or neglect to pay the said annuitys, yearly payments, summe or summes of money & portions at such time & times & in such manner as is above limited & appointed for the payment thereof, according to the true <intent> & meaning of this my will (due respect to be had on the contingences of my wife's refusall to accept of her said annuity on the terms aforesaid) then, & in every such case & cases, I do give full power & authority unto my said wife, daughter Mary, daughter Ann & sister Mary & to every of them to whom such faylure of payment shall happen or who shall want the moneys by me as before appointed to be paid according to the true & equitable meaning hereof, to enter into & upon all & every the messuages, farms, lands, tenements & hereditaments & to hold & enjoy the same untill full payment thereof be made, together with all reasonable charges about the same. Item I give unto my nephew Robert Deighton twenty pounds to be paid to him when he shall attaine to the age of one & twenty years or in the meanwhile if my sister shall think fit to put him apprentice to any trade. I will that my son shall pay the same or such part as is necessary for the putting my said nephew an apprentice & the remainder thereof at his full age. Item I give to my niece Ann Deighton thirty pounds to be paid to her at her full age of one & twenty years or her marriage whether shall first happen, yet so nevertheless that if my sister think fit to put my said niece to be apprentice to some simpstresse, millener or other convenient trade, then my will is that my said son shall pay the said thirty pounds or such part thereof as is necessary for the putting my said niece an apprentice & the remainder to be paid to her at her age or marriage. And I declare that that money my son shall pay for putting my said nephew & niece apprentices shall stand & be as such part of their respective legacies. Item I give to my wife twenty pounds to buy her mourning, and I give to her the best furniture I have at her choice to be taken by her for the furnishing of one roome. And I appoint that my son pay all my just debts and in and to my son & the lands I have given to him I give to him all the rest of my goods & chattells and personal estate & make him sole executor of this my

last will & testament & I do revoke & make voyd all former wills by me made. In witness whereof I have hereunto set my hand & seal this twelfth day of June in the year of our Lord God one thousand seaven hundred & seven.
Robert Raikes.[2]
Signed sealed and published by the testator Robert Raikes in our presence & our names subscribed as witnesses in his presence & by his directions & at his request. Witnesse our hands Thomas Forster, James Conyers, Henry Sayer, Thomas Crosfeild.

[1] The significance of the strokes here and elsewhere in this will is unclear; they may perhaps indicate interlineations in the original will of which the MS is a copy.

[2] Robert Raikes was buried on 23 March 1710, almost three years after making his will. For the memorial to Raikes in Northallerton parish church, see Ingledew, *History and Antiquities*, p. 167.

124. JANE GRIMSTON, WIDOW, 1710

BIA/67/10 [probate copy]

In the name of God, amen, I, Jane Grimston of North Allerton in the county of Yorke, widdow, being in health of body and of sound and perfect mind and memory, praised be God, doe make, publish and declare this my last will and testament in manner and forme following. First and principally I commit my soul into the hands of almighty God, hopeing through the merittorious death & passion of my dear saviour Jesus Christ to have and receive full and free remission and pardon for all my sins and as to such worldly estate as itt has pleased God to bless me with, far above my deserts, I give, devise, dispose and legate the same as followeth. Imprimis I give and devise unto my nephew George Meek, his heires and assignes all those my messuages, houses, lands, tenements and hereditaments whatsoever, as well freehold as leases for lives, scituate, standing and <lying> and being within the severall towns and towneshipps of North Allerton aforesaid and Romanby in the said county of Yorke, as also other messuages, houses, lands, tenements and hereditaments whatsoever scituate, standing, lying and being in the said county of Yorke, with all the title deeds and leases belonging to the same. Item I give and bequeath unto my nephew Thomas Meek the summe of eight hundred pounds to be paid unto him att his age of one and twenty yeares by my executors and trustees hereafter named, forth and out of my personall estate, and my will is that if itt so happen that my said nephew Thomas Meek dye before he shall attaine to his said age of one and twenty yeares, that then the said eight hundred pounds & the product thereof shall goe & be paid unto my said nephew George Meek. Item I give unto my neice Mary Meek, mother of my said nephews, the summe of fifty pounds to be paid by my executors att the end of twelve months next after my decease. Item I give unto my good friend Mr Neile,[1] present vicar of North Allerton, one guinea to buy him a mourning ring with. Item I give unto my cousin John Pye & his two sisters, each of them one guinea, to my cousin Elizabeth Pye, formerly Green, one guinea, unto my brother Simon Meek one guinea, unto my goddaughter Priest half a guinea to buy a ring with, to my cousin Dorothy Brown one guinea and alsoe the summe of tenn pounds which my mother in her last will desireing might be left unto her by me in case she survived me. Item I give unto my cousin Browne's two daughters, each of them halfe a guinea & unto her sister Rynoldson one guinea. Item I give unto my cousin Thomas Flower, his wife and son, each of them halfe a guinea. Item I give to be distributed to and amongst the poor of North Allerton three pounds, to the poor of Brompton fifteen shillings, to the poore of Romanby five shillings. Item my will is that my estate before bequeathed to my nephew George Meek shall be left & demised from time to time dureing the minority of my said nephew George Meek by my good friends Mr Robert Hilton & Mr Timothy Wright, both of Stockton in the county of Durham, and the rents thereof to be by them received and imployed as they shall think fitt towards the education, maintenance and bringing up of my said nephew George, and the overplus that shall spare after he is educated and maintained to be from time to time put forth to interest for his best advantage. Item my will is that my said good freinds Mr Hilton and Mr Wright & the survivor of them doe manage & put forth to interest the said eight hundred pounds to & for the best advantage of my said nephew Thomas Meek dureing his minority, from time to time untill he shall attaine his age of one and twenty yeares, deducting thereout for his education, maintenance & puting him forth either for imployment or trade and my will & desire is that my said freinds and trustees doe bring up and educate my said two nephews in such manner and to such imployment or trades as my said neice Mary Meek, their mother, shall direct if she shall be then living, if otherwise, as they or the survivor of them shall think fitt. Item my will is that my said trustees and the survivor of them shall deduct out of the rents of my said lands and the interest of the said money what summe & summes of money they, or either of them, shall disburse and lay out in and about in the mannagement of their said trust and what they

may reasonably deserve for their trouble. And my will is that my said trustees, or either of them, shall not be liable or answerable for the ability or abilityes of any person or persons as they or either of them shall att any time or times demise or lett the said lands unto, or for the ability or abilityes of any person or persons they or either of them shall lend the overpluss rents unto or the said eight hundred pounds or the improvement thereof, but shall onely be accountable for such summe or summes of money as they actually receive or comes to their hands. Item I give unto my said trustees for their fidelity in the mannagement of those affaires, each of them, the summe of tenn pounds. Item my <will> is that if my said personall estate fall short in paying my legacyes and the said eight hundred pounds, that then and in such case my said nephew Thomas Meek shall onely have what spares of my personall estate, my debts, legacies & funeral expences are paid and are discharged, and if otherwise that my personall estate happen to be more than will pay the said eight hundred pounds and my legacies and funerall expences, then I doe give the said overplus unto my said nephew George Meek. Item my will is that my funerall may be mannaged with discretion and decency and in such manner as my said neice Mary Meek shall direct. And lastly I doe hereby, as farr as in me lyes, make my said freinds Robert Hilton and Timothy Wright testamentary tutors of my said two nephews dureing their respective minoritys and I do hereby make, nominate and appoint them joynt executors in trust for the uses aforesaid of this my last will and testament. In testimoney whereof I have hereunto sett my hand and seal this fourth day of May in the yeare of our Lord one thousand seaven hundred and tenn.
Jane Grimston.[2]
Signed, sealed, published and declared in the presence of us who have hereunto subscribed our names hereunto in the presence of the testator. Timothy Wright, Matthew Dunn, Farrow Eden.

[1] For Charles Neile, vicar of Northallerton, see below [150].
[2] Jane Grimston was buried on 13 September 1710, four months after making her will. She was the daughter of Isabel Flower [73] and the widow of Richard Grimston [78].

125. WILLIAM ALLANSON, 1710

DPRI/6/B/1710/A1

A true and perfect inventory of William Allanson of North Allerton lately deceased appraised by us whose names are under written this 16th day of November 1710.[1]

	£	s	d
Inprimis his purse & apparrell	5	10	0
Goods in the fore house & kitchin	3	16	8
Goods in the parlour	2	10	0
Goods in the fore chamber	2	10	8
Goods in the best chamber	9	10	0
Goods in the entry chamber	2	10	6
Four cows & one gallaway	13	10	0
In stock of white and tanned leather	27	12	6
In stock of green hides	17	12	8
In allim salt spects and tallaw	17	19	9
In hay	8	10	0
In cheeses	2	10	0
Goods in the shop	2	2	6
	117	7	3
	[*recte* *116*	*5*	*3*]
Funerall charges	4	10	0
Debts owing to the deceased	12	0	0
Debts owing by the deceased to the landlord	20	0	0
to his neice	77	17	0
to his man	18	17	0
to John Carber	10	0	0
	106	10	0
	[*recte* *126*	*14*	*0*]
To John Wastell esquire	3	0	0

Henry Sayer, J. Tomes, Seb[astian] Cornforth, William Drybrough.

[1] William Allanson was buried at Hurworth-on-Tees, Co. Durham, on 12 November 1710.

126. WILLIAM HODSHON, MARINER, 1711

TNA/PROB/11/524 1537 [probate copy]

In the name of God, amen. I William Hodshon of Northallerton in the county of York, mariner, being in bodily health and of sound and disposing mind and memory and considering the perils and dangers of the sea and other uncertainties of this transitory life, doe, for avoiding controversies after my decease, make, publish and declare this my last will and testament in manner following, that is to say. First I recommend my soul to God that gave it and my body I commit to the earth or sea as it shall please God to order. And as for and concerning all my worldly estate I give, bequeath and

dispose thereof as followeth. That is to say all such pay, wages, sum and summs of money, lands, tenements, goods, chattels and estate whatsoever as shall be anyways due, owing or belonging to me at the time of my decease I doe give, devise and bequeath the same unto John Jones, citizen and inholder of London. And I doe hereby nominate and appoint the said John Jones sole executor of this my last will and testament, hereby revoking all former and other wills, testaments and deed of gift by me at any time heretofore made, and I doe ordain and ratify these present to stand and be for my only last will and testament. In witness whereof to this my said will I have sett my hand and seal the twelfth day of May anno domini 1707 and in the sixth year of the reign of her majesty Queen Ann over Great Britain etc.
William Hodshon.[1]
Signed, sealed and published in the presence of <us who subscribe our names in the presence of> the testator. John Swallow, Robert Lister, William Garrett.

[1] William Hodshon's will was proved at Canterbury in 1711, four years after it was made. The date of Hodshon's death has not been established.

127. LAWRENCE LOWCOCK, 1711

DPRI/6/T/1711/L1
Know all men that I Lowrence Lowcock of Northallerton do will & desier that George Lowcock my brother have all & every thing which doth belong to me both goods & moneys with what debt is oweing to me, only paying my father and my <mother> eatch of them 12 pence with a wegg allso to my father; allso I desier that Mary Hebdon may have my dreser; and my great cote and hatt to ~~be given~~ to Edward Ludley. I desier my brother to pay all my debt. This is my will & desier.
Laurence Lowcock [*signed*]
September 11th 1711

An appraisment made by us the 22nd of September 1711 of Laurence Lowcock who departed this life the 15th day of this instant.[1]

	£	s	d
Purse & apparell	2	0	0
Wood and timber	8	0	0
Summa	10	0	0

John Meriton, John Rimer, Samuell Meriton, John Whitton.

[1] Lawrence Locock was buried on 16 September 1711; he died four days after making his will.

128. THOMAS SWAILES, YEOMAN, 1711

DPRI/6/T/1711/T1

In the name of God, amen. I Thomas Swayles of North Allerton in the county of York, yeoman, being weak in body but of sound and perfect mind and memory, praise be therefore given to almighty God, do make and ordain this my present last will and testament in manner and form following (that is to say): first and principally I commend my soul unto the hands of almighty God hoping through the meritts, death and passion of my saviour Jesus Christ to have full and free pardon and forgiveness of all my sins and to inheritt everlasting life, and my body I committ to the earth to be decently buried at the discretion of my executor hereafter named, and as touching the disposition of all such temporall estate as it hath pleased almighty God to bestow upon me, I give and dispose thereof as followeth. First I will that my debts and funerall charges shall be paid and discharged. Item give and bequeath unto Thomas Swayles, son of Robert Swayles, my grand child the summe of six pounds when he, the said Thomas Swayles my grand child, shall attain to the age of one and twenty years to be paid by my executeor. Item I give unto Anthony Wass and his wife and children the sume of two <&> six pence a peice. Item I give unto Richard Cummin the summe of tenn shillings. Item I give unto my son Robert Swayles one bedstead and bed and beding with all things thereto belonging with all other implement things which I have, and also I give unto my said son Robert Swayles one cow. All the rest and residue of my personall estate, goods and chattles whatsoever I do give and and bequeath unto my loving friend William Nodding of the said North Allerton whom I make my full and sole executor and likewise truste for my said grand child Thomas Swayles, and if my said executor William Nodding shall happen to be put to any charge in any matter of thing which may happen either in proving my will or with the commissary my will and pleasure is that any such charge shall be paid out of the four pounds which remains of the tenn pounds which I have out at use, out of which said tenn pounds my grand child Thomas Swayles [...],[1] and I desire that my body may be decently buried and I do hereby revoke disanull and make void

all former wills and testaments by me heretofore made. In wittness whereof I the said Thomas Swayles to this my last will and testament have sett my [hand] and seall this seventeenth day of October in the year of our Lord 1711.
Thomas Swayles his mark and seal.[2]
Signed, sealed and published in the presence of William Walker [*signed*], Isabell Flowar [*signed*], Ralph Haukswell [*signed*], Robert Young [*signed*].

An appraisement made of the goods and chattells of Thomas Swayles late of North Allerton this 20th day of October 1711.

	£	s	d
Inprimis his purse and apparrell	0	5	0
Item one bedstead & bed & curtains with all things thereto belonging	1	0	0
Item one long settle, 1 firm, 1 old chest, 1 old shelf	0	4	0
Item one table, one chair, 1 pott, 1 pan	0	2	0
Item one old churn, 1 pewter tankard, 1 pewter tumbler	0	0	8
	1	11	8

Appraised by us, Thomas Welbank, William Wright, Leonard Phillip his mark, Richard Cumming his mark.

[1] Sic. The text runs on but the sentence appears to be incomplete.
[2] Thomas Swailes was buried on 19 October 1711, two days after making his will.

129. MANN DOWSON, GENTLEMAN, 1711

DPRI/6/T/1712/D1

In the name of God, amen. I Mann Dowson of North Allerton in the county of York, gentleman, being sick in body but of sound, perfect and disposing mind and memory, praised be almighty God for the same, doe make and publish this to be and contein my last will and testament in manner and forme following (that is to say): Imprimis I give and bequeath my soul into the hands of almighty God my creator and my body to buried in decent manner at the discretion of my executors hereafter named. And as to the worldly estate wherewith it has pleased almighty God to bless me I give, devise and dispose thereof as followes (that is to say), I give devise and bequeath unto my trusty and well beloved friends George Dunn of North Allerton in the county of York, grocer, and Thomas Beckett of Hutton Bonville in the said county of York, clerk, and the survivor of them and the heires of the survivor of them all and singular my lands, tenements and hereditaments as well freehold as leasehold scituate lying and being within the township of Low Loftus and parish of Kirby Malzard in the said county of York, upon trust only and to the intent and purpose that they the said George Dunn and Thomas Beckett and the survivor of them and the heirs of the survivor of them shall and may (as soon as possible after my decease or as soon as a convenient chapman can be met with or found for the same) sell and dispose of all and singular the said lands, tenements and hereditaments and out of the money thereby and by such sale to be raised, as also out of the rents and profitts of the said lands untill such sale be made, to pay discharge all and singular my just debts. And my mind and will is that if there shall be any surplusage or overplus of money soe to be raised more than shall discharge my just debts, my said trustees shall give and dispose thereof amongst my children, Anne Dowson, Man Dowson, Thomas Dowson, ~~Thomas~~ Sarah Dowson & John Dowson, share and share alike as they shall severally attain to their respective ages of twenty one years or be married, whatever shall first happen. And in case any of my said children shall dye before hee, her or they shall attain to the said age of twenty one years then my mind and will is that the share & shares of such child or children that shall soe happen to dye shall goe and be distributed to and amongst the rest of my said children, share and share alike, to be paid to them alsoe with their respective shares as aforesaid. Item I give devise and bequeath unto my dear and loveing wife Anne Dowson all and singular my lands tenements and hereditaments scituate, lying and being within the township and parish of North Allerton in the county of York for the terme of her naturall life, not doubting but that my said wife will carefully bring up and educate all my children. And after the decease of my said wife I give and devise the same unto my eldest son George Dowson charged and chargeable with the payments of […][1] fifty pounds apeice to each of my said younger children within one year next after the decease of my said wife. And in case any of my said younger children shall happen to dye without issue lawfully begotten before the said payments shall become due then my mind and will is that my ~~eldest son George~~ said Allerton estate shall only stand charged with the payments of fifty pounds apeice to such of my said children as shall be then liveing and unto the lawfull issue of the rest (if any such <issue> be left) and not otherwise. Item I give and devise all and singular my goods, chattells and personall estate unto my said loveing friends George Dunn and Thomas Beckett in trust alsoe to discharge my

debts and funeralls and to put and bind my said son George and alsoe my younger sons to convenient trades as my said loveing friends George Dunn and Thomas Beckett shall think fit and proper, and if there happen to be any surplusage or overplus thereof I give and devise the same unto my said younger children, Anne Dowson, Man Dowson, Thomas Dowson, Sarah Dowson and John Dowson, share and share alike. And I doe nominate and appoint the said George Dunn and Thomas Beckett executors of this my last will and testament. In witness whereof I have hereunto set my hand and seale this seaventeenth day of October in the year of our Lord God one thousand seaven hundred and eleaven.
Mann Dowson [*signed and sealed*][2]
Signed, sealed and published by the said Man Dowson the testator and our names subscribed as witnesses in his presence and at his request there being first three raisures made in the body of the will & the word issue first interlined. T. Crosfeild [*signed*], William Drybrough [*signed*], John Stringer [*signed*].

November the 1st 1711. An appraisement made of the goods & chattells of Mr Mann Dowson lately deceased by us whose names are underwritt.

	£	s	d
Imprimis his purse and apparrell	10	0	0
In the fore house two tables, 4 chairs with other implements	0	12	6
In the little parlour 1 table, 1 bed & six chairs	2	0	0
Chamber over the house, 2 beds & a table with four chaires. The back chamber, 1 bed	3	10	0
In the kitching, 2 kettles with a pott & other implements	1	0	0
A stack of oates and wheat	5	0	0
Carts, ploughs and other implements	1	1	6
Five cows and a calfe	13	0	0
Four horses	10	0	0
A haystack	4	0	0
Corne sowne downe	10	0	0
In all	60	4	0

Henry Sayer, John Ward, John Ruddock, William Drybrough.

1 Illegible erasure of approximately ten characters.
2 Mann Dowson was buried on 22 October 1711, five days after making his will.

130. JOHN MIDGLEY, YEOMAN, 1711

DPRI/6/T/1711/M1

In the name of God amen. I John Midgley of Jeckolow in the parish of North-Allerton in the county of Yorke, yeoman, being somewhat infirme in body but of good & perfect memory, praised be God, doe make & publish this my last will & testament in manner & forme following. First & principally I commend my soulle to almighty God, my body I committ to the earth from whence itt came to be buried in such sort as my executor hereafter named shall thinke fitt. And for the worldly estate wherewith God hath blessed me I give & dispose thereof as followeth. First I give & devise unto my son John Midgley all my leasehold messuages, closes, lands & tennements in Romanby in the county of Yorke with all the rights, member & appurtenances thereto belonging (excepting one parlour att the south end of the house with the chamber over itt[)] to hold the same unto my said sonne, his executors, administrators & assignes, with all my estate, interest, terme of years & tennant right of, in & to the same, and every part thereof together with all the originall leases, assignements & assurances by which I hold the same, upon condition that my said sonne, his executors, administrators & assignes shall & doe well & truely pay & satisfie unto my loveing wife Anne yearly & every year during her naturall life the summe of twenty shillings of lawfull Brittish money, the same to be paid to her [be]halphe yearly by equall payments from & after my decease. Item I give & devise my loveing wife the parlour and chamber before excepted to hold the same unto my said wife for the terme of ninty nine years if she shall soe long live, and continue sole & unmarried. But my mind and will is that when my said wife shall happen to dye or marry, that then & from thenceforth, immediately after her decease or marriage, the said parlour and chamber shall descend and come unto my said <son> John his executors, administrators or assignes. And I doe hereby give unto my loveing wife one bedstead which now standeth in the new parlour – with one feather bed and bed cloathes and hangings thereunto belonging. And I doe declare my mind and will to be that such my guifts, legacies & bequests to my said loveing wife shall be in full satisfaction of her dower & thirds and what else she could, can or might have, claime, challenge or demand forth or out of my estate. And I doe direct that my said wife [(]upon request & demand to her in that behalphe to be made by my said sonne) shall signe, sealle & execute a writeing to purport her being satisfied and contented with this my will, and to set forth her acceptance thereof and aquiescence therein accordingly, which if my said wife performe then I declare my mind and will to be; that in case my sonne shall neglect or faille to pay to my said wife the said yearly summe of twenty shillings dureing her life as aforesaid, that itt shall be lawfull to & for my said wife into all and every part or any of my said leasing lands and tennements to enter and to hold and enjoy the same untill full payment be made with reasonable charges. And in case my wife refuse to signe, sealle & execute such writeing, then my said guifts & legacies and authority to her given as aforesaid to be voide. And that then she shall only have five shillings in full of her widdow right. Item I give & bequeath unto my sonne Richard Midgley the summe of tenn pounds of lawfull Brittish money to be paide him within one yeare after my decease, which with what goods I have already given him I declare is to be in full of his child's part or portion. Item I give & bequeath unto my daughter Mary Midgley the summe of tenn pounds to be paid her att the age of fifteen years. Item I give unto my daughter Judith Midgley the summe of tenn pounds to be paid at her age of fifteen years. Item I give unto my sonne Abraham Midgley the summe of tenn pounds to be paid att his age of fifteen years. And I doe direct that my said sonne John shall[1] maintaine and keep all my three youngest children with all reasonable necessaries untill their severall legacies shall become due. And if my said son John shall refuse or neglect to maintaine any of my said three youngest children as aforesaid, that then & from thenceforth he shall immediately after such refusall pay unto every one of one them their full legacies and every one of them twenty shillings a year untill they doe respectively attaine to the age of fifteen years as before directed. And in case any of my children shall happen to die before their legacies shall become due, that then the portion or child's part soe dieing shall fall unto my son John. And I give the tuition of all my children unto my loveing wife for & dureing such time of their respective minorities, only as my said wife shall be & continue a widdow, sole & unmarried. And in case my said wife shall (after my death) marry or be wedd to any other man, then my mind & will is that then she shall be noe longer tutor or guardian to any of my said children. And I doe (in such a case) give and committ the tuition or guardianship of all my children for & during all the then residue of their respective minorities unto my said son John Midgley. Lastly I give all the rest, residue & remainder of my personall estate (my debts & funerall expences first paid and deducted) unto my said sonne John Midgley and doe make my said sonne John sole executor of this my last will. And I doe hereby revoke all & every former will & wills by me made and doe

declare this to be my last will. In witnesse whereof I have hereunto sett my hand & seall this ninteenth day of November in the yeare of our Lord 1711.
John Midgley [*signed and sealed*][2]
Signed, sealled & published by the testator and our names subscribed as witnesses in his presence and by his directiones. Witnesses, William Franckland [*signed*], Anthony Lawson [*signed*], Matt: Ludlow [*signed*].

A true and perfect inventory of all the goods and chattels and all other the personall estate which did belong to John Midgley of Jecklow[3] in parish of North-Allerton in the county of York deceased as followeth.

	£	s	d
Imprimis his purse and apparel	03	5	0
In the fore house one table, 6 pewter dishes, 2 chairs with other meterials	01	2	0
In the parlour one bedstead with bedding, one chest of drawers, 6 chairs	02	0	0
In the little parlour one bedstead with beding, one cupboard, one table	01	0	0
Two cows, 2 calves, one sterk	06	5	0
3 horses young and old	06	2	6
Corn	05	0	0
Debts owing to the deceased 44^{li} 10^{s}, he owing 36^{li} 15^{s}, therefore remains clear	07	15	0
Totall	32	9	6

1 'Shall' repeated in MS.
2 John Midgley was buried on 26 November 1711, a week after making his will.
3 Jeckelow Grange (SE 351 944), one mile west of Northallerton.

131. CUTHBERT MARSHALL, 1711

DPRI/6/B/1711/M1
An appraisment made of the goods & chattells of Cuthbert Marshall of North Allerton lately deceased made this eight day of November by us whose names are under written.[1]

	£	s	d
~~Inprimis his purse & apparrell~~			
Inprimis in the fore house			
1 table	0	5	0
1 dresser	0	5	0

ten puter dishes, 1 dozen & ½ of plates, 8 puter pints,			
1 puter chamber pott	1	15	0
1 warming pan	0	2	0
1 jack	0	4	0
half a dozen of chairs	0	3	6
1 long settle	0	1	6
8 trenchers, 4 cheney plates	0	1	6
1 puter possitt cup	0	1	6
4 stooles & 1 little chair	0	1	0
2 reckons, 1 pair of tongs, 1 fire shovell	0	3	0
	3	2	6
In the back parlor			
2 tables & six chairs	0	11	0
1 iron pott, 1 iron pan, 1 brass pan, 1 brass pott	0	5	0
1 pair of window curtains	0	1	0
	0	18	6
In the brewhouse one lead & brewing vessell	1	10	0
In the fore chamber			
1 wanded chair, 2 leather chairs, 2 wood chairs	0	4	0
2 trunks & three coffers	0	3	0
1 table cloth, 1 dozen of napkins, 2 pair of sheets,			
3 pillabears	0	10	0
2 wood chests	0	1	0
	0	18	0
In the back chambering			
2 bedsteads & beding	1	10	0
1 little table & 2 chairs, 1 oat tub	0	2	0
1 table & form	[1]	5	0[2]
In the seller			
1 half hogshead, 5 anchors, 2 half anchors, 1 kimbling	0	10	6
On the back-side, one gilt & 2 pigs	1	0	0
His purse & apparrell	0	10	0
In all	11	6	6

George Seton, William Boddy, Ralph Swailes, Michael Buck, Robert Young.

[1] Cuthbert Marshall was buried on 27 July 1711.

[2] The manuscript is torn at this point. However, as the total sum shows, the missing figure must be £1.

132. GEORGE HUDSON, 1712

DPRI/6/B/1712/H1

A true appraisment of the goods and chattells of George Hudson of North Allerton lately deceased, as followeth.[1]

	£	s	d
Inprimis his purse and apparrell	3	0	0
In the kitching and the seller			
in ale with a copper ~~& a stool~~, a maskfatt & a cooler & a stoan mill and other implement things	6	10	0
In the parlour one table & six chairs	0	12	0
In the fore house			
a cloke, 2 tables, 6 puter dishes, 1 dozen & a half of plates, a jack, a dresser and other implement things	8	0	0
In the back chamber			
a chest of drawers, one table and 11 chairs	2	10	0
In the midle chamber			
a panell chest and a close bed & beding	1	15	0
In the chamber over the fore house			
a chest of drawers, 2 tables and six chairs	2	0	0
In a garrett, 3 beds & other small things	2	0	0
In the malt kille, 50 quarters of malt[2]	50	0	0
Sew & 7 shotts	4	10	0
A horse	10	0	0
Goods in the shopp	12	10	0
In lining	3	0	0
Money owing by Edward Bastow esquire	7	0	0
In his shop book debts owing him	9	0	0
Owing for ale	3	10	0
Owing for malt by Michaell Loftis	3	0	0
Summe	128	17	0

Appraisors. Edward Woaller, George Trenholme, Robert Thompson, John Ruddock.

Debts owing by George Hudson deceased			
His funerall charges	5	10	0
Debts owing by him to tradsmen & others as faer 9 years the now debts <expected> to be demanded[3]	41	8	0
	46	18	0
	[81	*19*	*0]*[4]

[1] George Hudson was buried on 29 March 1712.

[2] In margin at this point: '125-17-08'.

[3] Probably to be interpreted as '... going as far back as 9 years, the debts are now expected to be demanded'.
[4] Net sum of inventory after deduction of debts.

133. JOHN JINSON, YEOMAN, 1712

DPRI/6/T/1712/J1

In the name of God amen. I John Jinson, in the parish of North Allerton in the county of York, yeoman, being in good, sound and perfect mind and memory, praise be therefore given to almighty God, do make and ordaine this my last will and testament in manner and form following (that is to say): first and principally I commend my soul into the hands of almighty God hoping through the merits, death and passion of my saviour Jesus Christ to have full and free pardon and forgiveness of all my sins and to inherit everlasting life; and my body to be decently buried at the discretion of my executor hereafter named; and as touching the disposition of all such temporall estate as it hath pleased almighty God to bestow on me I give and dispose thereof as followeth. First I will that my debts and funerall charges shall be paid and discharged. Item I give unto my sister Dorothy Jinson the sume of one pound one shilling and sixpence of lawfull money of Great Brittain, as also one bedstead, one feather bed upon it, one pair of sheets, one pair of blankets, one boulster, one pillow, with hangings thereunto belonging, the said bedstead standing in the parlor at the back of the cubbard. And all the rest and residue of my personall estate, goods and chattles whatsoever I do give and bequeath to my loving sister Isabell Jinson, whom I make my full and sole executor of this my last will and testament, and I do hereby revoke, disanull and make void all former wills. In witness whereof I the said John Jinson to this my last will and testament have hereunto sett my hand and seal this thirtie first day of July anno domini 1712.
John Jhinson [*signed and sealed*]
Sealed, signed and delivered and published in the presence of, Ralph Humphray his mark, William Wilkinson his mark, Jane Buck [*signed*], Robert Young [*signed*].

An appraisment made this 22nd day of August 1712 of the goods and chattells of John Jinson the younger of the parish of North-Allerton late deceased by us whose names are under-written.

	£	s	d
Imprimis his purse & apparrell	1	0	0
In the forehouse			

1 little cupboard, 5 puter dishes, 5 puter plates, 1 table, 1 long settle, 2 chairs with other implements	1	10	0
In the parlour			
two bedsteads with beds & beding thereunto belonging, 1 pannell chest with other implements	3	0	0
In the milkhouse			
1 churn, 2 milking pales, 2 dozen of bowls, 1 kettle, 1 iron pott with other implements	1	5	0
Item five cows	15	0	0
1 two year old heifer	1	10	0
4 year old stirks	4	0	0
4 finger calves	2	10	0
2 horses	6	0	0
2 small piggs	0	10	0
Three acres of wheat in the township fields of North Allerton	4	10	0
7 acres of rye	8	15	0
6 acres of barley	6	0	0
Five acres of beans and oates	4	0	0
2 rucks of hay	4	0	0
1 cart, 1 plough with other implements of husbandry gear	2	0	0
	64	10	0
	26	1	6[1]
In all	38	8	6[2]
Deducting rents which is now due to pay	20	0	0
Also legacies sett to my syster Dorothy by my father & brother by their wills	6	1	6
	26	1	6

Witness our hands, Peter Johnson, John Squire, Ralph Humphrey his marke, Robert Young.

[1] This sum represents the sum of deductions (rents and legacies) shown below.
[2] Net total of inventory after deduction of rents and legacies.

134. JOHN PREST, BLACKSMITH, 1713

DPRI/6/T/1713/P1

In the name of God, amen, I, John Prest of North Allerton in the county of York, blacksmith, being somwhat weak in body but of sound and disposeing mind and memory, praized be almighty God for the same, doe make and ordain this my last will and testament in manner and forme following (that is to say): I give and bequeath my soul into the hands of almighty God, and my body to be buried in decent manner at the will of my executors <hereafter> named. And as touching my worldly estate I give and devise the same as followeth, (videlicet) I give and devise all and singular my messuages, burgages, lands, tenements and hereditaments whatsoever and wheresoever with their and every of their appurtenances unto my trusty friends Thomas Nixon of Brompton Moor near North Allerton aforesaid, yeoman, and Edward Kilvington of Thirsk in the county of York aforesaid, butcher, their heirs and assignes upon trust and to the intent and purpose that the said Thomas Nixon and Edward Kilvington their heirs and assignes shall and may stand seized of and in all and singular my said messuages, burgages, lands, tenements and hereditaments with their appurtenances to and for the severall uses, interests and purposes in this my last will and testament hereafter expressed, limited and appointed, and to and for none other use, interest or purpose whatsoever (that is to say), that they my said trustees their heirs and assignes shall stand seized of <and in> all and singular my messuages, burgages, lands, tenements and heraditaments with the appurtenances to the use and behoofe of my son Stephen Prest for and during his naturall life without impeachment of or for any manner of waste and (after the decease of my said son) I doe give and devise all that my messuage or tenement (being two burgages) in North Allerton aforesaid called the Blew House and all that close or parcell of ground called North Moor Close which I purchased of John Scott with the appurtenances to the said messuage or burgages and close belonging to the use and behoofe of my grandaughter Elizabeth Prest for her heirs and assignes for ever (except that part of the said messuage or burgage wherein Robert Straker now dwells which I give to the use and behoofe of my daughter Jane for and during her naturall life in case my daughter shall happen to survive my said son her husband[)]; and after the decease of my said daughter then to the use and behoofe of my grandaughter Elizabeth, her heirs and assignes for ever. Item my mind and will is and I doe give and devise (after the decease of my said son) all that my messuage or tenement wherein I now dwell and all those three closes called North Moor Closes which I purchased of John Abbott and James Appleby, with the appurtenances to the said last mentioned messuage and closes belonging to the use and behoofe of my grandaughter Isabell Prest her heirs and assignes for ever. And as to all and singular my goods, chattells and personall estate I give and devise the same unto my said two grandaughters Elizabeth

Prest and Isabell Prest equally to be divided betwixt them share and share alike. And all such moneys or summes of money as my said personall estate shall amount unto or shall or may be raised thereby I doe will and desire that my said trustees may put out the same at interest for my said grandaughters untill they shall respectively attain to the age of twenty one yeares or be married whether shall first happen. And my mind and will further is that my said trustees shall pay and satisfie unto my said grandaughters their respective shares or proportions of my said personall estate when they my said grandaughters shall respectively attain to the age of twenty one yeares or be married and not before. And I doe make and appoint the said Thomas Nixon and Edward Kilvington executors of this my last will and testament and I doe hereby revoke all former wills by me made. In witness whereof I have to this my last will and testament set my hand and seale this twelfth day of March in the year of our Lord one thousand seaven hundred and twelve [*12 Mar. 1713*].

John Prest [*signed and sealed*][1]

Signed, sealed, declared and published by the said John Prest to be his last will and testament in the presence of us, the word hereafter being first interlined, T. Crosfield [*signed*], Michael Buck junior [*signed*], Richard Harling [*signed*].

May the 8th 1713.

An appraisment made of the goods of <John> Prest of North-Allerton lately deceased.

	£	s	d
Imprimis his purse and apparell	5	0	0
In the forehouse			
2 tables, 2 cuberts, 6 chairs, 2 forms	0	10	0
12 dublers, 11 plates with small puter	1	0	0
2 kettles, 3 potts, 3 pans, 1 iron pan, 1 warming pan, 3 brass candlesticks with other implements of brass	1	3	0
1 driping pan, 12 sheets, 1 pair of rax, 1 iron pan and other implements	0	6	0
In the little parlour, 1 bedstead & beding with other implements	1	0	4
In the milkhouse, 3 shelves	0	1	0
In the garitt, 2 bedsteads & beding with curtains, 2 panell chests, 1 kimblin with other implements	2	0	0
9 pair of sheets	1	16	0
1 linn sheet	0	2	6

2 dozen of napkins, 2 table cloths, 12 pillibears	0	15	4
2 milk kine	5	0	0
In moneys	20	0	0
Summa	38	14	2
For the funerall charges deducted off	8	14	2
Summa	30	0	0

By us whose names are under written,
James Coates, George Dunn, John Kendrow, Edward Wooller.

[1] John Prest was buried on 4 May 1713, seven weeks after making his will.

135. JOHN RYMER, GLOVER, 1713

DPRI/6/T/1713/R1

In the name of God, amen, the fourth day of Aprell in the year of our Lord 1713, I, John Rymer of Northallerton in the county of York, glover, being sick and weak in body, but of perfect mind and memory, thanks be given unto God theirfore, calling unto mind the mortality of my body, and knowing that it is appointed for all men once to die, I do make and ordain this my last will and testament, that is to say principally, and first of all, I give and recommend my soul into the hands of God that gave it, and for my body I recommend it to the earth, to be buried in a Christian like <& desent> maner, at the discretion of my executors, nothing doubting but at the generall resurrection I shall receive the same againe by the mighty power of God, and as touching such worldly estate, wherewith it hath pleased God to bless me in this life, I give, devise and dispose of the same in the following manner and form. Imprimis: I give and bequeath to Alise my dearly beloved wife the summ of fower pounds and the back parte of my house, that part that Margret Hutton now lives in, dureing her life, over and above her joynter I made her before marridg. Item I give to my nephey Thomas Marshall twenty shilings to be payd when he comes att fourteen years of age to put him prentis withall, and to my neece Jone Marshell twenty shilings, and to my neece Ann twenty shilings, and to my nepheu Cuthbert Marshell twenty shilings, to be payd to them when thay come att one and twenty yers of age, in case any of them die to be divided amongst the other. Item I give to my well-beloved daughter Esabell Darbey whome I likewise constitute, make and ordain my only and sole executrix of this my last will and testament, all and singular my lands, messuages and tenements[1] by her and her heirs freely to be possessed and enjoyed for ever. Item when my granson John Darbey

comes at one and twenty years of age, to receive five pounds yearly from his mother, provided she live so long, otherwise to enter of the estate <then to pay his father five pounds yearly for his life>. And I do hereby disalow, revoke and disannul all and every other former testaments, wills and legacies, requests and executors, by me in any ways before this time named, willed and bequeathed, ratifying and confirming this, and no other, to be my last will and testiment. In witness whereof I have hereunto sett my hand and seal, the day and year above written. Signed, sealed, published, pronounced and declared by the said John Rymer, as his last will testament, in the presence of us the subscribers.
John Rymer his mark [*sealed*][2]
John Stringer [*signed*], Jno. Tomes [*signed*], George Shemeld [*signed*], John Thompson [*signed*].

An appraisment of John Rymer's goods of North-Allerton deceased, praised by us whose names are subscribed May the 5th 1713.

	£	s	d
His purse and apparell	2	0	0
Eight dozen and eight skins of leather	1	10	0
Gloves att	0	8	0
One bay mare att	2	0	0
Total	5	18	0

Christopher Robinson, Thomas Robinson his marke, George Shemeld.

[1] 'all and singular my lands, messuages and tenements' repeated in MS.
[2] John Rymer was buried on 4 May 1713, one month after making his will.

136. JOHN LOFTIS, CARPENTER, 1713

DPRI/6/T/1713/L1

In the name of God, amen. The thurd day of May one thousand seven hundred and thurteen. I, John Loftis of Northallerton in the county of York, house carpenter, being very sick and wake in body but of perfect mind and memory, thanks be given unto God theirfor, calling unto mind the mortality of my body, and knowing that it is appointed for all men once to die, do make and ordaine this my last will and testament, that is to say: prencipally and first of all I give and recommend my soul into the hands of God that gave it; and for my body I recommend it to the earth to be buried in a Christian like and deacent manner at the discretion of my exectrix, not doubting but at the generall resurrection I shall receive the same again by the mighty power of God; and as touching such worldly estate wherewith it hath pleased God to bless me in this life I give, devise and dispose of the same in the following manner and form. Imprimis I give and bequeath to my brother Mickel Loftis the house I now live in after the death of my mother, and at the death of my mother to pay to my sister Marthay Pybas the sume of tenn pounds; and to all my nepheys and neeses twelve pence a pece; and all the rest of goods moveable and imovable to my mother my exetrix; and I do hereby disallow, revoke and disannul all and every other former testaments, wills and legacies, requests and executors by me in any ways before this time named, willed and bequeathed, retifying and confirming this and no other to be my last will and testament, in witness whereof I have hereunto set my hand and seal, the day and year a bove written.

John Loftis his mark [*sealed*][1]

Signed, sealed, published, pronounced and declared by the said John Loftis as his last will and testament in the presence of us the subscribers, Marke Nelson [*signed*], John Ruddock [*signed*], Geo: Shemeld [*signed*].

May the 18th 1713. A true appraisment of the goods and chattells of John Loftus lately deceased of North-Allerton.

	£	s	d
2 cows	6	0	0
2 whyes	4	0	0
1 calfe	0	10	0
3 ewes	1	10	0
6 hogs	2	0	0
13 axeltrees at 9d. a peice	0	9	9
3 ganges of speakes	0	7	6
Offell wood	0	5	0
Work tooles and other implement things	0	10	0
Boards and sparrs	0	8	0
Other loose wood	0	8	0
Summa	16	8	3

Appraised by us, John Ruddock, Thomas Burton, Samuel Meriton.

[1] John Loftis (or Loftus) was buried on 16 May 1713, 13 days after making his will.

137. FRANCIS KAYE, GENTLEMAN, 1714

DPRI/6/T/1714/K1

In the name of God, amen, I, Francis Kay of North Allerton in the county of Yorke, gentleman, being sick & week in body but of a sound & disposeing mind & memory doe make, ordain & publesh this my last will & testament in manner & forme following. (That is to say), first and principally I committ my soul into the hands of almighty God (my maker), assuredly trusting to receive remission & pardon of all my sins through the meritts of Jesus Christ my saviour, and my body to the earth from whence itt was taken, to be buryed in such decent manner as my executor, herein after named, shall think meet & convenient. And as to the setling of my temporall estate, wherewithall itt hath pleased God to bless me, I give bequeath and dispose of the same in manner following. Imprimis I give, devise & bequeath unto my trusty & well beloved freind Thomas Crosfeild of North Allerton aforesaid, gentleman, and to his heires & assignes for ever all that my mesuage, house or tenement wherein <I> now live, scituate, standing & being in North Allerton aforesaid with all the rights, members & appurtenances thereunto belonging, and also all that my close or parcell of ground scituate, lying & being in Northmoore within the paresh of North Allerton aforesaid and now in the possession or occupacion of Richard Peirson, as <also> all other my mesuages, houses, lands, tenements and hereditaments whatsoever and wheresoever within the said county of Yorke, in trust that the said Thomas Crosfeild shall with all convenient speed after my decease, by mortgage or sale thereof and out of the profitts thereof till such time as such mortgage or sale cann be made, pay discharge & satifye all my just debts and particularly the debt now due & oweing by me unto my kind freind Mr Nicholas Hall of London and after all my just debts shall be paid and satisfyed and fully discharged, I give and bequeath and my mind and will is that all the rest, residue and remainder of all my reall and personall estate whatsoever shall by my said trustee and executor herein after named be equally divided and distributed amongst my brothers and sisters by even and equall shares and proporcions and none to have a greater share or preference then the other. And I doe make, nominate and appoint the said Thomas Crosfeild sole executor of this my last will and testament and doe hereby revoke, disanull and for ever make void all other wills and testaments by me heretofore made and doe declare this onely to be my last will and testament. In witness whereof I have hereunto sett my hand & seale this seaventeenth day

of March in the year of our Lord one thousand seaven hundred and thirteen [*17 Mar. 1714*].
Fr: Kaye [*signed and sealed*][1]
Signed, sealed, published & declared by the above named testator in our presence, who sett our names as witnesses hereunto in the testator's presence. James Conyers [*signed*], Mar: Sidgswick [*signed*], P. Consett [*signed*].

A true & perfect inventory of the goods, chattells & personall estate of Francis Kaye, late of North-Allerton in the county of Yorke, gentleman deceased. Appraized by us whose names are under-written this twenty fifth of March 1714.

	£	s	d
Imprimis his purse & apparell	08	00	00
His books	01	00	00
One cane & sword & belt	00	06	00
One saddle and bridle	00	04	00
A nest of boxes, one small old desk & one coffer or oaken box	00	08	00
Debts owing to the deceased a great part of which appearing to be desperate	10	00	00
One pair of spurres	00	01	00
Summa	19	19	00

James Conyers, Marmaduke Sidgswick, Thomas Corney, William Sedgwick.

[1] Francis Kaye was buried on 24 March 1714, seven days after making his will.

138. JOHN WHITTON, MERCHANT, 1715

DPRI/6/T/1715/W1

In the name of God, amen, I, John Whitton of North Allerton in the county of York, merchant, being sick and weak in body but of sound and disposing mind and memory (praised be almighty God for the same[)], doe make and ordain my last will and testament in manner and forme following, (that is to say): imprimis I committ my soul into the hands of almighty God, and my body to be buried in decent manner at the discretion of my executor hereinafter named. And as to my worldly estate I give and devise the same as follows, (that is to say). I give and devise unto my brother James Whitton his heirs and assignes for ever all that messuage, burgage or tenement wherein I now dwell with all and singular the ediffices, buildings, garth,

garden and appurtenances to the same belonging and all my estate, right, title, interest, claime and demand whatsoever in possession, revertion, remainder and expectancy of, in and to the same. Item I give all my goods, chattells and personall estate (after my just debts and funerall expences shall be discharged) unto my said brother James Whitton and to my two sisters, Susanna Whitton and Elizabeth Whitton, equally to be devided amongst my said brother and sisters share and share alike. And I doe make and appoint my said brother James Whitton executor of this my last will and testament. In witness whereof I have hereunto set my hand and seale this thirteenth day of December in the yeare of our Lord one thousand seaven hundred and fourteen.
John Whitton [*signed and sealed*][1]
Signed, sealed and published by the testator John Whitton in our presence and our names subscribed as witnesses in his presence and at his request. Thomas Crosfield [*signed*], Eluen Hardcasell [*signed*], John Rayne [*signed*] juratus.

1 John Whitton was buried on 3 January 1715, three weeks after making his will.

139. JOHN CARVER, BUTCHER, 1715

DPRI/6/T/1715/C1
I, John Carver of Northallerton in the county of York, butcher, doe hereby give and bequeath unto my dear wife Mary Carver and to my trusty brother George Trenholme of Northallerton in the said county, yeoman, all my lands, tenements and heraditaments scituate, lying and being in the township of Brompton untill John Carver, my son and heire apparent attaine to the age of six and twenty years, at what time I do order and direct my said son John to pay unto my said dear wife and unto my said brother George Trenholme the sume of six score pounds to be devided equally, shaire and shaire like a mongst my three younger sons, George, Thomas and Robert, for their portions; and my mind and will further is that my said dear wife shall have a pouer to charge my said lands in Brompton with any sume or sums of money further for the use of my said three younger sons, George, Thomas and Robert, not exceeding twenty pound if she at any time shall so think fit; and I do also order and direct that my son John shall when he attaines unto his full age of one and twenty years surrender all his interest, right and [title][1] which he hath or shall have in that close called Stephensons Close in the township of Northallerton unto Margret Carver and Mary Carver, my daughters,

and to theire heires forever according to the costome of the mannor of Northallerton. But if my said son John shall when he attaines his full age of one and twenty years refuse to surrender all his interest in the above said close to my said daughters as aforesaid, and refuse also to pay unto my said dear wife and to George Trenholme the sume of six score pound as above for the portion of my said three younger sons and also the further sume of twenty pounds if my dear wife think fit to charge the said lands at Brompton with it, I do hereby give all my said lands and tenements in Brompton to my dear wife and to her heires forever, she paying unto my severall children when they attaine unto their severall ages of one and twenty, that is to Margrett and Mary each ten pound and to George, Thomas and Robert each twenty pound over and above the six score pounds above mentioned. And as for the rest of my personal estate I do give and bequeath unto my said dear wife whom I do hereby make sole executrix of this my last will and testament and do order her to pay all my debts and funerall expences and to give unto my two daughters Joan and Jane twenty pound a peice within two years after my decease, and also to pay unto my father John Carver the sume of twenty shillings a year for five years if he so long live and if need require it. In witness whereof I have hereunto set my hand and seale this seaventh day of January 1714 [*7 Jan. 1715*].
John Carver [*signed and sealed*][2]
Signed, sealed, published and declared in the presence of us, Edward Wooller [*signed*], George Reveley [*signed*], Michael Buck junior, [*signed*].

[1] MS reads 'tithe' but 'title' is presumably meant.
[2] John Carver was buried on 29 June 1715.

140. GEORGE DUNN, GROCER, 1715

DPRI/6/T/1714/D1
In the name of God, amen, I, George Dunn of North Allerton in the county of York, grocer, being in perfect health and of sound and disposing mind and memory (praised be God for the same), but being mindfull of my mortality doe make and ordain my last will and testament in manner and forme following, (that is to say[)]. Imprimis I give and devise unto my son George Dunn all and singular my lands, tenements and hereditaments scituate, lying and being within the township and territories of North Allerton aforesaid to have and to hold the same with the appurtenances unto my said son George his heirs and assignes for ever, charged and chargable nevertheless

with the severall portions to my two daughters as are by this my last will and testament hereafter given and appointed. Item I give unto my son John Dunn and to his executors, administrators and assignes all and singular my lands and tenements lying and being within the township of Brompton near North Allerton aforesaid being or reputed to be two oxgang and an halfe of leasehold land and now in the tenure or occupation of Thomas Langdale. Item I give unto my daughter Anne Dunn the summe of two hundred and fifty pounds to be paid with interest for the same within one yeare next after my decease. Item I give unto my daughter Isabell Dunn the summe of two hundred and fifty pounds to be paid with interest for the same within one year next after my decease. And I doe charge all and singular my said lands and tenements given as aforesaid unto my son George with the payment of the said severall summes of two hundred and fifty pounds unto my said daughters respectively. And my mind and will is that (in case of failer of payment of the said severall summes of two hundred and fifty pounds to my said daughters respectively as aforesaid) they my said daughters or either of them their or either of their executors, administrators and assignes shall and may enter into and upon all or any part of the lands and tenements given to my son George as aforesaid and the same have and hold and enjoy untill by the rents and profitts thereof or otherwise they shall respectively receive or have satisfied the respective portions or summes given to them by this my will as aforesaid. Item I give unto my dear and loveing wife Jane Dunn all the furniture in the chamber or lodgeing where I lye. And I doe make and appoint my said son George sole executor of this my last will and testament hereby revokeing all former wills by me made. In witness whereof I have hereunto set my hand and seale this thirtieth day of May in the year of our Lord one thousand seaven hundred and thirteen.

Memorandum that I doe alsoe give unto my said two daughters all my linning to be equally divided betwixt them share and share alike.

George Dunn [*signed and sealed*][1]

Signed, sealed, declared and published by the said George Dunn the testator to be and contain his last will and testament and our names subscribed as witnesses in his presence and at his request, and be it remembered that the memorandum relateing to the linning given to the two daughters was added or subjoined <to> the will before sealing. James Conyers [*signed*], Joseph Dunn [*signed*], Thomas Crosfield [*signed*].

[1] George Dunn was buried on 6 January 1715, 18 months after making his will.

141. SIMON MEEKE, GENTLEMAN, 1715

DPRI/6/T/1715/M1

I, Simon Meeke of Northallerton in the county of Yorke, gentleman, do hereby give and bequeath unto my son Edmund Meeke and his heires forever all my lands, tenements and herredetaments scituate, lying and being in Anderby Steeple now in the possession of Christopher Meynell my tenant. And as to my burgage house in Northallerton which I bought of Christopher Hudson and Jane Hudson and my Milne Close and paddock in Northallerton which I hold under the bishop of Durham for the heires therein mentioned I give and bequeath unto my daughter Jane Prest of Northallerton and to her heires forever, she paying unto my son Simond the sume of thurty pound lawfull money within twelve months after my decease and twenty pound further which was borrowed of my daughter Meeke for my said son Simon's use, and also ten pound of lawfull money to Simon Pattison my grandson when he attaines unto his full age of one and twenty years; and I do also create my said daughter Jane Prest sole executrix of this my last will and testament. In witnes whereof I have hereunto sett my hand and seale eighteenth day of January anno domini 1714 [*18 Jan. 1715*].

Simon Meeke [*signed and sealed*][1]

Sealed, signed, published and declared in the presence of us, E. Barstow [*signed*], John Hogg [*signed*], Chris. Ducket [*signed*].

[1] Simon Meeke was buried on 21 February 1716, more than a year after making his will.

142. THOMAS FLOWER, BUTCHER, 1716

DPRI/6/T/1716/F1

In the name of God, amen, I, Thomas Flower of North Allerton in the county of York, butcher, being sick and week in body but of sound and perfect mind and memory, praised be God for the same, doe make and publish this my last will and testament in manner and forme following, (that is to say): imprimiss I committ my soul to God who gave it, and my body to the earth from whence it came to be buried in such decent manner as my executrix hereafter named shall think fitt; and as to the worldly goods wherewith God hath blessed me I give, devise and bequeath thereof in manner and forme following. Imprimiss I give and bequeath unto Mrs Elizabeth Markland, the wife of Mr Markland of Nottingham, the sum of five pounds of good and lawfull moneys of Great Brittane to be paid to her by my executrix immediately after my decease or to her or her husband's assignes. Item I give and bequeath unto Jane Golling, widow, the sum of two shillings sixpence of like lawfull moneys of Great Brittane to be paid to her by my executrix after my decease or to her assignes. And for all the rest and residue of my parsonall estate, goods and chattels movable and immovable, mortgages, bills, bonds and writings whatsoever I do give and bequeath unto my loving wife Ann Flower, whom I make my full and sole executrix of this my last will and testament, disannulling and making void all former wills and writings. In witness whereof I have hereunto sett my hand and seal this nineteenth day of March anno domini 1715/16.

Thomas Flower his mark & seal [*sealed*][1]

Signed, sealed, published and declared in the presence of William Huthwate [*signed*], Mary Surbert her mark, Robert Young [*signed*].

An appraisement made this ninth day of Aprill 1716 of the goods and chattles of Thomas Flower butcher late of North Allerton deceassed.

	£	s	d
Imprimis his purse and apparell	2	0	0
In the forehouse two tables, three chairs and one stoole with other implements	0	13	0
In the parlar one bed stead with bedding thereunto belonging	1	0	0
In the milkhouse 1 brass kettle, 2 puther dishes with other implements	0	13	4
In the field, three kine	10	0	0
	14	6	4

Appraised by us J. Tomes [*signed*], Wm Huthwate [*signed*], Tho: Peckit [*signed*], Robert Young [*signed*].

[1] Thomas Flower was buried on 1 April 1716, 13 days after making his will.

143. JAMES CONYERS, APOTHECARY, 1716

BIA/71/119 [probate copy]

In the name of God, amen, I, James Conyers, of North Allerton in the county of Yorke, apothecary, being nowe very infirme in body but (praised be God) of a perfect, sound and disposing mind and memory and being sensible of the uncertainty of human life and willing to order & settle my worldly estate, do make and ordaine this my last will and testament in manner & forme following (that is to say). I give and devise all and singular my lands, tenements & heraditaments whatsoever and wheresoever (except such as were <hereto>fore settled in joynture or otherwise upon my marriage with my late wife Jane Conyers) unto my son James Conyers & daughter Jane Conyers, their heirs & assignes, to have and to hold the same to the said James Conyers & Jane Conyers, their heirs & assignes for ever as tenants in common and not as joynt tenants. Item whereas by the beforementioned joynture there is sufficient provisions made for my eldest son Richard Conyers and I have paid unto my daughter Dorothy, now wife of Robert Raine of Scarbrough in the said county of Yorke, apothecary, her filialls or child's portcion att the time of her marriage, and whereas by the aforesaid joynture deed there is power given or referred to me to charge the landes, tenements & heraditaments therein mencioned or some part thereof with the summe of one hundred pounds, I doe therefore (according to the power wich is given or referred to me) give and bequeath unto my said sonn & daughter James Conyers and Jane Conyers the said summe of one hundred pounds equally to be divided betwixt them, share & share alike, and I do charge the aforesaid lands & tenements settled in joynture as aforesaid with the payment thereof. Item all the rest & residue of my goods, chattells and personall estate whatsoever I give and bequeath unto my said son & daughter James Conyers & Jane Conyers equally to be divided betwixt them, but my mind & will is that such part share or proporcion of my lands & tenements or goods & chattells or personall estate or legacy which I have hereby given, devised or bequeathed unto my said son James Conyers shall not come into his hands, power or possession or be paid unto him untill he shall attain the age of four and twenty yeares, but that the same & every part thereof shall remain and be in the hands & power or possession of my beloved brother Richard Conyers of Yarme in the said county of Yorke, apothecary, whom I have hereafter named joynt executor with my said daughter, Jane Conyers, but in trust onely for my said son James Conyers untill he shall attain the age of four & twenty years. And my will & desire is that my said brother shall putt and place out at interest all such summe or summes as shall come into his hands by vertue of this trust aforesaid and the interest or proceeds thereof shall yearly pay unto my said son James Conyers untill he shall attaine to the age of twenty four yeares as aforesaid. And I do hereby nominate and appointe my said daughter Jane Conyers and my said brother Richard Conyers joynt executors of this my last will and testament hereby revoking all former and other wills by me att any time heretofore made, and publishing & declareing this to be my onely last will and testament. In witness whereof I have hereunto sett my hand & seale this sixteenth day of July in the year of our Lord God one thousand seven hundred and sixteen.

James Conyers.[1]
Signed sealed published and declared by the testator James Conyers & our names sett & subscribed as witnesses thereto in the presence & att the request of the said testator (after the interlineation of the word (one) and (James Conyers)[)]. Clifton Wintringham, Cuthbert Mitford, P. Consett.

[1] James Conyers was buried on 18 July 1716, two days after making his will.

144. THOMAS GAMBLE, 1716

DPRI/6/T/1717/G1
In the name of God, amen. I, Thomas Gamble of North Allerton in the county of York being sick and week in body but of sound and perfect memory, praised be almighty God for the same, do make this my last will and testament in manner and form following. Imprimis I bequeath my soul to God who gave it and my body to the ground from whence it came, to be buried in decent order as my executrix hereafter shall seem fitt. Item I give and bequeath unto my son Thomas Gamble the dwelling house that I now live in, with all the back housing and garth thereunto belonging, to him and his heires and assignes for ever. Item I give and bequeath to my loving wife Elizabeth Gamble, whom I make my sole executrix, all my goods and chattles movable and immovable together with the rest and residue of my personall estate, making her my full and sole executrix of this my last will and testament and I do hereby revoke, disanull and make void all former wills and testaments by me heretofore made. In witness whereof I, the said Thomas Gamble, have hereunto set my hand and seal this twenty fifth day of October anno domini 1716.
Thomas Gamble <his mark & seal>[1]
Signed, sealed, published and declared in the presence of Edward Ludlow <his mark>, John Appleby <his mark>, Thomas Lowson [*signed*], Robert Young [*signed*].

An appraisement made this 23 day of November 1716 of the goods and chattles of Thomas Gamble of North Allerton, late deceased, appraised by us whose names are underwritten.

	£	s	d
Imprimis his purse and apparell	2	5	0
In the fore house 1 cubbard, 1 table, 4 chaires, 4 puther dishes, 1 long settle with other implements	1	7	6

In the parlor 1 bedstead, bed and bedding thereto belonging, 1 little table	1	0	0
In the chamber 1 panell chist and 3 little boxes	0	5	0
In the field 1 cow and 2 whies	5	0	0
	9	17	6

John Appleby his marke, Robert Young [*signed*], Thomas Lowson [*signed*], Edward Londlay [*signed*], Robert Straker [*signed*].

[1] Thomas Gamble was buried on 15 November 1716, three weeks after making his will.

145. MICHAEL TAYLOR, TALLOW CHANDLER, 1717

DPRI/6/T/1717/T1

In the name of God, amen, I, Michaell Taylor of North Allerton in the county of Yorke, tallow chandler, being now in perfect health of body and of a sound and perfect mind and memory (praised be God for the same), and calling to mind the uncertain state of this transitory life and that all mankind is mortall, and being desirous to settle my worldly affairs so as to prevent controversies, differences and disputes amongst my relacions for or about the same after my decease, doe make, publish and declare this my last will and testament in manner following, (that is to say). First and principally I committ my soul into the hands of almighty God my creator, assuredly trusting through the meritorious death and passion of my saviour Jesus Christ to receive remission and pardon for all my sinns and my body to the earth from whence itt came to be decently buryed att the discrecion of my executrix hereafter named. And as to the settling and disposeing <the> temporall estate wherewithall itt hath pleased God to bless me, I give bequeath and dispose of the same as follows. Imprimis, I give and bequeath unto my dearly beloved wife the summe of five pounds to be paid unto her immediately after my decease, as also all and all manner of household goods or household stuff whatsoever which were hers or came to me upon her account att our marriage, and a silver cupp. Item I give unto my said wife the annuall or yearly summe or rent charge of tenn pounds, to be paid her half yearly upon the feasts of St Martin the Bishopp in winter and St Phillip and Jacob, by even and equall porcions for and dureing her naturall life, the first payment to beginn and be made att or upon the first of the said feasts which shall happen or be next after my decease, which said annuall or yearly summe or rent charge of tenn pounds my will is shall be paid unto my said wife out of my houses, lands and tenements or out of my personall estate or both of them, and that free and clear of and from and without any manner of deduccion or abatement of or for any taxes assessments or other charge or incumbrance whatsoever, and upon failure of payment of the said annuity or rent charge or any part thereof att the times appointed for the payment thereof, that my said wife have full power to enter upon my houses, lands or tenements and distress or distresses there to make and the same to take, carry away, sell or dispose of till the said annuity or rent charge of tenn pounds be fully saitisfyed and paid and all the arrears thereof. And my will is that the said annuity or rent charge <and legacys> shall be in full recompence and liew of my said wife's dower, title of dower, thirds or other claime or demand whatsoever which <she> cann or may have, claime or otherwise demand out of my reall or personall estate. Item I give unto my kinswoman Dorothy Taylor, who is dumb, the annuall or yearly summe of twenty shillings to be paid her half yearly upon the beforemencioned feasts for and dureing her naturall life by even and equall porcions, the first payment to beginn and be made upon the first of the said feasts which shall happen next after my decease, for the due payment whereof I likewise charge all my houses, lands, tenements and personall estate as aforesaid. Item I give unto Mary Consett, formerly called Mary Shipton, the summe of tenn pounds to buy her mourning. Item I give unto Ralph Hopton junior the summe of five pounds. All the rest and residue of my reall and personall estate whatsoever and wheresoever I give and devise unto my beloved sister Elizabeth Raine, wife of William Rayne, to be by her by will, writeing or otherwise disposed of as she shall think fitt. And I doe hereby make, constitute and appoint my said sister Elizabeth sole executrix of this my last will and testament, hereby revokeing, disanulling and for ever makeing void all former and other wills & testaments by me heretofore made, and I doe declare this onely to be my last will and testament. In wittness whereof I have hereunto sett my hand and seale this twenty eighth day of December in the twelfth year of the reign of our soveraigne lady Anne, by the grace of God Queen of Brittain, France and Ireland, defender of the faith &c. annoque domini 1713.

Michael Taylor [*signed and sealed*][1]

Signed, sealed, published and declared in the presence of us who subscribed our names as wittnesses hereunto in the presence of the testator (after the interlineacion of the words (the), (and legacyes), (she)[)]. Ralph Hopton [*signed*], Mary Danby [*signed*], P. Consett [*signed*] juratus.

A true and perfect inventory of the goods and chattells of Michaell Taylor, late of North Allerton in the county of Yorke, chandler, taken and appraised by us whose names are here under subscribed this fourth day of May 1717.

	£	s	d
Imprimis. His purse and apparrell	10	0	0
Quick goods			
two milch cowes	8	0	0
3 oxen	12	0	0
one year[l]ing storke	1	1	6
two horses	10	0	0
7 ews and lambs	4	0	0
6 weather hoggs and a guelt ewe	3	10	0
one sewe and eight pigges	2	0	0
Husbandry geere			
carts, plows, harrows and other utensills & husbandry geere	3	10	0
Corne cut			
one hundred stooks of rye	12	10	0
one hundred stooks of oates	5	0	0
one hundred bushells of pease and beanes	10	0	0
Corne standing & growing & hay			
five acres of wheat sown down	7	10	0
hay	2	10	0
In the shopp			
one large copper	3	0	0
9 dozen of candles	2	14	0
candle mowles and other utensills in the shopp	1	0	0
In the forehouse			
3 large pewter dishes	0	12	0
4 leather chairs in the kitching	0	12	0
5 other pewter dishes and a dozen and halfe of pewter plates	1	10	0
In the great chamber			
one feather bedd, bedstead, bolster, pillowbers, blankets, hangings and other furniture thereunto belonging	7	0	0
half a dozen black wood chairs	0	12	0
one ovall table and one looking glass	0	10	6
a little square table and one chest of drawers	1	0	0
In the little chamber			
one leather trunk with drawers	0	5	0

Linnen			
two huggaback table cloaths and two dozen of napkins of the same sort	1	12	0
three pair of sheets and half a dozen pillowbears	1	0	0
Plate			
one silver cupp	2	10	0
Brass & iron &c.			
one jacke, copper kettle, spitts, racke and other brass, iron and copper utensils & implements	2	0	0
	117	9	0

4to Maii 1717. Appraised by us P. Consett [*signed*], Edward Wooller [*signed*], John Jhinson [*signed*], Christopher Appleton [*signed*].

[1] Michael Taylor was buried on 1 April 1717, more than three years after making his will.

146. WILLIAM SIMPSON, WEAVER, 1717

DPRI/6/T/1717/S1

Memorandum that William Simpson late of Northallerton, being sick of the sickness whereof he dyed, and haveing a mind to make his will nuncupative or by word of mouth did one the third day of May in the yeare of our Lord on thousand seaven hondered and seaventene, in his dwelling house in the saides Northallerton did declare, say or explaine him selfe in the forme of words following, or in words to the same purpose or effeckt videlicet the money which I have in house I give it to George Rimer of the saide Northallerton, he bringing me forth as he thinks fitt. And I did desiare us whose names are here unto subscribed to bere witness that the same should stand & be his last will & testament nuncupative. In witness whereof we have here unto set our hands this seaventh day of May anno domini 1717.
Robert Kay [*signed*], Elizabeth Galloway [*signed*] juratus, Thomas Lee [*signed*] juratus, Ann Heckley hir mark juratus.
Coram Carolo Neile surrogat'.

An inventory of all and singular the goods and chattles of William Simpson, late of <North> Allerton in the countie of Yorke, weaver, deaceased.

	£	s	d
Imprimis a bed and bedstead	0	7	6
Item a litle chist cupboard	0	1	6
Item a very ordinarie table	0	1	0

Item a litle pott	0	1	0
Item a clogg chaire	0	0	6
Item his wearing apparel	0	6	6
Item money in his purse	4	15	6
Sum of the inventory	5	13	6

Appraised by us Leonard Galloway [*signed*], Thomas Lee [*signed*], the mark of Robert Hutton, the mark of George Greathead.

147. STEPHEN PREST, TALLOW CHANDLER, 1717

DPRI/6/T/1717/P1

I, Stephen Prest of Northallerton in the county of Yorke, tallow chandler, doe hereby give and bequeath unto my dearly beloved wife Jone Prest and to her heires and assignes forever all my messuage, burgage or tenement in Northallerton with the appurtenances wherein Robert Straker now dweleth and do create my said dear wife sole executrix of this my last will and testament, she discharging all my debts & funerall expences. In witnes whereof I have hereunto set my hand and seale this fourteenth day of January anno domini 1714 [*14 Jan. 1715*].

Ste: Prest [*signed and sealed*][1]

Sealed, signed, published and delivered in the presence of us, Elli' Barstow [*signed*], E. Barstow [*signed*], Rosamind Shaw her marke.

A true and perfect inventory of the goods and chattells of Stephen Prest late of North Allerton in the county of Yorke, tallow chandler, deceased, taken the elleaventh day of October one thousand seaven hundred and seaventeen and appraized by us whose names are hereunto subscribed as followeth

	£	s	d
Imprimis his purse and apparell	05	00	00
In the Wairebanc Close			
five cowes	15	00	00
two calves	01	00	00
a ruck of hay	07	00	00
In the Spire Close			
one ruck of hay	03	00	00
In the Milne Close			
two twinter calves	02	10	00
two goakes of hay	04	10	00
In the yard			
fower sowes & fower piggs	03	00	00

two horses, a foale, a cart	06	00	00
an a[c]re and a halfe of hard corne	03	00	00
fower acres of beanes	03	00	00
In the fore house			
twenty pewter dishes	02	00	00
fower dozen & a halfe of plates	01	07	00
twenty pewter flaggins	00	10	00
one dresser, two tables & six chaires	01	06	00
brasse, a jack and a clock	03	00	00
In the fore parler			
three tables	01	00	00
fowerteen chaires	01	08	00
silver plate	08	00	00
In the little clozett			
one bedd, a cupboard & other implements	02	10	00
In Stelling parler			
one bedd and two tables	01	00	00
In the fore chamber			
one beddstead with hangings and other matters thereunto belonging	04	00	00
one paire of drawers	01	00	00
one dozen of chaires	01	16	00
three tables	01	00	00
a lookeing glass	00	05	00
In the chamber called Stare Chamber			
thre beddes with hangings and other appertenances thereunto belonging	10	00	00
two tables and six chaires	00	16	00
a lookeing glasse	00	01	06
In the back chamber			
three bedds with hangings and other appertenances to the same belonging	06	00	00
two tables, three chaires, one firme	00	14	00
In the stare head chamber			
two bedds with theire appertenances	02	10	00
a table and a lookeing glasse	00	07	00
In the woorke house			
a melting copper,[2] with trowes, candlecase, knives, scailes, weights and other matters belonging to the traid	04	00	00
In the back kitching			
one copper, a pann in a firnice, one cowler with tubbs and other brewing vessell	03	00	00

a hand milne	01 00 00
lining of all sorts	04 00 00
	115 10 06

Appraisers. Edward Wooller [*signed*], George Dunn, [*signed*], Robert Straker [*signed*], Geo: Pemberton [*signed*].

1 Stephen Prest was buried on 26 September 1717, two years and nine months after making his will.

2 'a pann in a firnice one cowler' erased – presumably a copying error from the following entry.

148. THOMAS FOGGITT, 1717

BIA/72/185

9ber 24th 1717

The words of Thomas Foggitt which he desired to be putt into writeing after his death, being his last will. First he desired that his just debts might be paid and that after his debts were paid he likewise desired that there might be forty pounds laid out in the house for Elizabeth Foggitt, his said wife, to live in & if such house cannot be bought then the summe of forty pounds is to be putt out & his said wife is to receive the interest during her life, and att her death the said summe of forty pounds to be equally divided among his childer if living, or to so many as shall be living. And all his said goods to be sold and what remains over & above the forty pounds to be equally divided among his eight childer and his said wife if living, and every respective summ or summes to be paid when they attaine to the age of fore and twenty, and if any one shall dye before that age then that said summe to be divided among the remainder of his childer and his wife. And he further said that there was twenty pounds ten shillings oweing to his brother John Robinson for which said debt he ordered him to have two kine and a bull att seaven pound ten shillings and a mare and her foale att other seaven pounds ten shillings and five pounds ten shillings which makes up his summ of twenty pound ten shillings. And likewise he said there was a son with him of his brother Abraham Foggitt's which he designed to putt to a trade and that there was a pair of buckskin bretches, the which his brother Abraham eldest son, the dyer, should have.

Attested by us whose names are underwritten, J. Tomer, Edward Flunders, Joseph Flunders.

149. HENRY BANISTER, MASON, 1718

DPRI/6/T/1718/B1

In the name of God, amen, the twenty fifth day of June anno domini one thousand seaven hundred and fowerteen. I, Henry Banister of North Allerton in the county of Yorke, mayson, being somewhat infirme and weake but of good and perfect memory (praised be God), doe hereby make and publish this my last will and testament in manner and forme following, revoakeing and absolutely anulling all and every will and wills, testament and testaments by these presents heretofore by me made and declared. First I give and bequeath my sole to almighty God my maker and redeamer and my bodye to be buried in such decent manner as my executrix, hereafter named, shall thinke fitt and convenient. And as touching such temporall estate of houses, goods, chattells and debts as the Lord has beene pleased to bestow upon me, I doe order, give, devise, bequeath and dispose of the same in manner and forme following. Imprimis I give and bequeath unto my nephew John Banister, sonne of Robert Banister, the summe of tenn poundes. Item I give and bequeath unto my neice Margarett Ouseman, one of the daughters of Robert Banister, the sume of tenn poundes. Item I give and bequeath unto my neice Jane Banister, another of the dawghters of Robert Banister, the summe of tenn poundes. Item I give & bequeath unto Anne Waller, another of the dawghters of Robert Banister, the summe of tenn poundes. Item I give and bequeath unto Robert Banister, sonne of Robert Banister, the summe of tenn poundes. Item I give & bequeath unto Jane Banister, daughter of William Banister, the summe of tenn poundes. Item I give and bequeath unto my nephew John Bramley the summe of tenn poundes. Item I give and bequeath unto my nephew Robert Bramley the summe of tenn poundes. Item I give and bequeath unto my nephew William Bramley the summe of thirty poundes. Item I give and bequeath unto my nephew Ralph Banister the summe of one hundred and fourty poundes. Item all the rest of my goods and chattells moveable and imoveable, debts, house and household stuff and other matters and things of what kinde or nature whatsoever I give, devise and bequeath unto my deare wife who I doe hereby nominate, constitute and appoint sole executrix of this my last will and testament. In witness whereof I have hereunto sett my hand and seale the day and yeare first above written.

The marke and seale of Henry Banister.[1]

Signed, sealed and published in our presence and our names

subscribed in his presence and by and with his consent. George Dunn [*signed*], George Robinson [*signed*], Geo: Pemberton [*signed*].

A true and perfect inventory of the goods and chattells of Henry Banister late of North-Allerton in the county of Yorke, mayson, deceased, taken the twelfth day of January in the yeare of our Lord God one thousand seaven hundred and seaventeen [*12 Jan. 1718*] and appraized by us whose names are underwritten as followeth

	£	s	d
Imprimis his purse and apparrell	02	10	00
Item one bedstead with fetherbed, curtings, blanckettes &c.	02	10	00
Item six pewter dishes	00	15	00
Item one pewter flaggon, a tankard and two candlesticks	00	03	00
Item one ovell table	00	04	00
Item two square tables	00	08	00
Item a cuppboard	00	05	00
Item six wood chaires	00	10	00
Item a dripping pann & a warmeing pan	00	07	06
Item a spitt and a reikin	00	03	00
Item a paire of tongues & a ~~warming pan~~ fire shovell	00	02	00
Item a brass pot, a kettle & a pan	01	00	00
Item a paile, a siall and a barrell	00	04	00
Item a lookeing glasse	00	01	00
Item a silver tumbler	00	13	00
Item two stooles	00	02	00
Item a paire of bellas & a salt pye	00	01	00
Item a pannell chest & a coffer	00	05	00
Totall	08	03	06
Moneyes owing to the testator upon bonds and other securityes	400	00	00
Moneyes owing & inventory	408	03	06
	[*recte* *410*	*03*	*06*]
Legacyes bequeathed to severall persons	260	00	00
Funerall expences	11	00	00
Debts owing	04	00	00
Legacyes, funerall expences & debts	275	00	00
Due to the executrix	133	03	06
	[*recte* *135*	*03*	*06*]

Appraizers: George Robinson [*signed*], John Yates [*signed*], Geo: Pemberton [*signed*], John Ruddock [*signed*].

[1] Henry Banister was buried on 9 January 1718, three and a half years after making his will.

150. CHARLES NEILE, CLERK, 1718

DPRI/6/T/1718/N1

In the name of God, amen, I, Charles Neile of North Allerton in the county of York, clerk, being sick and weak in body but of sound and disposing mind and memory (praised be almighty God), doe make and ordaine my last will and testament touching my worldly estate in manner following, (that is to say), I give and devise all and singular my lands, tenements and heraditaments scituate, lying and being within the township of Romanby in the county of York, not only my freehold or leasehold lands and tenements there but alsoe (as much as in me lyes) my copyhold with the appurtenances unto my trusty friends George Lawson of Harlesey in the said county esquire and Timothy Mauleverer of Arncliffe in the said county, esquire, and the survivour of them and the heirs of such survivour to and for the uses, intents and purposes only following, (that is to say), to the use and behoofe of my niece Mrs Dorothy Davile and her assignes for and during her naturall life, and after her decease to the use and behoofe of my niece Mrs Elizabeth Jackson for and during the naturall life of my said niece Elizabeth, and after the decease of my said two nieces, to the use and behoofe of my nephew Charles Jackson for and during his naturall life and after the decease of them my said nieces and nephew my mind and will is that my said trustees and the survivour of them and the heirs of such survivour shall stand and be seized of and in the premisses aforesaid to and for the use of such poor widow of some clergy man of the Church of England as shall for that purpose be named by the viccar of North Allerton and approved of by the Dean and Chapter of Durham for the time being, it being my mind and will that the viccar of North Allerton aforesaid for the time being shall name two such widows, one of which to be within the North Riding of the county of York, and the other within the bishoprick of Durham, and that the <said> Dean and Chapter shall appoint which of such two they shall think most needfull; and so from time to time for ever hereafter upon the death of every such widow which shall be so appointed, another such widow shall be named and appointed after the same manner, and to and for no other use, intent or purpose shall my said trustees or either of them or their heirs stand seized of the said lands and tenements but only for the uses aforesaid. Item I give unto my said niece Jackson the summe of thirty pounds, and unto her son my said nephew Charles the summe of ten pounds, and unto my servant Robert Smith forty shillings to buy him mourning. Item all the rest of my goods, chattells and personall estate I give unto my said niece Mrs Dorothy Davile and doe make her, the said Mrs Dorothy Davile, sole executrix of this my last will and testament, revoking all former wills by me made. In witness whereof I have hereunto set my hand and seale this first day of September in the year of our Lord one thousand seven hundred and eighteen.

Charles Neile [*signed and sealed*][1]

Signed, sealed and published by the testator Mr Neile in our presence and our names subscribed as witnesses in his presence and at his request. William Dobson [*signed*], Cuthbert Mitford [*signed*], Thomas Crosfield [*signed*].

[1] Charles Neile (or Neale) was educated at Peterhouse College, Cambridge, and gained his MA in 1690. From 1689 to 1694 he was rector of St Mary-le-Bow, Durham and then vicar of Northallerton. He was buried on 3 September 1718, two days after making his will. Venn and Venn, *Alumni Cantabrigienses*.

151. ROBERT STRINGER, YEOMAN, 1719

DPRI/6/T/1719/S2

In the name of God, amen, I, Robert Stringer of North Allerton in the county of York, yeoman, of sound and perfect mind and memory (praised be God), do make, ordain and constitute this my last will and testament in manner and form following, that is to say, imprimis I recommend to God allmighty, my maker and redeemer, and my body to be buried in such decent manner as my executor, hereafter named, shall think fit and convenient. And as for the real and personal estate which God has been pleased to bestow upon me, I bequeath, give and dispose thereof in manner and form following. Imprimis I give and bequeath unto my grandson William Stringer all that fore part of my messuage, burgage or tenement in North Allerton (butting or bounding on the south upon the tenement now or late in the possession of George Smith and on the north upon the messuage or tenement now in the possession of Jane Prist) and wherin one William Green now dwelleth, together with his shop and another shop in the possession of John Thompson with two chambers over the same; and also the great stable on the backside therof and also half of the garth on the said backside with ingress, egress and regress to him my said grandson his heires and assignes for ever. Item my will and pleasure is that my daughter in law Elisabeth Stringer, mother of my said grandson, shall have and enjoy all that backpart of my house wherein I now dwell together with two parlers and one lesser stable and little house, now in the possession of John Carver, and the other half part of the garth, to hold the same for the term of her natural life only <with ingress egress and regress>. Item I give unto my said grandson William Stringer my two closes called by the name of Windmill Flatt which I hold by lease under the bishopp of Durham for three lives, scituate and being within the precincts of Northallerton aforesaid. But in case my said grandson William Stringer die before he attains the full age of one and twenty years, my will is that the said two closes shall be sold for the payment of the debt whereof and wherewith they are chargeable and now stand mortgaged for, and the surplussage that may and will arise over and above the discharging of the said debt I give and dispose as follows, that is to say, it shall be divided into thre equall parts or moyeties, and one half part or moyety, the three equal moyeties I give unto the children of William Maltby, Mr John Jackson of Bromton and my nephew William Stringer to be equally divided among them share & share like, and the said half moyety to be equally divided amongst the daughters of Lennard Taylor of Danby, to the due performance wherof I do nominate, ordain and constitue Mr Richard Hutchinson in the parish of Mawnby and Mr John Jackson of Bromton, aforesaid feoffees in trust with full power, good, right and lawfull authority to dispose of and sell and securities to give and make in as firm and ample manner as if I myself was personally present, and due dividends of such summ or summs of mony as shall arise from such sale, over and above the discharging the said mortgage, to be made in due proportion to the parties aforesaid severally as above mentioned. And also upon my said granson's discease, not having attained unto the age of one and twenty years, I then give all that part of my house, stable and halfe garth, before bequeathed unto my aforesaid grandson, unto William Stringer, the only son of my nephew William Stringer aforesaid, he paying three pounds a year out of the rents thereof unto my said daughter in law Elizabeth Stringer at Mayday and Martinmass by equal payments for the time and terme of her natural life; but after her descease also, then the said William Stringer, son of my said nephew, shall have, possess and enjoy all my said burgage house, stables, garth and and there appurtenances to him, his heirs and assignes for ever. Item I give unto my nephew John Stringer one shilling. Item I give unto my sister's two sonns, Francis Lownsdale and William Lownsdale, each one shilling. And I do hereby solely nominate, constitute and appoint my said granson William Stringer executor of this my last will and testament, revoking all other wills by me made. In wittness whereof

I have hereunto set my hand and seal this twenty eight day of May annoque domini 1718.
Robert Stringer his yester[1] [*sealed*][2]
Signed, sealed and published by the testator in the presence of Michael Gibson [*signed*], William Green [*signed*] juratus, John Todd [*signed*].

[1] The reading is not in doubt: 'marke' is presumably meant.
[2] Robert Stringer was buried on 21 March 1719, ten months after making his will.

152. CHRISTOPHER ROBINSON, FELLMONGER, 1719

BIA/73/248
In the name of God, amen, I, Christopher Robinson of North Allerton in the county of Yorke, fellmonger, being somewhat infirme but of sound and perfect memory, praised be God, doe make and publish this my last will and testament in manner following (that is to say[)]: first I recamend my sole to almighty God my maker and redeemer, and my bodye to be buried in such decent manner as my executer hereafter named shall thinke fitt. And as touching such worldly matters as God has been pleased to bestow upon me, I give, devise, dispose and bequeath thereof as followeth. Imprimis I give and bequeath unto my deare wife the summe of fourty poundes to be paid within twelve months after my decease. Item I give and bequeath unto my sonne Mathew Robinson the summe of thirty poundes over and above the summe of tenn poundes I am justly indebted unto him, to be paid by my executer within twelve months next after my decease. Item I give and bequeath unto my sonne Christopher Robinson the summe of fourty poundes to be paid unto him three yeares after my decease and alsoe the yearly summe of thirty shillings as consideracion thereof untill the same become due to him. Item I give and bequeath unto my daughter Dorothy Robinson the summe of fourty poundes to be paid unto her when she attaines to the age of eighteen yeares and also consideracion for the same until the same become due. Item my will and pleasure is that in case any of my said children shall happen to dye before theire porcions become due to them, that the moneyes soe bequeathed unto them shall be divided equally amongst all my said children. Item all the rest of estate of what kinde or nature soever I give and bequeath unto my sonne Thomas Robinson <juratus> whoe I doe nominate and appoint sole executer of this my last will and and testiament.

Item my will and pleasure is that my deare wife shall have all my household stuffe over and above the fourty poundes bequeathed unto her. In witness whereof I have hereunto sett my hand and seale the eighteenth day of March anno domini 1718 [*18 Mar. 1719*]
Christopher Robinson [*signed and sealed*][1]
Signed, sealed and published in the presence of us Samuell Button [*signed*], George Thompson [*signed*] <juratus>, George Pemberton [*signed*].

A true and perfect inventory of the goods & chattels of Christopher Robinson late of North Allerton, fellmonger, deceased, valued and apprized by us whose names are underwritten
April 14th 1719

	£	s	d
Imprimis his purse & apparel	2	3	4
In the fore house			
one dresser, 1 table, 1 long setle with other implements	1	2	6
pewter	0	15	0
In the little parlour			
2 bedsteads with beding, livery cupboard & one panel chest	3	0	0
In the great parlour			
one bedstead with beding, one chest of drawers, 2 little tables, ½ dozen chairs	3	4	8
In the chamber over the house			
1 bedstead with beding & 1 panell chest	0	18	4
In the great chamber			
a parcel of wooll	6	13	4
In the workhouse			
leather wrought & unwrought	3	6	1
One cow & two working horses & 2 stags	11	13	4
In linen	1	1	4
Debts owing to the testator	30	10	6
	64	12	5
Debts owing by the testator	28	6	8

J. Winer, George Robinson, W. Husthwaite, Edward Flunders.

[1] Christopher Robinson was buried on 28 March 1719, ten days after making his will.

153. MICHAEL BUCK, BLACKSMITH, 1719

BIA/73/246 [probate copy]

In the name of God, amen, I, Michael Buck of North Allerton in the county of York, blacksmith, being sick and weake in body but of sound and perfect mind and memory, praised be almighty God for the same, do make and ordaine this my last will and testament in manner and form following (that is to say). First and principally I commend my soul into the hands of almighty God and my body I commit to the earth to be decently buried at the discretion of my executors hereafter named. And as concerning the disposition of all such temporall estate and goods as it hath pleased almighty God to bestow upon me, I give and dispose thereof as followeth. Imprimis I give and bequeath unto my eldest son Michael Buck the sum of five shillings of good and lawful money of Great Britain, to be paid unto him by my executors within twelve months of my decease, he giving my executors a receipt for the same in full for his share of what he might have out of my estate and goods. Item I give and bequeath unto my third son John Buck the value of a guinea to be paid him by my executors within twelve months next after my decease, he giving my executors a receipt for the same in full for his share out of my estate and goods. Item I give and bequeath unto my daughter Elizabeth Buck the sum of twenty pounds of good and lawful money of Great Britain to be paid unto her by my executors within twelve months next after my decease, she giving my executors a discharge for the same. And also I give unto my said daughter one bedstead and bed and bedding thereunto belonging. Item I give and bequeath unto my daughter Jane Buck the sum of ten pounds ten shillings of good and lawful money of Great Britain to be paid her by my executors when she shall attain to the age of one and twenty years. Item I give and bequeath unto my loving wife Jane Buck and to my youngest son Thomas Buck all that my borrow house which Henry Atkinson now liveth within, standing and being on the West Row of the said town of North Allerton aforesaid and after my said wife's decease I give unto my said son Thomas Buck, his heirs and assigns for ever. And all the residue of my personal estate, goods, chattels, bonds, bills, writings and debts whatsoever, I give and bequeath unto my said loving wife and my said son Thomas Buck whom I make my full, sole and joint executors of this my last will and testament, they paying my debts, legacies and funeral expenses. And I do hereby revoke, disanull and make void all former wills and testaments and writings by me heretofore made. In witness thereof I have hereunto

set my hand and seal the twenty seventh day of November anno domini 1718.
Michael Buck.[1]
Signed, sealed, published and declared in the presence of Leonard Galloway, William Boddy, Robert Young, Christopher Robinson.

[1] Michael Buck was buried on 14 April 1719, five months after making his will.

GLOSSARY

This glossary offers explanations of unfamiliar words in the wills and inventories. Some are local dialect words; others are obsolete words which have passed out of use. Significant variant spellings are noted below but minor variations are not. Meanings are drawn from the *Oxford English Dictionary*; J. Wright, *The English Dialect Dictionary*, (6 vols, London 1898–1905); and the glossaries provided in J. A. Atkinson *et al.* (eds), *Darlington Wills, 1600–1625*, Surtees Society 201 (1993) and J. Briggs *et al.* (eds), *Sunderland Wills and Inventories, 1601–1650*, Surtees Society 214 (2010).

alamode: thin, light, glossy black silk.
andiron: moveable iron plates to reduce the size of a grate.
anker (anchor): cask.
ark: box, chest or coffer.
axle tree: axle or spindle on which the wheels of a cart revolve.
backsettle: outshot at the back of a building.
bakan: bacon.
ballons: valance (q.v.).
belies: from the context, presumably leather from the belly of an animal.
bellas(s) (bellice): bellows.
bends: (of leather), thickest and strongest pieces of leather, used for the soles of boots and shoes.
board chest: chest made from boards pegged or pinned together rather than jointed.
boule: a boll; measure of quantity of grain, varying in northern England from 2 to 6 bushels.
boulting (bouting) house: place where meal is sifted.
boulting tub: bowl used for the process of sifting meal to separate flour from husk.
brake: an instrument for breaking flax.
brake: bridle or snaffle for horses.
broash: broach; tapered spike on which to stick candles.
broyling: grilling.

buffet stool/form: low stool; footstool; or a form for use at table.
bussy leather chairs: exact significance of 'bussy' has not been traced.
caddices: worsted tape or binding; ribbon.
callimankers: a glazed Flemish-wool/satin cloth, self-chequered or diamond pattern, for petticoats.
cambric: fine white linen originating from Cambrai in Flanders.
camlet: fine soft cloth of thin wool or fine wool and silk originally from the East but subsequently made of combinations of wool, hair, silk, cotton or linen.
caresey: *see* kersey.
carpet (carping cloth): woven wool cloth for table or dresser.
cart dogges: projecting ends of a cart.
chaff bed: mattress filled with chaff or corn husks.
chafing dish: small enclosed brazier for heating food.
chyney (cheney; cheanea): china.
clogg chair/form: furniture made from 'clogs' (thick planks or blocks of wood).
close bed: an enclosed bedstead or bunk with folding or sliding doors.
close stool: commode.
codds (kods): pillows or cushions.
codwar(e)s: pillow case.
coffin: small chest or box.
coop sole (coupe swoole): lower supporting timber frame of a 'coup' (a cart with closed sides).
counter: probably used in the sense of a dresser or table.
coup stanges: cart poles.
coverlet (coverlid): counterpane.
cowler: cooler, in which wort was cooled in brewing.
cushnett: cushionet; a little cushion or pincushion.
dack: (of leather), daker or dicker; a measure of leather consisting of a bundle of ten hides.
darnick: dornick, fabric used for hangings etc., originally manufactured in Flemish town of Doornick/Tournay.
defalcation: deduction; diminution; curtailment.
diaper (diber): twilled white linen cloth with geometric pattern.
dimothy: dimity; a heavy cotton dress or bed-hanging fabric, sprigged or with a raised stripe.
doubler (dubler): large plate or dish.
dreaping pan: dripping pan, placed beneath roasting meat.
dresser: a sideboard or table for preparing food.

duch bread: presumably 'Dutch bread' (the specific sense has not been established).

eller poules : alder poles.

emblements (empellments) : implements.

elwide: perhaps 'ell-wide' (an English ell was 45 inches).

fatham: fathom, i.e. as much as a person's arms can stretch around (6 feet).

felfs: *see* felloes.

felloes (phelkes; felfs): wooden segments forming the rim of a wheel.

ferrits: stout cotton or silk tape, often decorated (possibly for garters).

finger calves: sucking calves.

firdeeles (fur–; fyr–): planks of fir or other softwood, usually at least 6 feet long, 9 inches wide and 3 inches thick.

firkin: small cask, originally holding a quarter of a barrel.

firm: form; bench.

flacket (flakitt; flasket): small keg or flask. 'Flasket' can also refer to a long shallow basket.

fleak: flake; hurdle.

form (fourme; firme; furme): bench without back support.

fustion: heavy coarse cloth, made with linen warp and cotton weft, for working clothes.

galley balk (gallows balk): iron bar stretching across chimney from which pothooks were suspended.

Galloway: small, hardy horse of Scottish origin.

gallownes: galloon; narrow trimming of ribbon or braid, often of gold or silver.

ganges of speakes: sets of spokes.

gantree: gantry; a four-footed wooden stand for barrels.

garner: store house.

gate: abbreviation of 'cattlegate' or 'beastgate', a numerically limited grazing right or stint.

gavelock: iron crowbar.

geild (guelt): (of livestock) barren; without young.

gib (jib): stand for a barrel.

gille or frood: from the context, probably 'guile or fraud'.

glass case: either a glass-fronted cabinet or a looking glass.

goake: probably 'gowk', the inner part or core of a hay or straw stack.

graineing boards: probably boards on which the grain of leather was softened or raised.

green hides: untreated animal hides, before tanning.

grub: probably a rake or grubbing tool. In Scotland used of an iron harrow or scarifier.
grunstone: grindstone.
gyle-fat (guile fatt): vat in which malt is left to ferment.
halbot: perhaps 'halberd', a weapon consisting of a combination of a spear and a battle-axe.
hard corn: wheat or rye.
harden: coarse linen fabric used for cheap sheets.
heck: rack to hold fodder.
heckle: comb for combing out fibres of flax or hemp.
helme: shed in the fields to shelter cattle; a hovel or hut.
hogshead: cask for liquor, usually holding 63 old gallons (52½ imperial).
holland: fine linen fabric named from the province of Holland in the Netherlands.
horse lock: shackle for horse's foot; by extension any padlock.
howle: (of a dish), hollow; deep.
huggaback: huckaback, a strong linen fabric with roughened surface. Darlington was noted for the manufacture of this cloth.
indians: from the context, perhaps a category of silk.
inkle: linen tape.
jack (jake): device for turning a spit.
jarsay: jersey worsted.
jeystes: joists.
jib: *see* gib.
kass: probably 'cows'.
kersey: coarse, narrow cloth woven from long wool, usually ribbed.
kill: kiln.
kimlin (kimblin(g)): kimnel, a cask or tub made from hooped staves used for brewing/baking etc.
kine (key): cows.
kirn: churn.
kokes: perhaps 'cocks'.
lanthorn/lantron: lantern.
latts: laths; narrow strips of wood.
lead: large pot or cauldron.
leap: basket (for carrying seed).
linn (line): linen or flax; hence 'line wheel', small spinning wheel for flax.
livery cupboard: small food storage cupboard or an ornamental sideboard.
long settle: long bench with arms and a high back.

lorimer (lorrainer): maker of bits and metal mountings for horse bridles.
lutestring: a glossy silk fabric.
lynmer: limber, the shaft of a cart.
Manchester ware: cotton goods made in Manchester.
maner: manure.
mashleion: maslin; mixed grain, especially rye mixed with wheat.
maske fatt: vat for mashing malt with water to form wort.
mell: hammer or mallet.
milkness: milk products; dairying.
mowles: moulds (for candles).
offell wood: waste wood.
paragons: a kind of double camlet (q.v.); a stuff used in dress and upholstery.
peck: measure for dry goods (one-quarter of a bushel).
persell: perhaps 'parcel', in the sense of a measure.
phelkes: *see* felloes.
piggine (pigon): small wooden pail with one larger stave to serve as a handle.
pillion seat: small seat usually placed behind the main saddle; also a light saddle, usually used by women.
pillowbeare (pillowbee; pillowveare; pilliver): pillow case.
por: 'purr', a poker.
porringer/pottinger: dish (often covered) for porridge, soup etc.
posnet: small metal vessel with long handle and three short legs.
posset (posit) bowl: bowl for 'posset', milk curdled with liquor, spices etc.
pott kilp: iron hook to suspend a pot over the fire.
prentis: apprentice.
press: large cupboard.
puther (puder; powther; pouther): pewter.
pyke: small pointed stack.
quishions: cushions.
quy: heifer.
racken (reckon; reikin): rack supporting a pot over the fire.
randle balk: wooden beam across a chimney from which the pot-hook was suspended.
raper: perhaps rapier, a long pointed sword.
rook: a rick of hay.
runlet: a cask.
safe: food cupboard with ventilation.

safeguard: outer skirt or petticoat to protect a woman's dress when riding.
salt: a salt cellar; a **salt pie** is a salt box.
salt spects: saltpetre.
samron: cloth with a texture between linen and hemp.
scotch cloth: presumably cloth from Scotland. A specific meaning was cloth made from nettle fibre, akin to coarse linen.
scummer/skimmer: perforated ladle for skimming liquids.
searge: serge, a durable woollen fabric.
set work: embroidery.
sew (swe): sow.
shockalees: a kind of fabric or haberdashery; exact meaning has not been ascertained. Also occurs in Blake Tyson (ed.), *Estate and Household Accounts of Sir Daniel Fleming of Rydal Hall, Westmorland: 1688–1701* (Kendal, 2001), p. 335 (purchase of '2 yards of shocolees').
shots: young pigs.
showell: shovel.
sile: a sieve or strainer, particularly for milk.
sinker: circular lid of cheese press, a weight for pressing cheese.
skeel (skeall): wooden tub or bucket for milk or water.
slear: slay; an instrument used in the weaving process to beat up the weft.
speakes: spokes of a wheel.
speet: spit.
spetch: patch, specifically a strip of leather or a piece of undressed leather.
stackbar: hurdle; used to fence off haystacks.
stagg: young horse.
stand-heck: rack for fodder.
stee: ladder.
steele: steel rod for sharpening knives.
stem(p)ses: *see* tem(p)se.
stirk (storke; sturk): young bullock or heifer.
stott (stoat): bullock; young ox; less commonly a heifer.
stowell: stool.
struell: meaning not ascertained; perhaps related to 'strail', a woollen bed covering or blanket.
stuffe: worsted cloth without nap.
swill: large shallow basket.
tan tubs: tan pits, in which leather was steeped.
teame: harness chain for horses or oxen.
tearse: tierce; a cask or vessel holding 42 gallons.

tem(p)se (stem(p)s): strainer or fine sieve for flour.
tenter: frame on which cloth was stretched to dry.
tester: canopy over a four-poster bed.
tiffeney: thin, transparent silk; fine-meshed gauze used for sieves.
towe: flax or hemp.
trencher: flat platter from which food was eaten.
troughill: trowel.
truckle bed (trunckle; trunnle; trinnell): bedstead on wheels which could be pushed under a standing bed.
twinter: a young animal of two winters.
valance: short curtain, specifically drapery around the canopy or frame of a bed.
vise, pair of: a vice.
voyder: tray or basket; or a vessel into which something is emptied.
wain (wayne): wagon.
wainscot: panelled.
wanded chair: wickerwork chair.
ware corn: spring corn.
warming pan: long-handled pan containing live coals for warming a bed.
weather hogg: young castrated male sheep.
why (whey; wye; quy): heifer up to three years which has not calved.
window (winder; windring) cloth: winnowing cloth.

INDEX OF NAMES

Page numbers in **bold** refer to wills and/or inventories of individuals of that name. Places are identified by county, using the following abbreviations: Du: Co. Durham; YN: Yorkshire North Riding; YW: Yorkshire West Riding. Field-names in Northallerton township are indicated by the abbreviation f.n.

SUBJECT INDEX